To my wife Miriam, for your love, patience, and support.

—Arnold Robbins

Sixth Edition

Learning the vi Editor

Sixth Edition

Linda Lamb and Arnold Robbins

O'REILLY®

Beijing · Cambridge · Farnham · Köln · Paris · Sebastopol · Taipei · Tokyo

Learning the vi Editor, Sixth Edition
by Linda Lamb and Arnold Robbins

Published by O'Reilly & Associates, Inc., 101 Morris Street, Sebastopol, CA 95472.

Editor: Tim O'Reilly

Update Editor: Gigi Estabrook

Production Editor: Nicole Gipson Arigo

Printing History:

February 1986:	First edition, by Linda Lamb.
April 1986:	Second edition, with minor corrections.
August 1987:	Third edition; revised and enlarged, index added, by Walter Gallant. Revised page design by Linda Lamb and Dale Dougherty.
June 1988:	Fourth edition; updated, minor corrections by Tim O'Reilly.
October 1990:	Fifth edition; revised and enlarged by Daniel Gilly.
November 1998:	Sixth edition; updated, added coverage of vi clones, new index.

ISBN: 1-56592-426-6
[M]

[8/00]

Table of Contents

Preface

Text editing is one of the most common uses of any computer system, and *vi* is one of the most useful standard text editors on your system. With *vi* you can create new files or edit any existing UNIX text file.

Scope of This Handbook

This book consists of twelve chapters and five appendixes, divided into three parts. Part I, *Basic and Advanced vi*, is designed to get you started using *vi* quickly, and to follow up with advanced skills that will let you use it effectively.

The first two chapters, *The vi Text Editor* and *Simple Editing*, present some simple *vi* commands with which you can get started. You should practice these until they are second nature. You could stop at the end of Chapter 2, *Simple Editing*, having learned some elementary editing tools.

But *vi* is meant to do a lot more than rudimentary word processing; the variety of commands and options enables you to shortcut a lot of editing drudgery. Chapter 3, *Moving Around in a Hurry*, and Chapter 4, *Beyond the Basics*, concentrate on easier ways to do tasks. During your first reading, you'll get at least an idea of what *vi* can do and what commands you might harness for your specific uses. Later, you can come back to these chapters for further study.

Chapter 5, *Introducing the ex Editor*, Chapter 6, *Global Replacement*, and Chapter 7, *Advanced Editing*, provide tools that help you shift more of the editing burden to the computer. They introduce you to the *ex* line editor underlying *vi*, and show you how to issue *ex* commands from within *vi*.

Part II, *Extensions and Clones*, describes extensions to "standard" *vi* that are commonly available in many or all of the *vi* clones.

Chapter 8, *vi Clones Feature Summary*, covers multiwindow editing, GUI interfaces, extended regular expressions, facilities that make editing easier, and several other features.

Chapter 9, *nvi—New vi*, through Chapter 12, *vile—vi Like Emacs*, cover the various *vi* clones—*nvi, elvis, vim,* and *vile*—showing you how to use their extensions to *vi* and discussing the features that are specific to each one.

Part III, *Appendixes*, provides useful reference material.

Appendix A, *Quick Reference*, lists all *vi* and *ex* commands, sorted by function.

Appendix B, *ex Commands*, is an alphabetical list of *ex* commands.

Appendix C, *Setting Options*, lists `set` command options.

Appendix D, *Problem Checklists*, consolidates checklists found in the book.

Appendix E, *vi and the Internet*, describes *vi*'s place in the larger UNIX and Internet culture.

How the Material Is Presented

The philosophy of this handbook is to give you a good overview of what we feel are *vi* survival materials for the new user. Learning a new editor, especially an editor with all the options of *vi*, can seem like an overwhelming task. We have made an effort to present basic concepts and commands in an easy-to-read and logical manner. The following sections describe the conventions used in this handbook.

Discussion of vi Commands

A picture of a keyboard button, like the one on the left, marks the main discussion of that particular keyboard command or of related commands. You will find a brief introduction to the main concept before it is broken down into task-oriented sections. We then present the appropriate command to use in each case, along with a description of the command and the proper syntax for using it.

Conventions

In syntax descriptions and examples, what you would actually type is shown in the `Courier` font, as are all command names. Variables (which you would not type literally, but would replace with an actual value when you typed the command) are shown in *Courier italic*. Brackets indicate that a variable is optional. For example, in the syntax line:

```
vi [filename]
```

filename would be replaced by an actual filename. The brackets indicate that the vi command can be invoked without specifying a filename at all. The brackets themselves are not typed.

Certain examples show the effect of commands typed at the UNIX shell prompt. In such examples, what you actually type is shown in **Courier Bold** to distinguish it from the system response. For example:

```
$ ls
ch01.sgm ch02.sgm ch03.sgm ch04.sgm
```

In examples, *italic* indicates a comment which is not to be typed. Otherwise, *italic* emphasizes special terms and indicate the names of files.

The owl icon designates a note, which is an important aside to its nearby text. For example . . .

 When you see the owl icon, you know the text beside it is a note, like this.

Keystrokes

Special keystrokes are shown in a box. For example:

```
iWith a ESC
```

Throughout the book, you will also find columns of *vi* commands and their results:

Keystrokes
zz

Results

```
"practice" [New file] 6 lines, 320 characters
```

Give the write and save command, zz. Your file is saved as a regular UNIX file.

In the example above, the command ZZ is shown in the left column. In the window to the right is a line (or several lines) of the screen that show the result of the command. Cursor position is shown by an underscore. In this instance, since ZZ saves and writes the file, you see the status line shown when a file is written; the cursor position is not shown. Below the window is an explanation of the command and its result.

Sometimes *vi* commands are issued by pressing the CTRL key and another key simultaneously. In the text, this combination keystroke is written within a box (for example, CTRL-G). In examples, it is written by preceding the name of the key with a caret (^). For example, ^G means to hold down CTRL while pressing the G key.

Problem Checklist

A problem checklist is included in those sections where you may run into some trouble. You can skim these checklists and go back to them when you actually encounter a problem. All of the problem checklists are also collected in Appendix D, for ease of reference.

What You Need to Know Before Starting

This book assumes you have already read *Learning the UNIX Operating System* or some other introduction to UNIX. You should already know how to:

*   Log in and log out
*   Enter UNIX commands
*   Change directories
*   List files in a directory
*   Create, copy, and remove files

Familiarity with *grep* (a global search program) and wildcard characters is also helpful.

Although *vi* can run on almost any terminal, it must know what kind of terminal you are using. The terminal type is usually set in your *.profile* or *.login* file. See your system administrator if you are not sure whether your terminal type is defined correctly. This will avoid possible confusion for you when you start experimenting with *vi*.

Comments and Questions

Please address comments and questions concerning this book to the publisher:

> O'Reilly & Associates, Inc.
> 101 Morris Street
> Sebastopol, CA 95472
> 1-800-998-9938 (in the U.S. or Canada)
> 1-707-829-0515 (international or local)
> 1-707-829-0104 (FAX)

You can send us messages electronically. To be put on the mailing list or request a catalog, send email to:

> *info@oreilly.com*

To ask technical questions or comment on the book, send email to:

> *bookquestions@oreilly.com*

About the Previous Edition

In the fifth edition of this book, the *ex* editor commands were first discussed more fully. In Chapters 5, 6, and 7, the complex features of *ex* and *vi* were clarified by adding more examples, in topics such as regular expression syntax, global replacement, *.exrc* files, word abbreviations, keyboard maps, and editing scripts. A few of the examples were drawn from articles in *UNIX World* magazine. Walter Zintz wrote a two-part tutorial* on *vi* that taught us a few things we didn't know, and that also had a lot of clever examples illustrating features we did already cover in the book. Ray Swartz also had a helpful tip in one of his columns.† We are grateful for the ideas in these articles.

Preface to the 6th Edition

The 6th edition of *Learning the vi Editor* brings the book into the late 1990s. In particular, besides the "original" version of *vi* that comes as a standard part of every UNIX system, there are now a number of freely available "clones," or work-alike editors. Many of them have improvements over the original *vi*. One could thus say that there is now a "family" of *vi* editors, and this book's goal is to teach you what you need to know to use them.

---

* "*vi* Tips for Power Users," *UNIX World*, April 1990; and "Using *vi* to Automate Complex Edits," *UNIX World*, May 1990. Both articles by Walter Zintz.

† "Answers to UNIX," *UNIX World*, August 1990.

What's New

The following features are new for this edition:

- Many minor corrections and additions have been made to the basic text.

- For each chapter where it's appropriate, there is a command summary at the end.

- New chapters cover each *vi* clone, the features and/or extensions common to two or more of the clones, and multiwindow editing.

- The chapter for each *vi* clone describes a bit of that program's history and goals, its unique features, and where to get it.

- The new appendix describes *vi*'s place in the larger UNIX and Internet culture.

Versions

The following programs were used for testing out various *vi* features:

- The Solaris 2.6 version of *vi* for a "reference" version of UNIX *vi*

- Version 1.79 of Keith Bostic's *nvi*

- Version 2.0 of Steve Kirkendall's *elvis*

- Versions 5.0 and 5.1 of Bram Moolenaar's *vim*

- Versions 7.4 and 8.0 of *vile*, by Kevin Buettner, Tom Dickey, and Paul Fox

Acknowledgments

First and foremost, thanks to my wife Miriam for taking care of the kids while I was working on this book, particularly during the "witching hours" right before meal times. I owe her large amounts of quiet time and ice cream.

Paul Manno, of the Georgia Tech College of Computing, provided invaluable help in pacifying my printing software. Len Muellner and Erik Ray of O'Reilly & Associates helped with the SGML software. Jerry Peek's *vi* macros for SGML were invaluable.

Although all of the programs were used during the preparation of the new and revised material, most of the editing was done with *vim* versions 4.5 and 5.0 under GNU-Linux (Redhat 4.2).

Thanks to Keith Bostic, Steve Kirkendall, Bram Moolenaar, Paul Fox, Tom Dickey, and Kevin Buettner, who reviewed the book. Steve Kirkendall, Bram Moolenaar, Paul Fox, Tom Dickey, and Kevin Buettner also provided important parts of Chapters 8 through 12.

Without the electricity being generated by the power company, doing anything with a computer is impossible. But when the electricity is there, you don't stop to think about it. So too when writing a book—without an editor, nothing happens, but when the editor is there doing her job, it's easy to forget about her. Gigi Estabrook at O'Reilly is a true gem. It's been a pleasure working with her, and I appreciate everything she's done and continues to do for me.

Finally, many thanks to the production team at O'Reilly & Associates.

Arnold Robbins
Ra'anana, ISRAEL
June 1998

I

Basic and Advanced vi

Part I is designed to get you started with *vi* quickly and to provide the advanced skills that will let you use *vi* most effectively. This part contains the following chapters:

- Chapter 1, *The vi Text Editor*
- Chapter 2, *Simple Editing*
- Chapter 3, *Moving Around in a Hurry*
- Chapter 4, *Beyond the Basics*
- Chapter 5, *Introducing the ex Editor*
- Chapter 6, *Global Replacement*
- Chapter 7, *Advanced Editing*

I

Basic and Advanced al

1

The vi Text Editor

UNIX has a number of editors that can process the contents of text files, whether those files contain data, source code, or sentences. There are line editors, such as *ed* and *ex*, which display a line of the file on the screen; and there are screen editors, such as *vi* and *emacs*, which display a part of the file on your terminal screen. Text editors based on the X Window System are also commonly available, and are becoming increasing popular. Both GNU *emacs* and its derivative *xemacs* provide multiple X windows; an interesting alternative is the *sam* editor from Bell Labs. All but one of the *vi* clones described in Part II of this book also provide X-based interfaces.

vi is the most useful standard text editor on your system. (*vi* is short for *vi*sual editor and is pronounced "vee-eye.") Unlike *emacs*, it is available in nearly identical form on almost every UNIX system, thus providing a kind of text-editing *lingua franca*.* The same might be said of *ed* and *ex*, but screen editors are generally much easier to use. With a screen editor, you can scroll the page, move the cursor, delete lines, insert characters, and more, while seeing the results of your edits as you make them. Screen editors are very popular, since they allow you to make changes as you read through a file, like you would edit a printed copy, only faster.

To many beginners, *vi* looks unintuitive and cumbersome—instead of using special control keys for word processing functions and just letting you type normally, it uses all of the regular keyboard keys for issuing commands. When the keyboard keys are issuing commands, *vi* is said to be in *command mode*. You must be in a special *insert mode* before you can type actual text on the screen. In addition, there seem to be so many commands.

---

* Actually, these days, GNU *emacs* is pretty much the universal version of *emacs*; the only problem is it doesn't come standard with most commercial UNIX systems; you must retrieve and install it yourself.

3

Once you start learning, however, you realize that *vi* is well designed. You need only a few keystrokes to tell *vi* to do complex tasks. As you learn *vi*, you learn shortcuts that transfer more and more of the editing work to the computer—where it belongs.

vi (like any text editor) is not a "what you see is what you get" word processor. If you want to produce formatted documents, you must type in codes that are used by another formatting program to control the appearance of the printed copy. If you want to indent several paragraphs, for instance, you put a code where the indent begins and ends. Formatting codes allow you to experiment with or change the appearance of your printed files, and in many ways, give you much more control over the appearance of your documents than a word processor. UNIX supports the *troff* formatting package.* The TEX and LATEX formatters are popular, commonly available alternatives.

(*vi* does support some simple formatting mechanisms. For example, you can tell it to automatically wrap when you come to the end of a line, or to automatically indent new lines.)

As with any skill, the more editing you do, the easier the basics become, and the more you can accomplish. Once you are used to all the powers you have while editing with *vi*, you may never want to return to any "simpler" editor.

What are the components of editing? First, you want to *insert* text (a forgotten word or a missing sentence), and you want to *delete* text (a stray character or an entire paragraph). You also need to *change* letters and words (to correct misspellings or to reflect a change of mind about a term). You might want to *move* text from one place to another part of your file. And, on occasion, you want to *copy* text to duplicate it in another part of your file.

Unlike many word processors, *vi*'s command mode is the initial or "default" mode. Complex, interactive edits can be performed with only a few keystrokes. (And to insert raw text, you simply give any of the several "insert" commands and then type away.)

One or two characters are used for the basic commands. For example:

i   insert

cw   change word

Using letters as commands, you can edit a file with great speed. You don't have to memorize banks of function keys or stretch your fingers to reach awkward

---

* *troff* is for laser printers and typesetters. Its "twin brother" is *nroff*, for line printers and terminals. Both accept the same input language. Following common UNIX convention, we refer to both with the name *troff*.

combinations of keys. Most of the commands can be remembered by the letter that performs them, and nearly all commands follow similar patterns and are related to each other.

In general, *vi* commands:

- Are case-sensitive (uppercase and lowercase keystrokes mean different things; I is different from i).

- Are not shown (or "echoed") on the screen when you type them.

- Do not require a RETURN after the command.

There is also a group of commands that echo on the bottom line of the screen. Bottom-line commands are preceded by different symbols. The slash (/) and the question mark (?) begin search commands, and are discussed in Chapter 3, *Moving Around in a Hurry*. A colon (:) begins all *ex* commands. *ex* commands are those that are used by the *ex* line editor. The *ex* editor is available to you when you use *vi*, because *ex* is the underlying editor, and *vi* is really just its "visual" mode. *ex* commands and concepts are discussed fully in Chapter 5, *Introducing the ex Editor*, but this chapter introduces you to the *ex* commands to quit a file without saving edits.

Opening and Closing Files

You can use *vi* to edit any text file. *vi* copies the file to be edited into a *buffer* (an area temporarily set aside in memory), displays the buffer (though you can see only one screenful at a time), and lets you add, delete, and change text. When you save your edits, *vi* copies the edited buffer back into a permanent file, replacing the old file of the same name. Remember that you are always working on a *copy* of your file in the buffer, and that your edits will not affect your original file until you save the buffer. Saving your edits is also called "writing the buffer," or more commonly, "writing your file."

Opening a File

 vi is the UNIX command that invokes the *vi* editor for an existing file or for a brand new file. The syntax for the vi command is:

```
$ vi [filename]
```

The brackets shown on the above command line indicate that the filename is optional. The brackets should not be typed. The $ is the UNIX prompt. If the filename is omitted, *vi* will open an unnamed buffer. You can assign the name when you write the buffer into a file. For right now, though, let's stick to naming the file on the command line.

A filename must be unique inside its directory. On older System V UNIX systems, it cannot exceed 14 characters in length (most common UNIX systems allow much longer names). A filename can include any 8-bit character except a slash (/), which is reserved as the separator between files and directories in a pathname, and ASCII NUL, the character with all zero bits. You can even include spaces in a filename by typing a backslash (\) before the space. In practice, though, filenames generally consist of any combination of uppercase and lowercase letters, numbers, and the characters dot (.) and underscore (_). Remember that UNIX is case-sensitive: lowercase letters are distinct from uppercase letters. Also remember that you must press RETURN to tell UNIX that you are finished issuing your command.

When you want to open a new file in a directory, give a new filename with the vi command. For example, if you want to open a new file called *practice* in the current directory, you would enter:

```
$ vi practice
```

Since this is a new file, the buffer is empty and the screen appears as follows:

```
~
~
~
"practice" [New file].
```

The tildes (~) down the left-hand column of the screen indicate that there is no text in the file, not even blank lines. The prompt line (also called the status line) at the bottom of the screen echoes the name and status of the file.

You can also edit any existing text file in a directory by specifying its filename. Suppose that there is a UNIX file with the pathname */home/john/letter*. If you are already in the */home/john* directory, use the relative pathname. For example:

```
$ vi letter
```

brings a copy of the file *letter* to the screen.

If you are in another directory, give the full pathname to begin editing:

```
$ vi /home/john/letter
```

Problems Opening Files

✓ *When you invoke* vi, *the message* [open mode] *appears.*

Your terminal type is probably incorrectly identified. Quit the editing session immediately by typing :q. Check the environment variable $TERM. It should be set to the name of your terminal. Or ask your system administrator to provide an adequate terminal type setting.

✓   *You see one of the following messages:*

```
Visual needs addressable cursor or upline capability
Bad termcap entry
Termcap entry too long
terminal:  Unknown terminal type
Block device required
Not a typewriter
```

Your terminal type is either undefined, or there's probably something wrong with your *terminfo* or *termcap* entry. Enter :q to quit. Check your $TERM environment variable, or ask your system administrator to select a terminal type for your environment.

✓   *A* [new file] *message appears when you think a file already exists.*

You are probably in the wrong directory. Enter :q to quit. Then check to see that you are in the correct directory for that file (enter pwd at the UNIX prompt). If you are in the right directory, check the list of files in the directory (with ls) to see whether the file exists under a slightly different name.

✓   *You invoke* vi, *but you get a colon prompt (indicating that you're in* ex *line-editing mode).*

You probably typed an interrupt before *vi* could draw the screen. Enter *vi* by typing vi at the *ex* prompt (:).

✓   *One of the following messages appears:*

```
[Read only]
File is read only
Permission denied
```

"Read only" means that you can only look at the file; you cannot save any changes you make. You may have invoked *vi* in *view mode* (with view or vi -R), or you do not have write permission for the file. See the section "Problems Saving Files" below.

✓   *One of the following messages appears:*

```
Bad file number
Block special file
Character special file
Directory
Executable
Non-ascii file
file non-ASCII
```

The file you've called up to edit is not a regular text file. Type :q! to quit, then check the file you wish to edit, perhaps with the file command.

✓   *When you type* `:q` *because of one of the above difficulties, the message appears:*

> ```
> No write since last change (:quit! overrides).
> ```

You have modified the file without realizing it. Type `:q!` to leave *vi*. Your changes from this session will not be saved in the file.

Modus Operandi

As mentioned earlier, the concept of the current "mode" is fundamental to the way *vi* works. There are two modes, *command mode* and *insert mode*. You start out in command mode, where every keystroke represents a command. In insert mode, everything you type becomes text in your file.

Sometimes, you can accidentally enter insert mode, or conversely, leave insert mode accidentally. In either case, what you type will likely affect your files in ways you did not intend.

Press the ESC key to force *vi* to enter command mode. If you are already in command mode, *vi* will beep at you when you press the ESC key. (Command mode is thus sometimes referred to as "beep mode.")

Once you are safely in command mode, you can proceed to repair any accidental changes, and then continue editing your text.

Saving and Quitting a File

You can quit working on a file at any time, save your edits and return to the UNIX prompt. The `vi` command to quit and save edits is `ZZ`. Note that `ZZ` is capitalized.

Let's assume that you do create a file called *practice* to practice *vi* commands, and that you type in six lines of text. To save the file, first check that you are in command mode by pressing ESC and then enter `ZZ`.

Keystrokes   **Results**
`ZZ`

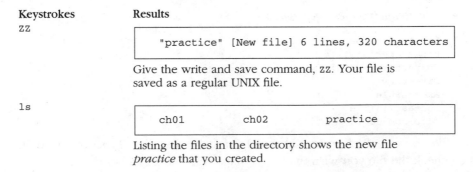

> ```
> "practice" [New file] 6 lines, 320 characters
> ```

Give the write and save command, `zz`. Your file is
saved as a regular UNIX file.

`ls`

> ```
> ch01          ch02          practice
> ```

Listing the files in the directory shows the new file
practice that you created.

You can also save your edits with *ex* commands. Type `:w` to save your file but not quit *vi*; type `:q` to quit if you haven't made any edits; and type `:wq` to both save your edits and quit. (:wq is equivalent to ZZ.) We'll explain fully how to use commands in Chapter 5, *Introducing the ex Editor*; for now, you should just memorize a few commands for writing and saving files.

Quitting Without Saving Edits

When you are first learning *vi*, especially if you are an intrepid experimenter, there are two other *ex* commands that are handy for getting out of any mess that you might create.

What if you want to wipe out all of the edits you have made in a session and then return to the original file? The command:

:e! RETURN

returns you to the last saved version of the file, so you can start over.

Suppose, however, that you want to wipe out your edits and then just quit *vi*? The command:

:q! RETURN

quits the file you're editing and returns you to the UNIX prompt. With both of these commands, you lose all edits made in the buffer since the last time you saved the file. *vi* normally won't let you throw away your edits. The exclamation point added to the :e or :q command causes *vi* to override this prohibition, performing the operation even though the buffer has been modified.

Problems Saving Files

✓ *You try to write your file, but you get one of the following messages:*

```
File exists
File file exists - use w!
[Existing file]
File is read only
```

Type :w! *file* to overwrite the existing file, or type :w *newfile* to save the edited version in a new file.

✓ *You want to write a file, but you don't have write permission for it. You get the message "Permission denied."*

Use :w *newfile* to write out the buffer into a new file. If you have write permission for the directory, you can use mv to replace the original version with your copy of it. If you don't have write permission for the directory, type :w *pathname/file* to write out the buffer to a directory in which you do have write permission (such as your home directory, or */tmp*).

✓   *You try to write your file, but you get a message telling you that the file system is*
    full.

Type `:!rm junkfile` to delete a (large) unneeded file and free some space.
(Starting an *ex* command with an exclamation point gives you access to
UNIX.)

Or type `:!df` to see whether there's any space on another file system. If
there is, choose a directory on that file system and write your file to it with `:w`
`pathname`. (`df` is the UNIX command to check a *d*isk's *f*ree space.)

✓   *The system puts you into open mode and tells you that the file system is full.*

The disk with *vi's* temporary files is filled up. Type `:!ls /tmp` to see
whether there are any files you can remove to gain some disk space.* If there
are, create a temporary UNIX shell from which you can remove files or issue
other UNIX commands. You can create a shell by typing `:sh`; type
CTRL-D or `exit` to terminate the shell and return to *vi*. (On most UNIX systems, when using a job-control shell, you can simply type CTRL-Z to suspend
vi and return to the UNIX prompt; type `fg` to return to *vi*.) Once you've freed
up some space, write your file with `:w!`.

✓   *You try to write your file, but you get a message telling you that your disk quota*
    has been reached.

Try to force the system to save your buffer with the *ex* command `:pre` (short
for `:preserve`). If that doesn't work, look for some files to remove. Use
`:sh` (or CTRL-Z if you are using a job-control system) to move out of *vi* and
remove files. Use CTRL-D (or `fg`) to return to *vi* when you're done. Then
write your file with `:w!`.

Exercises

The only way to learn *vi* is to practice. You now know enough to create a new file
and to return to the UNIX prompt. Create a file called *practice*, insert some text,
and then save and quit the file.

Open a file called *practice* in the current directory: `vi practice`
Insert text: `i any text you like`
Return to command mode: ESC
Quit *vi*, saving edits: `ZZ`

---

* Your *vi* may keep its temporary files in */usr/tmp*, */var/tmp*, or your current directory; you may need
to poke around a bit to figure out where exactly you've run out of room.

2

Simple Editing

This chapter introduces you to editing with *vi*, and it is set up to be read as a tutorial. In it you will learn how to move the cursor and how to make some simple edits. If you've never worked with *vi*, you should read the entire chapter.

Later chapters show you how to expand your skills to perform faster and more powerful edits. One of the biggest advantages for an adept user of *vi* is that there are so many options to choose from. (One of the biggest *disadvantages* for a newcomer to *vi* is that there are so many different editor commands.)

You can't learn *vi* by memorizing every single *vi* command. Start out by learning the basic commands introduced in this chapter. Note the patterns of use that the commands have in common.

As you learn *vi*, be on the lookout for more tasks that you can delegate to the editor, and then find the command that accomplishes it. In later chapters you will learn more advanced features of *vi*, but before you can handle the advanced, you must master the simple.

This chapter covers:

- Moving the cursor

- Adding and changing text

- Deleting, moving, and copying text

- More ways to enter insert mode

vi Commands

vi has two modes: command mode and insert mode. As soon as you enter a file, you are in command mode, and the editor is waiting for you to enter a command. Commands enable you to move anywhere in the file, to perform edits, or to enter insert mode to add new text. Commands can also be given to exit the file (saving or ignoring your edits) in order to return to the UNIX prompt.

You can think of the different modes as representing two different keyboards. In insert mode, your keyboard functions like a typewriter. In command mode, each key has a new meaning or initiates some instruction.

There are several ways to tell *vi* that you want to begin insert mode. One of the most common is to press i. The i doesn't appear on the screen, but after you press it, whatever you type *will* appear on the screen and will be entered into the buffer. The cursor marks the current insertion point. To tell *vi* that you want to stop inserting text, press ESC . Pressing ESC moves the cursor back one space (so that it is on the last character you typed) and returns *vi* to command mode.

For example, suppose you have opened a new file and want to insert the word "introduction". If you type the keystrokes iintroduction, what appears on the screen is:

    introduction

When you open a new file, *vi* starts in command mode and interprets the first key-stroke (i) as the insert command. All keystrokes made after the insert command are considered text until you press ESC . If you need to correct a mistake while in insert mode, backspace and type over the error. Depending on the type of termi-nal you are using, backspacing may erase what you've previously typed or may just back up over it. In either case, whatever you back up over will be deleted. Note that you can't use the backspace key to back up beyond the point where you entered insert mode.

vi has an option that lets you define a right margin and provides a carriage return automatically when you reach it. For right now, while you are inserting text, press RETURN to break the lines.

Sometimes you don't know whether you are in insert mode or command mode. Whenever *vi* does not respond as you expect, press ESC once or twice to check which mode you are in. When you hear the beep, you are in command mode.

Moving the Cursor

You may spend only a small amount of time in an editing session adding new text in insert mode; much of the time you will be making edits to existing text.

In command mode you can position the cursor anywhere in the file. Since you begin all basic edits (changing, deleting, and copying text) by placing the cursor at the text that you want to change, you want to be able to move the cursor to that place as quickly as possible.

There are *vi* commands to move the cursor:

- Up, down, left, or right—one *character* at a time

- Forward or backward by blocks of *text* such as words, sentences, or paragraphs

- Forward or backward through a file, one *screen* at a time

In Figure 2-1, an underscore marks the present cursor position. Circles show movement of the cursor from its current position to the position that would result from various *vi* commands.

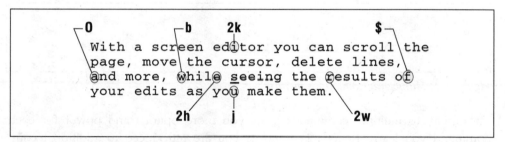

Figure 2-1: Sample movement commands

Single Movements

The keys h, j, k, and l, right under your fingertips, will move the cursor:

h   left, one space

j   down, one line

k   up, one line

l   right, one space

You can also use the cursor arrow keys (←, ↓, ↑, →), + and – to go up and down, or the RETURN and BACKSPACE keys, but they are out of the way, and the arrow keys are not supported by all terminals. At first, it may seem awkward to use letter keys instead of arrows for cursor movement. After a short while, though, you'll find it is one of the things you'll like best about *vi*—you can move around without ever taking your fingers off the center of the keyboard.

Before you move the cursor, press ESC to make sure that you are in command mode. Use h, j, k, and l to move forward or backward in the file from the current cursor position. When you have gone as far as possible in one direction, you hear a beep and the cursor stops. For example, once you're at the beginning or end of a line, you cannot use h or l to wrap around to the previous or next line; you have to use j or k.* Similarly, you cannot move the cursor past a tilde (˜) representing a line without text, nor can you move the cursor above the first line of text.

Numeric Arguments

You can precede movement commands with numbers. Figure 2-2 shows how the command 4l moves the cursor four spaces to the right, just as if you had typed l four times (llll).

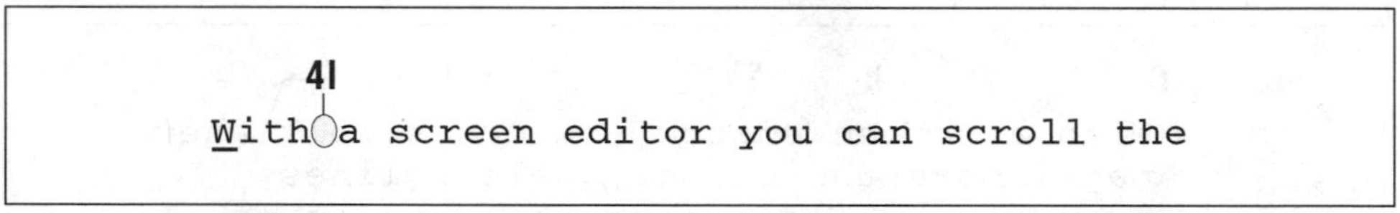

```
              4l
     With◯a screen editor you can scroll the
```

Figure 2-2: Multiplying commands by numbers

The ability to multiply commands gives you more options and power for each command you learn. Keep it in mind as you are introduced to additional commands.

Movement Within a Line

When you saved the file *practice*, *vi* displayed a message telling you how many lines are in that file. A *line* is not necessarily the same length as the visible line (often limited to 80 characters) that appears on the screen. A line is any text entered between newlines. (A *newline* character is inserted into the file when you press the RETURN key in insert mode.) If you type 200 characters before pressing RETURN , *vi* regards all 200 characters as a single line (even though those 200 characters visibly take up several lines on the screen).

---

* *vim* version 4.x, and *vim* version 5.x with nocompatible set, allow you to "space past" the end of the line to the next one with l or the spacebar.

As we mentioned, *vi* has an option that allows you to set a distance from the right margin at which *vi* will automatically insert a newline character. This option is `wrapmargin` (its abbreviation is `wm`). You can set a wrapmargin at 10 characters:

```
:set wm=10
```

This command doesn't affect lines that you've already typed. We'll talk more about setting options in Chapter 7, *Advanced Editing*. (This one really couldn't wait!)

If you do not use *vi*'s automatic `wrapmargin` option, you should break lines with carriage returns to keep the lines of manageable length.

0 Two useful commands that involve movement within a line are:

0   Move to beginning of line.

$ Move to end of line.

In the example below, line numbers are displayed. (Line numbers can be displayed in *vi* by using the `number` option, which is enabled by typing `:set nu` in command mode. This operation is described in Chapter 7.)

```
1 With a screen editor you can scroll
  the page
2 move the cursor, delete lines, insert
  characters, and more, while seeing the
  results of your edits as you make them.
3 Screen editors are very popular.
```

$ The number of logical lines (3) does not correspond to the number of visible lines (6) that you see on the screen. If the cursor were positioned on the *d* in the word *delete*, and you entered $, the cursor would move to the period following the word *them*. If you entered 0, the cursor would move back to the letter *m* in the word *move*, at the beginning of line two.

Movement by Text Blocks

w You can also move the cursor by blocks of text: words, sentences, paragraphs, etc. The w command moves the cursor forward one word at a time, counting symbols and punctuation as equivalent to words. The line below shows cursor movement by w:

```
cursor, delete lines, insert characters,
```

You can also move by word, not counting symbols and punctuation, using the W command. (You can think of this as a "large" or "capital" *W*ord.)

Cursor movement using W looks like this:

    cursor, delete lines, insert characters,

To move backward by word, use the b command. Capital B allows you to move backward by word, not counting punctuation.

As mentioned previously, movement commands take numeric arguments; so, with either the w or b commands you can multiply the movement with numbers. 2w moves forward two words; 5B moves back five words, not counting punctuation.

We'll discuss movement by sentences and by paragraphs in Chapter 3, *Moving Around in a Hurry*. For now, practice using the cursor movement commands that you know, combining them with numeric multipliers.

Simple Edits

When you enter text in your file, it is rarely perfect. You find typos or want to improve on a phrase; sometimes your program has a bug. Once you enter text, you have to be able to change it, delete it, move it, or copy it. Figure 2-3 shows the kinds of edits you might want to make to a file. The edits are indicated by proofreading marks.

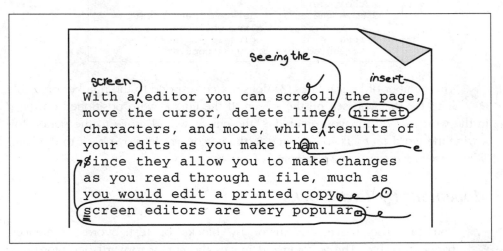

Figure 2-3: Proofreading edits

In *vi* you can perform any of these edits with a few basic keystrokes: i for insert (which you've already seen); a for append; c for change; and d for delete. To move or copy text, you use a pair of commands. You move text with a d for delete, then a p for put; you copy text with a y for "yank," then a p for put. Each type of edit is described in this section. Figure 2-4 shows the *vi* commands you use to make the edits marked in Figure 2-3.

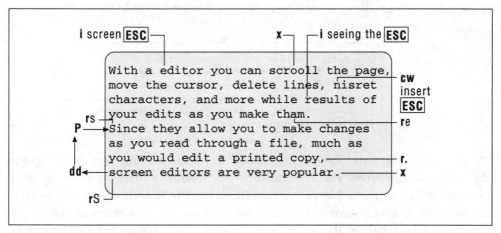

Figure 2-4: Edits with vi commands

Inserting New Text

You have already seen the insert command used to enter text into a new file. You also use the insert command while editing existing text to add missing characters, words, and sentences. In the file *practice*, suppose you have the sentence:

```
you can scroll
the page, move the cursor, delete
lines, and insert characters.
```

with the cursor positioned as shown. To insert *With a screen editor* at the beginning of the sentence, enter the following:

Keystrokes

2k

Results

```
you can scroll
the page, move the cursor, delete
lines, and insert characters.
```

Move the cursor up two lines with the k command, to the line where you want to make the insertion.

```
iWith a
```

```
With a_you can scroll
the page, move the cursor, delete
lines, and insert characters.
```

Press i to enter insert mode and begin inserting text.

```
screen editor
ESC
```

```
With a screen editor_you can scroll
the page, move the cursor, delete
lines, and insert characters.
```

Finish inserting text, and press ESC to end the insert
and return to command mode.

On the screen shown in the example above, *vi* pushes existing text to the right as
the new text is inserted. That is because we are assuming that you are using *vi* on
an "intelligent" terminal that can rewrite the screen with each character you type.
An insert on a "dumb" terminal (such as an *adm3a*) will look different. The terminal itself cannot handle the overhead of updating the screen for each character
typed (without a tremendous sacrifice of speed), so *vi* doesn't rewrite the screen
until after you press ESC . On a dumb terminal, the same insert would appear:

Keystrokes   **Result**
```
iWith a
```

```
With an scroll
the page, move the cursor, delete
lines, and insert characters.
```

Press i to enter insert mode and begin inserting text.
The dumb terminal appears to overwrite the existing
text on the line.

```
screen editor
```

```
With a screen editor_
the page, move the cursor, delete
lines, and insert characters.
```

The insertion appears to have overwritten existing text.

```
ESC
```

```
With a screen editor_you can scroll
the page, move the cursor, delete
lines, and insert characters.
```

After you have finished inserting text, press ESC to
end the insert and return to command mode. *vi* now
rewrites the line, so that you see all existing text.

Appending Text

a You can append text at any place in your file with the append command **a**. **a** works in almost the same way as **i**, except that text is inserted *after* the cursor rather than *before* the cursor. You may have noticed that when you press **i** to enter insert mode, the cursor doesn't move until after you enter some text. On the other hand, when you press **a** to enter insert mode, the cursor moves one space to the right. When you enter text, it appears *after* the original cursor position.

Changing Text

c You can replace any text in your file with the change command, **c**. In order to tell **c** how much text to change, you combine **c** with a movement command. In this way, a movement command serves as a *text object* for the **c** command to affect. For example, **c** can be used to change text from the cursor:

cw to the end of a word.

c2b
   back two words

c$ to the end of line

c0 to the beginning of line.

After issuing a change command, you can replace the identified text with any amount of new text, with no characters at all, with one word, or with hundreds of lines. **c**, like **i** and **a**, leaves you in insert mode until you press the ESC key.

When the change only affects the current line, *vi* marks the end of the text that will be changed with a $, so that you can see what part of the line is affected. (See the example for **cw**, below.)

Words

c **w** To change a word, combine the **c** (change) command with **w** for word. You can replace a word (**cw**) with a longer or shorter word (or any amount of text). **cw** can be thought of as "delete the word marked and insert new text until ESC is pressed."

Suppose you have the following line in your file *practice*:

```
With an editor you can scroll the page,
```

and want to change *an* to *a screen*. You need to change only one word:

Keystrokes   **Results**

w

> With a̲n editor you can scroll the page,

Move with w to the place you want the edit to begin.

cw

> With a̲$ editor you can scroll the page,

Give the change word command. The end of the text
to be changed will be marked with a $ (dollar sign).

a screen

> With a scree̲n editor you can scroll the page,

Type in the replacement text, and then press ESC to
return to command mode.

cw also works on a portion of a word. For example, to change *spelling* to *spelled*,
you can position the cursor on the *i*, type cw, then type *ed*, and finish with ESC .

Lines

To replace the entire current line, there is the special change command,
cc. cc changes an entire line, replacing that line with any amount of
text entered before pressing ESC . It doesn't matter where the cursor is located on
the line; cc replaces the entire line of text.

A command like cw works differently from a command like cc. In using cw, the
old text remains until you type over it, and any old text that is left over (up to the
$) goes away when you press ESC . In using cc, though, the old text is wiped
out first, leaving you a blank line on which to insert text.

The "type over" approach happens with any change command that affects less
than a whole line, whereas the "blank line" approach happens with any change
command that affects one or more lines.

C replaces characters from the current cursor position to the end of the line.
It has the same effect as combining c with the special end-of-line indicator $
(c$).

General Form of vi Commands

In the change commands we've mentioned up to this point, you may have noticed the following pattern:

> (*command*)(*text object*)

command is the change command c, and *text object* is a movement command (you don't type the parentheses). But c is not the only command that requires a text object. The d command (delete) and the y command (yank) follow this pattern as well.

Remember also that movement commands take numeric arguments, so numbers can be added to the text objects of c, d, and y commands. For example, d2w and 2dw are commands to delete two words. With this in mind, you can see that most *vi* commands follow a general pattern:

> (*command*)(*number*)(*text object*)

or the equivalent form:

> (*number*)(*command*)(*text object*)

Here's how this works. *number* and *command* are optional. Without them, you simply have a movement command. If you add a *number*, you have a multiple movement. On the other hand, combine a *command* (c, d, or y) with a *text object* to get an editing command.

When you realize how many combinations are possible in this way, *vi* becomes a powerful editor indeed!

The commands cc and C are really shortcuts for other commands, so they don't follow the general form of *vi* commands. You'll see other shortcuts when we discuss the delete and yank commands.

Characters

One other replacement edit is given by the r command. r replaces a single character with another single character. You do *not* have to press ESC to return to command mode after making the edit. There is a misspelling in the line below:

```
Pith a screen editor you can scroll the page,
```

Only one letter needs to be corrected. You don't want to use cw in this instance because you would have to retype the entire word. Use r to replace a single character at the cursor:

Keystrokes   **Results**
rW

> <u>W</u>ith a screen editor you can scroll the page,

Give the replace command r, followed by the replacement character *W.*

Substituting text

s Suppose you want to change just a few characters, and not a whole word. The substitute command (s), by itself, replaces a single character. With a preceding count, you can replace that many characters. As with the change command (c), the last character of the text will be marked with a $ so that you can see how much text will be changed.

S The S command, as is usually the case with uppercase commands, lets you change whole lines. In contrast to the C command, which changes the rest of the line from the current cursor position, the S command deletes the entire line, no matter where the cursor is. *vi* puts you in insert mode at the beginning of the line. A preceding count replaces that many lines.

Both s and S put you in insert mode; when you are finished entering new text, press ESC .

R The R command, like its lowercase counterpart, replaces text. The difference is that it simply enters overstrike mode. The characters you type replace what's on the screen, character by character, until you type ESC . You can only overstrike a maximum of one line; as you type RETURN , *vi* will open a new line, effectively putting you into insert mode.

Changing Case

~ Changing the case of a letter is a special form of replacement. The tilde (~) command will change a lowercase letter to uppercase, or an uppercase letter to lowercase. Position the cursor on the letter whose case you want to change, and type a ~. The case of the letter will change, and the cursor will move to the next character.

In older versions of *vi,* you cannot specify a numeric prefix or text object for the ~ to affect. Modern versions do allow a numeric prefix.

If you want to change the case of more than one line at a time, you must filter the text through a UNIX command like `tr`, as described in Chapter 7.

Deleting Text

 You can also delete any text in your file with the delete command `d`. Like the change command, the delete command requires a text object (the amount of text to be operated on). You can delete by word (`dw`), by line (`dd` and `D`), or by other movement commands that you will learn later.

With all deletions, you move to where you want the edit to take place, then give the delete command (`d`) and the text object, such as `w` for word.

Words

  Suppose you have the following text in the file:

```
Screen editors are are very popular,
since they allowed you to make
changes as you read through a file.
```

with the cursor positioned as shown. You want to delete one *are* in the first line.

Keystrokes   **Results**
2w

```
Screen editors are are very popular,
since they allowed you to make
changes as you read through a file.
```

Move the cursor to where you want the edit to begin
(*are*).

dw

```
Screen editors are very popular,
since they allowed you to make
changes as you read through a file.
```

Give the delete word command (`dw`) to delete the
word *are*.

`dw` deletes a word beginning where the cursor is positioned. Notice that the space following the word is deleted.

dw can also be used to delete a portion of a word. In this example:

```
since they allowed you to make
```

you want to delete the *ed* from the end of *allowed*.

Keystrokes   **Results**
dw

```
since they allowyou to make
```

Give the delete word command (dw) to delete the
word, beginning with the position of the cursor.

dw always deletes the space before the next word on a line, but we don't want to
do that in the previous example. To retain the space between words, use **de**,
which will delete only to the end of a word. Typing **dE** will delete to the end of a
word, including punctuation.

You can also delete backward (**db**) or to the end or beginning of a line (**d$** or
d0).

Lines

The **dd** command deletes the entire line that the cursor is on. **dd** will
not delete part of a line. Like its complement **cc**, **dd** is a special command. Using the same text as in the previous example, with the cursor positioned
on the first line as shown below:

```
Screen editors are very popular,
since they allow you to make
changes as you read through a file.
```

you can delete the first two lines:

Keystrokes   **Results**
2dd

```
changes as you read through a file.
```

Give the command to delete two lines (2dd). Note that
even though the cursor was not positioned on the
beginning of the line, the entire line is deleted.

If you are using a "dumb" terminal* (or a very slow one), line deletions look different. The dumb terminal will not redraw the screen until you scroll past the bottom of the screen. On a dumb terminal the deletion looks like this:

Keystrokes   **Results**
2dd

```
@
@
changes as you read through a file.
```

Give the command to delete two lines (2dd). An @
symbol "holds the place" of the deleted line, until *vi*
redraws the entire screen.

D The D command deletes from the cursor position to the end of the line. (D is a shortcut for d$.) For example, with the cursor positioned as shown:

```
Screen editors are very popular,
since they allow you to make
changes as you read through a file.
```

you can delete the portion of the line to the right of the cursor.

Keystrokes   **Results**
D

```
Screen editors are very popular,
since they allow you to make
changes_
```

Give the command to delete the portion of the line to
the right of the cursor (D).

Characters

x Often you want to delete only one or two characters. Just as r is a special change command to replace a single character, x is a special delete command to delete a single character. x deletes only the character the cursor is on. In the line below:

```
zYou can move text by deleting text and then
```

---

* Dumb terminals are rather rare these days. Most of the time, you will run *vi* inside a terminal emulator on a bitmapped screen.

you can delete the letter *z* by pressing x.* A capital X deletes the character before the cursor. Prefix either of these commands with a number to delete that number of characters. For example, 5x will delete the five characters under and to the right of the cursor.

Problems with deletions

✓ *You've deleted the wrong text and you want to get it back.*

There are several ways to recover deleted text. If you've just deleted something and you realize you want it back, simply type u to undo the last command (for example, a dd). This works only if you haven't given any further commands, since u only undoes the most recent command. On the other hand, a U will restore the line to its pristine state; the way it was before *any* changes were applied to it.

You can still recover a recent deletion, however, by using the p command, since *vi* saves the last nine deletions in nine numbered deletion buffers. If you know, for example, that the third deletion back is the one you want to restore, type:

    "3p

to "put" the contents of buffer number 3 on the line below the cursor.

This works only for a deleted *line*. Words, or a portion of a line, are not saved in a buffer. If you want to restore a deleted word or line fragment, and u won't work, use the p command by itself. This restores whatever you've last deleted. The next few subsections will talk more about the commands u and p.

Moving Text

In *vi*, you move text by deleting it and then placing that deleted text elsewhere in the file, like a "cut and paste." Each time you delete a text block, that deletion is temporarily saved in a special buffer. Move to another position in your file and use the put command (p) to place that text in the new position. You can move any block of text, although moving is more useful with lines than with words.

p The put command (p) puts the text that is in the buffer *after* the cursor position. The uppercase version of the command, P, puts the text *before* the cursor. If you delete one or more lines, p puts the deleted text on a new line(s) below the cursor. If you delete less than an entire line, p puts the deleted text on the current line, after the cursor.

---

* The mnemonic for x is that it is supposedly like "x-ing out" mistakes with a typewriter. Of course, who uses a typewriter any more?

Suppose in your file *practice* you have the text:

```
You can move text by deleting it and then,
like a "cut and paste",
placing the deleted text elsewhere in
the file.
each time you delete a text block.
```

and want to move the second line, *like a "cut and paste",* below the third line. Using delete, you can make this edit.

Keystrokes   Results
dd

```
You can move text by deleting it and then,
placing the deleted text elsewhere in
the file.
each time you delete a text block.
```

With the cursor on the second line, delete that line. The text is placed in a buffer (reserved memory).

p

```
You can move text by deleting it and then,
placing that deleted text elsewhere in
the file.
like a "cut and paste",
each time you delete a text block.
```

Give the put command, p, to restore the deleted line at the next line below the cursor. To finish reordering this sentence, you would also have to change the capitalization and punctuation (with r) to match the new structure.

 Once you delete text, you must restore it before the next change command or delete command. If you make another edit that affects the buffer, your deleted text will be lost. You can repeat the put over and over, so long as you don't make a new edit. In Chapter 4, *Beyond the Basics*, you will learn how to save text you delete in a named buffer so you can retrieve it later.

Transposing two letters

You can use xp (delete character and put after cursor) to transpose two letters. For example, in the word *mvoe*, the letters *vo* are transposed (reversed). To correct a transposition, place the cursor on *v* and press x, then p. By coincidence, the word *transpose* helps you remember the sequence xp; x stands for *trans*, and p stands for *pose*.

There is no command to transpose words. The section "More Examples of Mapping Keys" in Chapter 7 discusses a short sequence of commands that transposes two words.

Copying Text

y Often you can save editing time (and keystrokes) by copying a part of your file to use in other places. With the two commands y (for yank) and p (for put), you can copy any amount of text and put that copied text in another place in the file. A yank command copies the selected text into a special buffer, where it is held until another yank (or deletion) occurs. You can then place this copy elsewhere in the file with the put command.

As with change and delete, the yank command can be combined with any movement command (yw, y$, 4yy). Yank is most frequently used with a line (or more) of text, because to yank and put a word usually takes longer than simply to insert the word.

The shortcut yy operates on an entire line, just as dd and cc do. But the shortcut Y, for some reason, does not operate the way D and C do. Instead of yanking from the current position to the end of the line, Y yanks the whole line. Y does the same thing as yy.

Suppose you have in your file *practice* the text:

```
With a screen editor you can
scroll the page.
move the cursor.
delete lines.
```

You want to make three complete sentences, beginning each with *With a screen editor you can*. Instead of moving through the file, making this edit over and over, you can use a yank and put to copy the text to be added.

Keystrokes   **Results**
yy

```
With a screen editor you can
scroll the page.
move the cursor.
delete lines.
```

Yank the line of text that you want to copy into the buffer. The cursor can be anywhere on the line you want to yank (or on the first line of a series of lines).

2j

```
With a screen editor you can
scroll the page.
move the cursor.
delete lines.
```

Move the cursor to where you want to put the yanked
text.

P

```
With a screen editor you can
scroll the page.
With a screen editor you can
move the cursor.
delete lines.
```

Put the yanked text above the cursor line with P.

jp

```
With a screen editor you can
scroll the page.
With a screen editor you can
move the cursor.
With a screen editor you can
delete lines.
```

Move the cursor down a line and put the yanked text
below the cursor line with p.

Yanking uses the same buffer as deleting. Each new deletion or yank replaces the
previous contents of the yank buffer. As we'll see in Chapter 4, up to nine previous yanks or deletions can be recalled with put commands. You can also yank or
delete directly into up to 26 named buffers, which allows you to juggle multiple
text blocks at once.

Repeating or Undoing Your Last Command

Each edit command that you give is stored in a temporary buffer until you give the
next command. For example, if you insert *the* after a word in your file, the command used to insert the text, along with the text that you entered, is temporarily
saved.

Repeat

Any time you make the same editing command over and over, you can save
time by duplicating it with the repeat command, the period (.). Position the
cursor where you want to repeat the editing command, and type a period.

Suppose you have the following lines in your file:

```
With a screen editor you can
scroll the page.
With a screen editor you can
move the cursor.
```

You can delete one line, and then, to delete another line, simply type a period.

Keystrokes   **Results**
dd

```
With a screen editor you can
scroll the page.
move the cursor.
```

Delete a line with the command dd.

```
With a screen editor you can
scroll the page.
```

Repeat the deletion.

Older versions of *vi* had problems repeating commands. For example, such versions may have difficulty repeating a long insertion when **wrapmargin** is set. If you have such a version, this bug will probably bite you sooner or later. There's not a lot you can do about it after the fact, but it helps to be forewarned. (Modern versions do not seem to have this problem.) There are two ways you can guard against a potential problem when repeating long insertions. You can write your file (:w) before repeating the insertion (returning to this copy if the insertion doesn't work correctly). You can also turn off **wrapmargin** like this:

```
:set wm=0
```

In the section "More Examples of Mapping Keys", we'll show you an easy way to use the wrapmargin solution. In some versions of *vi*, the command CTRL-@ repeats the most recent insertion. CTRL-@ is typed in *insert* mode and returns you to command mode.

Undo

As mentioned earlier, you can undo your last command if you make an error. Simply press u. The cursor need not be on the line where the original edit was made.

To continue the example above, showing deletion of lines in the file *practice*:

Keystrokes   **Results**
u

```
With a screen editor you can
scroll the page.
move the cursor.
-
```

u undoes the last command and restores the deleted line.

U, the uppercase version of u, undoes all edits on a single line, *as long as the cursor remains on that line*. Once you move off a line, you can no longer use U.

Note that you can undo your last undo with u, toggling between two versions of text. u will also undo U, and U will undo any changes to a line, including those made with u. (A tip: the fact that u can undo itself leads to a nifty way to get around in a file. If you ever want to get back to the site of your last edit, simply undo it. You will pop back to the appropriate line. When you undo the undo, you'll stay on that line.)

More Ways to Insert Text

You have inserted text before the cursor with the sequence:

    i*text to be inserted*ESC

You've also inserted text after the cursor with the **a** command. There are other insert commands for inserting text at different positions relative to the cursor:

A   Append text to end of current line.

I   Insert text at beginning of line.

o   Open blank line below cursor for text.

O   Open blank line above cursor for text.

s   Delete character at cursor and substitute text.

S   Delete line and substitute text.

R   Overstrike existing characters with new characters.

All of these commands place you in insert mode. After inserting text, remember to press ESC to escape back to command mode.

A (append) and I (insert) save you from having to move your cursor to the end or beginning of the line before invoking insert mode. (The A command saves one keystroke over $a. Although one keystroke might not seem like much of a saving, the more adept—and impatient—an editor you become, the more keystrokes you will want to omit.)

o and O (open) save you from having to insert a carriage return. You can type these commands from anywhere within the line.

s and S (substitute) allow you to delete a character or a whole line and replace the deletion with any amount of new text. s is the equivalent of the two-stroke command c SPACE and S is the same as cc. One of the best uses for s is to change one character to several characters.

R ("large" replace) is useful when you want to start changing text, but you don't know exactly how much. For example, instead of guessing whether to say 3cw or 4cw, just type R and then enter your replacement text.

Numeric Arguments for Insert Commands

Except for o and O, the above insert commands (plus i and a) take numeric prefixes. With numeric prefixes, you might use the commands i, I, a, and A to insert a row of underlines or alternating characters. For example, typing 50i* ESC inserts 50 asterisks, and typing 25a*- ESC appends 50 characters (25 pairs of asterisk and hyphen). It's better to repeat only a small string of characters.*

With a numeric prefix, r replaces that many characters with a repeated instance of a single character. For example, in C or C++ code, to change | | to &&, you would place the cursor on the first pipe character, and type 2r&.

You can use a numeric prefix with S to substitute several lines. It's quicker and more flexible, though, to use c with a movement command.

A good case for using the s command with a numeric prefix is when you want to change a few characters in the middle of a word. Typing r wouldn't be correct, but typing cw would change too much text. Using s with a numeric prefix is usually the same as typing R.

There are other combinations of commands that work naturally together. For example, ea is useful for appending new text to the end of a word. It helps to train yourself to recognize such frequent combinations so that they become automatic.

Joining Two Lines with J

Sometimes while editing a file you will end up with a series of short lines that are difficult to scan. When you want to merge two lines into one, position the cursor anywhere on the first line, and press J to join the two lines.

---

* Very old versions of *vi* have difficulty repeating the insertion of more than one line's worth of text.

Suppose your file *practice* reads:

```
With a
screen editor
you can
scroll the page, move the cursor
```

Keystrokes   **Results**

J

```
With a screen editor
you can
scroll the page, move the cursor
```

J joins the line the cursor is on with the line below.

```
With a screen editor you can
scroll the page, move the cursor
```

Repeat the last command (J) with the . to join the
next line with the current line.

Using a numeric argument with J joins that number of consecutive lines. In the
example above, you could have joined three lines by using the command 3J.

Problem Checklist

✓ *When you type commands, text jumps around on the screen and nothing works
the way it's supposed to.*

Make sure you're not typing the J command when you mean j.

You may have hit the CAPS key without noticing it. *vi* is case-sensitive. That
is, uppercase commands (I, A, J, etc.) are different from lowercase commands
(i, a, j), so all your commands are being interpreted not as lowercase but as
uppercase commands. Press the CAPS key again to return to lowercase,
press ESC to ensure that you are in command mode, then type either U to
restore the last line changed or u to undo the last command. You'll probably
also have to do some additional editing to fully restore the garbled part of
your file.

Review of Basic vi Commands

Table 2-1 presents a few of the commands you can perform by combining the
commands c, d, and y with various text objects. The last two rows show additional commands for editing. Table 2-2 and Table 2-3 list some other basic commands. Table 2-4 summarizes the rest of the commands described in this chapter.

Table 2-1: Edit Commands

Text Object	Change	Delete	Copy
1 word	cw	dw	yw
2 words, not counting punctuation	2cW or c2W	2dW or d2W	2yW or y2W
3 words back	3cb or c3b	3db or d3b	3yb or y3b
1 line	cc	dd	yy or Y
To end of line	c$ or C	d$ or D	y$
To beginning of line	c0	d0	y0
Single character	r	x or X	yl or yh
Five characters	5s	5x	5yl

Table 2-2: Movement

Movement	Commands
←,↓,↑, →	h, j, k, l
To first character of next line	+
To first character of previous line	–
To end of word	e or E
Forward by word	w or W
Backward by word	b or B
To end of line	$
To beginning of line	0

Table 2-3: Other Operations

Operations	Commands
Place text from buffer	P or p
Start *vi*, open file if specified	vi *file*
Save edits, quit file	ZZ
No saving of edits, quit file	:q!

Table 2-4: Text Creation and Manipulation Commands

Editing Action	Command
Insert text at current position	i
Insert text at beginning of line	I
Append text at current position	a
Append text at end of line	A
Open new line below cursor for new text	o

Table 2-4: Text Creation and Manipulation Commands (continued)

Editing Action	Command
Open new line above cursor for new text	O
Delete line and substitute text	s
Overstrike existing characters with new text	R
Join current and next line	J
Toggle case	~
Repeat last action	.
Undo last change	u
Restore line to original state	U

You can get by in *vi* using only the commands listed in these tables. However, in order to harness the real power of *vi* (and increase your own productivity), you will need more tools. The following chapters describe those tools.

3

Moving Around in a Hurry

You will not use *vi* just to create new files. You'll spend a lot of your time in *vi* editing existing files. You rarely want to simply open to the first line in the file and move through it line by line. You want to get to a specific place in a file and start work.

All edits begin by moving the cursor to where you want to begin the edit (or, with *ex* line editor commands, by identifying the line numbers to be edited). This chapter shows you how to think about movement in a variety of ways (by screens, by text, by patterns, or by line numbers). There are many ways to move in *vi*, since editing speed depends on getting to your destination with only a few keystrokes.

This chapter covers:

- Movement by screens
- Movement by text blocks
- Movement by searches for patterns
- Movement by line number

Movement by Screens

When you read a book, you think of "places" in the book by page: the page where you stopped reading or the page number in an index. You don't have this convenience when you're editing files. Some files take up only a few lines, and you can see the whole file at once. But many files have hundreds of lines.

You can think of a file as text on a long roll of paper. The screen is a window of (usually) 24 lines of text on that long roll.

In insert mode, as you fill up the screen with text, you will end up typing on the bottom line of the screen. When you reach the end and press RETURN , the top line rolls out of sight, and a blank line appears on the bottom of the screen for new text. This is called scrolling.

In command mode, you can move through a file to see any text in it by scrolling the screen ahead or back. And, since cursor movements can be multiplied by numeric prefixes, you can move quickly to anywhere in your file.

Scrolling the Screen

CTRL **F** There are *vi* commands to scroll forward and backward through the file by full and half screens:

^F   Scroll forward one screen.
^B   Scroll backward one screen.
^D   Scroll forward half screen (down).
^U   Scroll backward half screen (up).

(In the list of commands above, the ^ symbol represents the CTRL key. ^F means to hold down the CTRL key and press the f key simultaneously.)

There are also commands to scroll the screen up one line (^E) and down one line (^Y). However, these two commands do not send the cursor to the beginning of the line. The cursor remains at the same point in the line as when the command was issued.

Repositioning the Screen with z

z If you want to scroll the screen up or down, but you want the cursor to remain on the line where you left it, use the z command.

z RETURN   Move current line to top of screen and scroll.
z.   Move current line to center of screen and scroll.
z-   Move current line to bottom of screen and scroll.

With the z command, using a numeric prefix as a multiplier makes no sense. (After all, you would need to reposition the cursor to the top of the screen only once. Repeating the same z command wouldn't move anything.) Instead, z understands a numeric prefix as a line number that it will use in place of the current line. For example, z RETURN moves the current line to the top of the screen, but 200z RETURN moves line 200 to the top of the screen.

Redrawing the Screen

CTRL **L** Sometimes while you're editing, messages from your computer system will display on your screen. These messages don't become part of your editing buffer, but they do interfere with your work. When system messages appear on your screen, you need to redisplay, or redraw, the screen.

Whenever you scroll, you redraw part of (or all of) the screen, so you can always get rid of unwanted messages by scrolling them off the screen and then returning to your previous position. But you can also redraw the screen without scrolling, by typing CTRL-L .

Movement Within a Screen

H You can also keep your current screen, or view of the file, and move around within the screen using:

H   Move to home—top line on screen.

M   Move to middle line on screen.

L   Move to last line on screen.

nH Move to *n* lines below top line.

nL Move to *n* lines above last line.

H moves the cursor from anywhere on the screen to the first, or "home," line. M moves to the middle line, L to the last. To move to the line below the first line, use 2H.

Keystrokes   **Results**
L

```
With a screen editor you can
scroll the page, move the cursor,
delete lines, insert characters, and more,
while seeing the results of your
edits as you make them.
Screen editors are very popular,
since they allow you to make changes
as you read through a file.
```

Move to the last line of the screen with the L command.

2H

```
With a screen editor you can
scroll the page, move the cursor,
delete lines, insert characters, and more,
while seeing the results of your
edits as you make them.
Screen editors are very popular,
since they allow you to make changes
as you read through a file.
```

Move to the second line of the screen with the 2H command. (H alone moves to the top line of the screen.)

Movement by Line

 Within the current screen there are also commands to move by line. You've already seen j and k. You can also use:

RETURN   Move to first character of next line.
+   Move to first character of next line.
–   Move to first character of previous line.

The above three commands move down or up to the first *character* of the line, ignoring any spaces or tabs. j and k, by contrast, move the cursor down or up to the first position of a line, even if that position is blank (and assuming that the cursor started at the first position).

Movement on the current line

Don't forget that h and l move the cursor to the left and right and that 0 and $ move the cursor to the beginning or end of the line. You can also use:

^   Move to first non-blank character of current line.

n| Move to column *n* of current line.

As with the line movement commands above, ^ moves to the first *character* of the line, ignoring any spaces or tabs. 0, by contrast, moves to the first position of the line, even if that position is blank.

Movement by Text Blocks

 Another way that you can think of moving through a *vi* file is by text blocks—words, sentences, paragraphs, or sections.

You have already learned to move forward and backward by word (w, W, b or B). In addition, you can use these commands:

e   Move to end of word.

E   Move to end of word (includes punctuation as part of word).

(Move to beginning of current sentence.

)   Move to beginning of next sentence.

{   Move to beginning of current paragraph.

}   Move to beginning of next paragraph.

[[Move to beginning of current section.

]] Move to beginning of next section.

To find the end of a sentence, *vi* looks for one of the punctuation marks ? . !. *vi* locates the end of a sentence when the punctuation is followed by at least two spaces or when it appears as the last non-blank character on a line. If you have left only a single space following a period, or if the sentence ends with a quotation mark, *vi* won't recognize the sentence.

A paragraph is defined as text up to the next blank line, or up to one of the default paragraph macros (.IP, .PP, .LP, or .QP) from the *troff* MS macro package. Similarly, a section is defined as text up to the next default section macro (.NH, .SH, .H 1, .HU). The macros that are recognized as paragraph or section separators can be customized with the :set command, as described in Chapter 7, *Advanced Editing*.

Remember that you can combine numbers with movement. For example, 3) moves ahead three sentences. Also remember that you can edit using movement commands: d) deletes to the end of the current sentence, 2y} copies (yanks) two paragraphs ahead.

Movement by Searches

One of the most useful ways to move around in a large file quickly is by searching for text, or more properly, a *pattern* of characters. Sometimes a search can be performed to find a misspelled word or to find each occurrence of a variable in a program.

The search command is the special character / (slash). When you enter a slash, it appears on the bottom line of the screen; you then type in the *pattern* that you want to find: /*pattern*.

A pattern can be a whole word or any other sequence of characters (called a "character string"). For example, if you search for the characters *red*, you will match *red* as a whole word, but you'll also match occur*red*. If you include a space before or after *pattern*, the spaces will be treated as part of the word. As with all bottom-line commands, press $\boxed{\text{RETURN}}$ to finish. *vi*, like all other UNIX editors, has a special pattern-matching language that allows you to look for variable text patterns; for example, any word beginning with a capital letter, or the word *The* at the beginning of a line.

We'll talk about this more powerful pattern-matching syntax in Chapter 6, *Global Replacement*. For right now, think of *pattern* simply as a word or phrase.

vi begins the search at the cursor and searches forward, wrapping around to the start of the file if necessary. The cursor will move to the first occurrence of the pattern. If there is no match, the message "Pattern not found" will be shown on the status line.*

Using the file *practice*, here's how to move the cursor by searches:

Keystrokes   **Results**

`/edits`

> With a screen editor you can scroll the
> page, move the cursor, delete lines, insert
> characters, and more, while seeing the
> results of your <u>e</u>dits as you make them.

Search for the pattern *edits*. Press $\boxed{\text{RETURN}}$ to enter.
The cursor moves directly to that pattern.

`/scr`

> With a <u>s</u>creen editor you can scroll the
> page, move the cursor, delete lines, insert
> characters, and more, while seeing the
> results of your edits as you make them.

Search for the pattern *scr.* Press $\boxed{\text{RETURN}}$ to enter.
Note that there is no space after *scr.*

The search wraps around to the front of the file. Note that you can give any combination of characters; a search does not have to be for a complete word.

To search backward, type a ? instead of a /:

     `?pattern`

---

* The exact messages will vary with different *vi* clones, but their meanings will be the same. In general, we won't bother noting everywhere that the text of a message may be different; in all cases the information conveyed will be the same.

In both cases, the search wraps around to the beginning or end of the file, if necessary.

Repeating Searches

n The last pattern that you searched for stays available throughout your editing session. After a search, instead of repeating your original keystrokes, you can use a command to search again for the last pattern.

n	Repeat search in same direction.
N	Repeat search in opposite direction.
/ RETURN	Repeat search forward.
? RETURN	Repeat search backward.

Since the last pattern stays available, you can search for a pattern, do some work, and then search again for the same pattern without retyping it by using n, N, / or ?. The direction of your search (/ is forward, ? is backward) is displayed at the bottom left of the screen.*

To continue with the example above, since the pattern *scr* is still available for search, you can:

Keystrokes   **Results**
n

```
    With a screen editor you can scroll the
    page, move the cursor, delete lines, insert
    characters, and more, while seeing the
    results of your edits as you make them.
```

Move to the next instance of the pattern *scr* (from *scr*een to *scr*oll) with the n (next) command.

?you

```
    With a screen editor you can scroll the
    page, move the cursor, delete lines, insert
    characters, and more, while seeing the
    results of your edits as you make them.
```

Search backward with ? from the cursor to the first occurrence of *you*. You need to press RETURN after typing the pattern.

---

* *nvi* 1.79 does not show the direction for the n and N commands. *vim* 5.x puts the search text into the command line too.

N

```
With a screen editor you can scroll the
page, move the cursor, delete lines, insert
characters, and more, while seeing the
results of your edits as you make them.
```

Repeat previous search for *you* but in the opposite
direction (forward).

Sometimes you want to find a word only if it is further ahead; you don't want the
search to wrap around earlier in the file. *vi* has an option, **wrapscan**, that controls whether searches wrap. You can disable wrapping like this:

```
:set nowrapscan
```

When **nowrapscan** is set and a forward search fails, the status line displays the
message:

```
Address search hit BOTTOM without matching pattern
```

When **nowrapscan** is set and a backward search fails, the message displays
"TOP" instead of "BOTTOM".

This section has given only the barest introduction to searching for patterns. Chapter 6 will teach you more about pattern matching and its use in making global
changes to a file.

Changing through searching

You can combine the / and ? search operators with the commands that change
text, such as c and d. Continuing with the previous example:

Keystrokes   **Results**
d?move

```
With a screen editor you can scroll the
page, your edits as you make them.
```

Delete from before the cursor up to and through the
word *move*.

Note how the deletion occurs on a character basis, whole lines are not deleted.

Current Line Searches

There are also miniature versions of the search commands that operate
within the current line. The command **f**x moves the cursor to the next
instance of the character *x* (where *x* stands for any character). The command **t**x
moves the cursor to the character *before* the next instance of *x*. Semicolons can
then be used repeatedly to "find" your way along.

The in-line search commands are summarized below. None of these commands will move the cursor to the next line.

f*x*   Find (move cursor to) next occurrence of *x* in the line, where *x* stands for any character.

F*x*   Find (move cursor to) previous occurrence of *x* in the line.

t*x*   Find (move cursor to) character *before* next occurrence of *x* in the line.

T*x*   Find (move cursor to) character *after* previous occurrence of *x* in the line.

;   Repeat previous find command in same direction.

,   Repeat previous find command in opposite direction.

With any of these commands, a numeric prefix *n* will locate the *n*th occurrence. Suppose you are editing in *practice*, on this line:

```
With a screen editor you can scroll the
```

Keystrokes   **Results**

fo

```
With a screen editor you can scroll the
```

Find the first occurrence of *o* in your current line with f.

;

```
With a screen editor you can scroll the
```

Move to the next occurrence of *o* with the ; command (find next *o*).

d f*x* deletes up to and including the named character *x*. This command is useful in deleting or yanking partial lines. You might need to use d f*x* instead of dw if there were symbols or punctuation within the line that made counting words difficult. The t command works just like f, except that it positions the cursor before the character searched for. For example, the command ct. could be used to change text up to the end of a sentence, leaving the period.

Movement by Line Number

Lines in a file are numbered sequentially, and you can move through a file by specifying line numbers.

Line numbers are useful for identifying the beginning and end of large blocks of text you want to edit. Line numbers are also useful for programmers, since compiler error messages refer to line numbers. Line numbers are also used by *ex* commands, which you will learn in the next chapters.

If you are going to move by line numbers, you must have a way to identify them. Line numbers can be displayed on the screen using the :set nu option described in Chapter 7. In *vi*, you can also display the current line number on the bottom of the screen.

The command CTRL-G causes the following to be displayed at the bottom of your screen: the current line number, the total number of lines in the file, and what percentage of the total the present line number represents. For example, for the file *practice*, CTRL-G might display:

```
"practice" line 3 of 6 --50%--
```

CTRL-G is useful either for displaying the line number to use in a command or for orienting yourself if you have been distracted from your editing session.

Depending upon the implementation of *vi* you're using, you may see additional information, such as what column the cursor is on, and an indication as to whether or not the file has been modified but not yet written out. The exact format of the message will vary as well.

The G (Go To) Command

G You can use line numbers to move the cursor through a file. The G (go to) command uses a line number as a numeric argument and moves directly to that line. For instance, **44G** moves the cursor to the beginning of line 44. G without a line number moves the cursor to the last line of the file.

Typing two backquotes (` `) returns you to your original position (the position where you issued the last G command), unless you have done some edits in the meantime. If you have made an edit, and then moved the cursor using some command other than G, ` ` will return the cursor to the site of your last edit. If you have issued a search command (/ or ?), ` ` will return the cursor to its position when you started the search. A pair of apostrophes (' ') works much like two backquotes, except that it returns the cursor to the beginning of the line instead of the exact position on that line where your cursor had been.

The total number of lines shown with CTRL-G can be used to give yourself a rough idea of how many lines to move. If you are on line 10 of a 1,000 line file:

```
"practice" line 10 of 1000 --1%--
```

and know that you want to begin editing near the end of that file, you could give an approximation of your destination with 800G.

Movement by line number is a tool that can move you quickly from place to place through a large file.

Review of vi Motion Commands

Table 3-1 summarizes the commands covered in this chapter.

Table 3-1: Movement Commands

Movement	Command
Scroll forward one screen.	^F
Scroll backward one screen.	^B
Scroll forward half screen.	^D
Scroll backward half screen.	^U
Scroll forward one line.	^E
Scroll backward one line.	^Y
Move current line to top of screen and scroll.	z RETURN
Move current line to center of screen and scroll.	z.
Move current line to bottom of screen and scroll.	z-
Redraw the screen.	^L
Move to home—top line of screen.	H
Move to middle line of screen.	M
Move to bottom line of screen.	L
Move to first character of next line.	RETURN
Move to first character of next line.	+
Move to first character of previous line.	-
Move to first non-blank character of current line.	^
Move to column *n* of current line.	n|
Move to end of word.	e
Move to end of word (ignore punctuation).	E
Move to beginning of current sentence.	(
Move to beginning of next sentence.	)
Move to beginning of current paragraph.	{
Move to beginning of next paragraph.	}
Move to beginning of current section.	[[
Move to beginning of next section.	]]
Search forward for pattern.	/pattern
Search backward for pattern.	?pattern
Repeat last search.	n
Repeat last search in opposite direction.	N
Repeat last search forward.	/
Repeat last search backward.	?

Table 3-1: Movement Commands (continued)

Movement	Command
Move to next occurrence of *x* in current line.	`fx`
Move to previous occurrence of *x* in current line.	`Fx`
Move to just before next occurrence of *x* in current line.	`tx`
Move to just after previous occurrence of *x* in current line.	`Tx`
Repeat previous find command in same direction.	`;`
Repeat previous find command in opposite direction.	`,`
Go to given line *n*.	`nG`
Go to end of file.	`G`
Return to previous mark or context.	`` `` ``
Return to beginning of line containing previous mark.	`' '`
Show current line (not a movement command).	`^G`

4

Beyond the Basics

In this chapter:
- *More Command Combinations*
- *Options When Starting vi*
- *Making Use of Buffers*
- *Marking Your Place*
- *Other Advanced Edits*
- *Review of vi Buffer and Marking Commands*

You have already been introduced to the basic *vi* editing commands, i, a, c, d, and y. This chapter expands on what you already know about editing. It covers:

- Description of additional editing facilities, with a review of general command form

- Additional ways to enter *vi*

- Making use of buffers that store yanks and deletions

- Marking your place in a file

More Command Combinations

In Chapter 2, *Simple Editing*, you learned the edit commands c, d, and y, as well as how to combine them with movements and numbers (such as 2cw or 4dd). In Chapter 3, *Moving Around in a Hurry*, you added many more movement commands to your repertoire. Although the fact that you can combine edit commands with movement is not a new concept to you, Table 4-1 gives you a feel for the many editing options you now have.

Table 4-1: More Editing Commands

Change	Delete	Copy	from Cursor to ...
cH	dH	yH	top of screen
cL	dL	yL	bottom of screen
c+	d+	y+	next line
c5|	d5|	y5|	column 5 of current line
2c)	2d)	2y)	second sentence following

Table 4-1: More Editing Commands (continued)

Change	Delete	Copy	from Cursor to ...
c{	d{	y{	previous paragraph
c/pattern	d/pattern	y/pattern	*pattern*
cn	dn	yn	next *pattern*
cG	dG	yG	end of file
c13G	d13G	y13G	line number 13

Notice how all of the above sequences follow the general pattern:

   (number)(command)(text object)

number is the optional numeric argument. *command* in this case is one of c, d, or y. *text object* is a movement command.

The general form of a *vi* command is discussed in Chapter 2. You may wish to review Table 2-1 and Table 2-2 as well.

Options When Starting vi

In this handbook, you have invoked the *vi* editor with the command:

   $ **vi** `file`

There are other options to the **vi** command that can be helpful. You can open a file directly to a specific line number or pattern. You can also open a file in read-only mode. Another option recovers all changes to a file that you were editing when the system crashed.

Advancing to a Specific Place

When you begin editing an existing file, you can call the file in and then move to the first occurrence of a *pattern* or to a specific line number. You can also specify your first movement by search or by line number right on the command line:*

$ **vi** +n `file`
   Opens *file* at line number *n*.

$ **vi** + `file`
   Opens *file* at last line.

---

* According to the POSIX standard, *vi* should use `-c command` instead of `+command` as shown here. Typically, for backwards compatibility, both versions are accepted.

$ **vi** *+/pattern file*

    Opens *file* at the first occurrence of *pattern*.

In the file *practice*, to open the file and advance directly to the line containing the word *Screen*, enter:

Keystrokes   **Results**

vi +/Screen practice

```
With a screen editor you can scroll
the page, move the cursor, delete
lines, and insert characters, while
seeing the results of your edits as
you make them.
Screen editors are
very popular, since they allow you
to make changes as you read
```

Give the vi command with the option *+/pattern* to
go directly to the line containing *Screen*.

As you see in the example above, your search pattern will not necessarily be positioned at the top of the screen. If you include spaces in the *pattern*, you must enclose the whole pattern within single or double quotes:*

    +/"you make"

or escape the space with a backslash:

    +/you\ make

In addition, if you want to use the general pattern-matching syntax described in Chapter 6, *Global Replacement*, you may need to protect one or more special characters from interpretation by the shell with either single quotes or backslashes.

Using *+/pattern* is helpful if you have to leave an editing session in the middle. You can mark your place by inserting a pattern such as ZZZ or HERE. Then when you return to the file, all you have to remember is /ZZZ or /HERE.

Normally, when you're editing in *vi*, the **wrapscan** option is enabled. If you've customized your environment so that **wrapscan** is always disabled,† you might not be able to use *+/pattern*. If you try to open a file this way, *vi* opens the file at the last line and displays the message "Address search hit BOTTOM without matching pattern."

---

* It is the shell that imposes the quoting requirement, not *vi*.

† See the section "Repeating Searches" in Chapter 3.

Read-only Mode

There will be times when you want to look at a file but want to protect that file from inadvertent keystrokes and changes. (You might want to call in a lengthy file to practice *vi* movements, or you might want to scroll through a command file or program). You can enter a file in read-only mode and use all the *vi* movement commands, but you won't be able to change the file.

To look at a file in read-only mode, enter either:

    $ **vi -R** *file*

or:

    $ **view** *file*

(The **view** command, like the **vi** command, can use any of the command-line options for advancing to a specific place in the file.)* If you do decide to make some edits to the file, you can override read-only mode by adding an exclamation point to the **write** command:

    :w!

or:

    :wq!

If you have a problem writing out the file, see the problem checklists summarized in Appendix D, *Problem Checklists*.

Recovering a Buffer

Occasionally there is a system failure while you are editing a file. Ordinarily, any edits made after your last write (save) are lost. However, there is an option, -r, which lets you recover the edited buffer at the time of a system crash.

When you first log on after the system is running again, you will receive a mail message stating that your buffer has been saved. In addition, if you type the command:

    $ **ex -r**

or:

    $ **vi -r**

you will get a list of any files that the system has saved.

---

* Typically view is just a link to vi.

Use the -r option with a file name to recover the edited buffer. For example, to recover the edited buffer of the file *practice* after a system crash, enter:

```
$ vi -r practice
```

It is wise to recover the file immediately, lest you inadvertently make edits to the file, and then have to resolve a version skew between the preserved buffer and the newly edited file.

You can force the system to preserve your buffer even when there is not a crash by using the command :pre. You may find it useful if you have made edits to a file, then discover that you can't save your edits because you don't have write permission. (You could also just write out a copy of the file under another name or into a directory where you do have write permission. See the section "Problems Saving Files" in Chapter 1, *The vi Text Editor*.)

Recovery for the various clones may work differently, and can change from version to version. It is best to check your local documentation. *vile* does not support any kind of recovery. The *vile* documentation recommends the use of the autowrite and autosave options. How to do this is described in the section "Customizing vi" in Chapter 7.

Making Use of Buffers

You have seen that while you are editing, your last deletion (d or x) or yank (y) is saved in a buffer (a place in stored memory). You can access the contents of that buffer and put the saved text back in your file with the put command (p or P).

The last nine deletions are stored by *vi* in numbered buffers. You can access any of these numbered buffers to restore any (or all) of the last nine deletions. (Small deletions, of only parts of lines, are not saved in numbered buffers, however. These deletions can only be recovered by using the p or P command immediately after you've made the deletion.)

vi also allows you to place yanks (copied text) in buffers identified by letters. You can fill up to 26 (a–z) buffers with yanked text and restore that text with a put command at any time in your editing session.

Recovering Deletions

Being able to delete large blocks of text at a single bound is all very well and good, but what if you mistakenly delete 53 lines that you need? There is a way to recover any of your past *nine* deletions, for they are saved in numbered buffers. The last delete is saved in buffer 1, the second-to-last in buffer 2, and so on.

To recover a deletion, type " (double quote), identify the buffered text by number, then give the put command. To recover your second-to-last deletion from buffer 2:

        "2p

The deletion in buffer 2 is placed after the cursor.

If you're not sure which buffer contains the deletion you want to restore, you don't have to keep typing "np over and over again. If you use the repeat command (.) with p after u, it automatically increments the buffer number. As a result, you can search through the numbered buffers as follows:

        "1pu.u.u *etc.*

to put the contents of each succeeding buffer in the file one after the other. Each time you type u, the restored text is removed; when you type a dot (.), the contents of the *next* buffer is restored to your file. Keep typing u and . until you've recovered the text you're looking for.

Yanking to Named Buffers

You have seen that you must put (p or P) the contents of the unnamed buffer before you make any other edit, or the buffer will be overwritten. You can also use y and d with a set of 26 named buffers (a–z) which are specifically available for copying and moving text. If you name a buffer to store the yanked text, you can retrieve the contents of the named buffer at any time during your editing session.

To yank into a named buffer, precede the yank command with a double quote (") and the character for the name of the buffer you want to load. For example:

        "dyy   *Yank current line into buffer* d.
        "a7yy   *Yank next seven lines into buffer* a.

After loading the named buffers and moving to the new position, use p or P to put the text back:

        "dP   *Put the contents of buffer* d *before cursor.*
        "ap   *Put the contents of buffer* a *after cursor.*

There is no way to put part of a buffer into the text—it is all or nothing.

In the next chapter, you'll learn to edit multiple files. Once you know how to travel between files without leaving *vi*, you can use named buffers to selectively transfer text between files.

You can also delete text into named buffers using much the same procedure:

    "a5dd   *Delete five lines into buffer* a.

If you specify a buffer name with a capital letter, your yanked or deleted text will be *appended* to the current contents of that buffer. This allows you to be selective in what you move or copy. For example:

"zd)

> Delete from cursor to end of current sentence and save in buffer **z**.

2)

> Move two sentences further on.

"Zy)

> Add the next sentence to buffer **z**. You can continue adding more text to a named buffer for as long as you like—but be warned: if you once forget, and yank or delete to the buffer without specifying its name in capitalized form, you'll overwrite the buffer, losing whatever you had accumulated in it.

Marking Your Place

During a *vi* session, you can mark your place in the file with an invisible "bookmark," perform edits elsewhere, then return to your marked place. In command mode:

m*x*

> Marks the current position with *x* (*x* can be any letter).

'*x*

> (apostrophe) Moves the cursor to the first character of the line marked by *x*.

`*x*

> (backquote) Moves the cursor to the character marked by *x*.

` `

> (backquotes) Returns to the exact position of the previous mark or context after a move.

' '

> (apostrophes) Returns to the beginning of the line of the previous mark or context.

> Place markers are set only during the current *vi* session; they are not stored in the file.

Other Advanced Edits

There are other advanced edits that you can execute with *vi*, but to use them you must first learn a bit more about the *ex* editor by reading the next chapter.

Review of vi Buffer and Marking Commands

Table 4-2 summarizes the command-line options common to all versions of *vi*. Table 4-3 and Table 4-4 summarize the buffer and marking commands.

Table 4-2: Command-Line Options

Option	Meaning
+n file	Open *file* at line number *n*.
+file	Open *file* at last line.
+/pattern file	Open *file* at first occurrence of *pattern*.
-c command file	Run *command* after opening file; usually a line number or search (POSIX version of +).
-R	Operate in read-only mode (same as using view instead of vi).
-r	Recover files after a crash.

Table 4-3: Buffer Names

Buffer Names	Buffer Use
1-9	The last nine deletions, from most to least recent.
a-z	Named buffers for you to use as needed. Uppercase letters append to the buffer.

Table 4-4: Buffer and Marking Commands

Command	Meaning
"b command	Do *command* with buffer *b*.
mx	Mark current position with *x*.
'x	Move cursor to first character of line marked by *x*.
`x	Move cursor to character marked by *x*.
` `	Return to exact position of previous mark or context.
' '	Return to beginning of the line of previous mark or context.

5

Introducing
the ex Editor

In this chapter:
- *ex Commands*
- *Editing with ex*
- *Saving and Exiting Files*
- *Copying a File into Another File*
- *Editing Multiple Files*

If this is a handbook on *vi*, why would we include a chapter on another editor? *ex* is not really another editor. *vi* is the visual mode of the more general, underlying line editor, *ex*. Some *ex* commands can be useful to you while you are working in *vi*, since they can save you a lot of editing time. Most of these commands can be used without ever leaving *vi*.*

You already know how to think of files as a sequence of numbered lines. *ex* gives you editing commands with greater mobility and scope. With *ex* you can move easily between files and transfer text from one file to another in a variety of ways. You can quickly edit blocks of text larger than a single screen. And with global replacement you can make substitutions throughout a file for a given pattern.

This chapter introduces *ex* and its commands. You will learn how to:

- Move around a file by using line numbers

- Use *ex* commands to copy, move, and delete blocks of text

- Save files and parts of files

- Work with multiple files (reading in text or commands, traveling between files)

ex Commands

Long before *vi* or any other screen editor was invented, people communicated with computers on printing terminals, rather than on today's CRTs (or bitmapped screens with pointing devices and terminal emulation programs). Line numbers were a way to quickly identify a part of a file to be worked on, and line editors

---

* *vile* is different from the other clones. Many of the more advanced *ex* commands simply don't work. Instead of noting each one, more details are provided in Chapter 12, *vile—vi Like Emacs*.

evolved to edit those files. A programmer or other computer user would typically print out a line (or lines) on the printing terminal, give the editing commands to change just that line, then reprint to check the edited line.

People don't edit files on printing terminals any more, but some *ex* line editor commands are still useful to users of the more sophisticated visual editor built on top of *ex*. Although it is simpler to make most edits with *vi*, the line orientation of *ex* gives it an advantage when you want to make large-scale changes to more than one part of a file.

Many of the commands we'll see in this chapter have filename arguments. Although it's possible, it is usually a very bad idea to have spaces in your files' names. *ex* will be confused to no end, and you will go to more trouble than it's worth trying to get the filenames to be accepted. Use underscores, dashes, or periods to separate the components of your file names, and you'll be much happier.

Before you start off simply memorizing *ex* commands (or worse, ignoring them), let's first take some of the mystery out of line editors. Seeing how *ex* works when it is invoked directly will help make sense of the sometimes obscure command syntax.

Open a file that is familiar to you and try a few *ex* commands. Just as you can invoke the *vi* editor on a file, you can invoke the *ex* line editor on a file. If you invoke *ex*, you will see a message about the total number of lines in the file, and a colon command prompt.

For example:

```
$ ex practice
"practice" 6 lines, 320 characters
:
```

You won't see any lines in the file unless you give an *ex* command that causes one or more lines to be displayed.

ex commands consist of a line address (which can simply be a line number) plus a command; they are finished with a carriage return. One of the most basic commands is p for print (to the screen). So, for example, if you type 1p at the prompt, you will see the first line of the file:

```
:1p
With a screen editor you can
:
```

In fact, you can leave off the p, because a line number by itself is equivalent to a print command for that line. To print more than one line, you can specify a range of line numbers (for example, 1,3—two numbers separated by a comma, with or without spaces in between). For example:

```
:1,3
With a screen editor you can
scroll the page, move the cursor,
delete lines, insert characters, and more,
```

A command without a line number is assumed to affect the current line. So, for example, the substitute command (s), which allows you to substitute one word for another, could be entered like this:

```
:1
With a screen editor you can
:s/screen/line/
With a line editor you can
```

Notice that the changed line is reprinted after the command is issued. You could also make the same change like this:

```
:1s/screen/line/
With a line editor you can
```

Even though you will be invoking *ex* commands from *vi* and will not be using them directly, it is worthwhile to spend a few minutes in *ex* itself. You will get a feel for how you need to tell the editor which line (or lines) to work on, as well as which command to execute.

After you have given a few *ex* commands on your *practice* file, you should invoke *vi* on that same file, so that you can see it in the more familiar visual mode. The command :vi will get you from *ex* to *vi*.

To invoke an *ex* command from *vi*, you must type the special bottom line character : (colon). Then type the command and press RETURN to execute it. So, for example, in the *ex* editor you move to a line simply by typing the number of the line at the colon prompt. To move to line 6 of a file using this command from within *vi*, enter:

```
:6
```

Press RETURN .

Following the exercise, we will discuss *ex* commands only as they are executed from *vi*.

Exercise: The ex Editor

At the UNIX prompt, invoke *ex* editor on a file called *practice*:	`ex practice`
A message appears:	`"practice" 6 lines, 320 characters`
Go to and print (display) first line:	`:1`
Print (display) lines 1 through 3:	`:1,3`
Substitute screen for line on line 1:	`:1s/screen/line`
Invoke *vi* editor on file:	`:vi`
Go to first line:	`:1`

Problem Checklist

✓ *While editing in* vi, *you accidentally end up in the* ex *editor.*

A Q in the command mode of *vi* invokes *ex*. Any time you are in *ex*, the command `vi` returns you to the *vi* editor.

Editing with ex

Many *ex* commands that perform normal editing operations have an equivalent in *vi* that does the job more simply. Obviously, you will use dw or dd to delete a single word or line rather than using the `delete` command in *ex*. However, when you want to make changes that affect numerous lines, you will find the *ex* commands more useful. They allow you to modify large blocks of text with a single command.

These *ex* commands are listed below, along with abbreviations for those commands. Remember that in *vi* each *ex* command must be preceded with a colon. You can use the full command name or the abbreviation, whichever is easier to remember.

`delete`	`d`	Delete lines.
`move`	`m`	Move lines.
`copy`	`co`	Copy lines.
	`t`	Copy lines (a synonym for co).

You can separate the different elements of an *ex* command with spaces, if you find the command easier to read that way. For example, you can separate line addresses, patterns, and commands in this way. You cannot, however, use a space as a separator inside a pattern or at the end of a substitute command.

Line Addresses

For each *ex* editing command, you have to tell *ex* which line number(s) to edit. And for the *ex* move and `copy` commands, you also need to tell *ex* where to move or copy the text to.

You can specify line addresses in several ways:

- With explicit line numbers

- With symbols that help you specify line numbers relative to your current position in the file

- With search patterns as *addresses* that identify the lines to be affected

Let's look at some examples.

Defining a Range of Lines

You can use line numbers to explicitly define a line or range of lines. Addresses that use explicit numbers are called *absolute* line addresses. For example:

`:3,18d`	Delete lines 3 through 18.
`:160,224m23`	Move lines 160 through 224 to follow line 23. (Like `delete` and `put` in *vi*.)
`:23,29co100`	Copy lines 23 through 29 and put after line 100. (Like `yank` and `put` in *vi*.)

To make editing with line numbers easier, you can also display all line numbers on the left of the screen. The command:

```
:set number
```

or its abbreviation:

```
:set nu
```

displays line numbers. The file *practice* then appears:

```
1  With a screen editor
2  you can scroll the page,
3  move the cursor, delete lines,
4  insert characters and more
```

The displayed line numbers are not saved when you write a file, and they do not print if you print the file. Line numbers are displayed either until you quit the *vi* session or until you disable the **set** option:

```
:set nonumber
```

or:

```
:set nonu
```

To temporarily display the line numbers for a set of lines, you can use the # sign. For example:

```
:1,10#
```

would display the line numbers from line one to line ten.

As described in Chapter 3, *Moving Around in a Hurry*, you can also use the CTRL-G command to display the current line number. You can thus identify the line numbers corresponding to the start and end of a block of text by moving to the start of the block, typing CTRL-G , then moving to the end of the block and typing CTRL-G again.

Yet another way to identify line numbers is with the *ex* = command:

`:=` Print the total number of lines.

`:.=`
   Print the line number of the current line.

`:/pattern/=`
   Print the line number of the first line that matches *pattern*.

Line Addressing Symbols

You can also use symbols for line addresses. A dot (.) stands for the current line; $ stands for the last line of the file. % stands for every line in the file; it's the same as the combination 1,$. These symbols can also be combined with absolute line addresses. For example:

`:.,$d`
   Delete from current line to end of file.

`:20,.m$`
   Move from line 20 through the current line to the end of the file.

`:%d`
   Delete all the lines in a file.

`:%t$`
   Copy all lines and place them at the end of the file (making a consecutive duplicate).

In addition to an absolute line address, you can specify an address relative to the current line. The symbols + and − work like arithmetic operators. When placed before a number, these symbols add or subtract the value that follows. For example:

`: ., .+20d`

Delete from current line through the next 20 lines.

`:226,$m.-2`

Move lines 226 through the end of the file to two lines above the current line.

`:.,+20#`

Display line numbers from the current line to 20 lines further on in the file.

In fact, you don't need to type the dot (.) when you use + or −, because the current line is the assumed starting position.

Without a number following them, + and − are equivalent to +1 and −1, respectively.* Similarly, + + and − − each extend the range by an additional line, and so on. The + and − can also be used with search patterns, as shown in the next section.

The number 0 stands for the top of the file (imaginary line 0). 0 is equivalent to 1−, and both allow you to move or copy lines to the very start of a file, before the first line of existing text. For example:

`:-,+t0`

Copy three lines (the line above the cursor through the line below the cursor) and put them at the top of the file.

Search Patterns

Another way that *ex* can address lines is by using search patterns. For example:

`:/pattern/d`

Delete the next line containing *pattern*.

`:/pattern/+d`

Delete the line *below* the next line containing *pattern*. (You could also use +1 instead of + alone.)

`:/pattern1/,/pattern2/d`

Delete from the first line containing *pattern1* through the first line containing *pattern2*.

---

* In a relative address, you shouldn't separate the plus or minus symbol from the number that follows it. For example, +10 means "10 lines following," but + 10 means "11 lines following (1 + 10)," which is probably not what you mean (or want).

`:.,/pattern/m23`

> Take the text from the current line (`.`) through the first line containing *pattern* and put it after line 23.

Note that patterns are delimited by a slash both *before* and *after*.

If you make deletions by pattern with *vi* and *ex*, there is a difference in the way the two editors operate. Suppose your file *practice* contains the lines:

```
With a screen editor you can scroll the
page, move the cursor, delete lines, insert
characters and more, while seeing results
of your edits as you make them.
```

Keystrokes   **Results**

`d/while`

```
With a screen editor you can scroll the
page, move the cursor, while seeing results
of your edits as you make them.
```

The *vi* delete to *pattern* command deletes from the cursor up to the word *while*, but leaves the remainder of both lines.

`:.,/while/d`

```
With a screen editor you can scroll the
of your edits as you make them.
```

The *ex* command deletes the entire range of addressed lines; in this case both the current line and the line containing the pattern. All lines are deleted in their entirety.

Redefining the Current Line Position

Sometimes, using a relative line address in a command can give you unexpected results. For example, suppose the cursor is on line 1, and you want to print line 100 plus the five lines below it. If you type:

`:100,+5 p`

you'll get an error message saying, "First address exceeds second." The reason the command fails is that the second address is calculated relative to the current cursor position (line 1), so your command is really saying this:

`:100,6 p`

What you need is some way to tell the command to think of line 100 as the "current line," even though the cursor is on line 1.

ex provides such a way. When you use a semicolon instead of a comma, the first line address is recalculated as the current line. For example, the command:

```
:100;+5 p
```

prints the desired lines. The +5 is now calculated relative to line 100. A semicolon is useful with search patterns as well as absolute addresses. For example, to print the next line containing *pattern*, plus the 10 lines that follow it, enter the command:

```
:/pattern/;+10 p
```

Global Searches

You already know how to use / (slash) in *vi* to search for patterns of characters in your files. *ex* has a global command, g, that lets you search for a pattern and display all lines containing the pattern when it finds them. The command :g! does the opposite of :g. Use :g! (or its synonym :v) to search for all lines that do *not* contain *pattern*.

You can use the global command on all lines in the file, or you can use line addresses to limit a global search to specified lines or to a range of lines.

:g/*pattern*
> Finds (moves to) the last occurrence of *pattern* in the file.

:g/*pattern*/p
> Finds and displays all lines in the file containing *pattern*.

:g!/*pattern*/nu
> Finds and displays all lines in the file that don't contain *pattern*; also displays the line number for each line found.

:60,124g/*pattern*/p
> Finds and displays any lines between lines 60 and 124 containing *pattern*.

As you might expect, g can also be used for global replacements. We'll talk about that in Chapter 6, *Global Replacement*.

Combining ex Commands

You don't always need to type a colon to begin a new *ex* command. In *ex*, the vertical bar (|) is a command separator, allowing you to combine multiple commands from the same *ex* prompt (in much the same way that a semicolon separates multiple commands at the UNIX shell prompt). When you use the |, keep track of the line addresses you specify. If one command affects the order of lines in the file, the next command does its work using the new line positions. For example:

```
:1,3d | s/thier/their/
```
Delete lines 1 through 3 (leaving you now on the top line of the file); then make a substitution on the current line (which was line 4 before you invoked the *ex* prompt).

```
:1,5 m 10 | g/pattern/nu
```
Move lines 1 through 5 after line 10, and then display all lines (with numbers) containing *pattern*.

Note the use of spaces to make the commands easier to read.

Saving and Exiting Files

You have learned the *vi* command ZZ to quit and write (save) your file. But you will frequently want to exit a file using *ex* commands, because these commands give you greater control. We've already mentioned some of these commands in passing. Now let's take a more formal look.

:w Writes (saves) the buffer to the file but does not exit. You can (and should) use :w throughout your editing session to protect your edits against system failure or a major editing error.

:q Quits the editor (and returns to the UNIX prompt).

:wq
Both writes the file and quits the editor. The write happens unconditionally, even if the file was not changed.

:x Both writes the file and quits (exits) the editor. The file is written only if it has been modified.*

vi protects existing files and your edits in the buffer. For example, if you want to write your buffer to an existing file, *vi* gives you a warning. Likewise, if you have invoked *vi* on a file, made edits, and want to quit *without* saving the edits, *vi* gives you an error message such as:

```
No write since last change.
```

These warnings can prevent costly mistakes, but sometimes you want to proceed with the command anyway. An exclamation point (!) after your command overrides the warning:

```
:w!
:q!
```

---

* The difference between :wq and :x is important when editing source code and using *make*, which performs actions based upon file modification times.

`:w!` can also be used to save edits in a file that was opened in read-only mode with `vi -R` or `view` (assuming you have write permission for the file).

`:q!` is an essential editing command that allows you to quit without affecting the original file, regardless of any changes you made in this session. The contents of the buffer are discarded.

Renaming the Buffer

You can also use `:w` to save the entire buffer (the copy of the file you are editing) under a new filename.

Suppose you have a file *practice*, which contains 600 lines. You open the file and make extensive edits. You want to quit but save *both* the old version of *practice and* your new edits for comparison. To save the edited buffer in a file called *practice.new*, give the command:

```
:w practice.new
```

Your old version, in the file *practice*, remains unchanged (provided that you didn't previously use `:w`). You can now quit editing the new version by typing `:q`.

Saving Part of a File

While editing, you will sometimes want to save just part of your file as a separate, new file. For example, you might have entered formatting codes and text that you want to use as a header for several files.

You can combine *ex* line addressing with the write command, w, to save part of a file. For example, if you are in the file *practice* and want to save part of *practice* as the file *newfile*, you could enter:

`:230,$w` *newfile*
> Saves from line 230 to end of file in *newfile*.

`:.,600w` *newfile*
> Saves from the current line to line 600 in *newfile*.

Appending to a Saved File

You can use the UNIX redirect and append operator (`>>`) with w to append all or part of the contents of the buffer to an existing file. For example, if you entered:

`:1,10w` *newfile*

then:

    :340,$w >>newfile

newfile would contain lines 1-10 and from line 340 to the end of the buffer.

Copying a File into Another File

Sometimes you want to copy text or data already entered on the system into the file you are editing. In *vi* you can read in the contents of another file with the *ex* command:

    :**read** filename

or its abbreviation:

    :**r** filename

This command inserts the contents of *filename* starting on the line after the cursor position in the file. If you want to specify a line other than the one the cursor's on, simply type the line number (or other line address) you want before the **read** or **r** command.

Let's suppose you are editing the file *practice* and want to read in a file called *data* from another directory called */home/tim*. Position the cursor one line above the line where you want the new data inserted, and enter:

    :r /home/tim/data

The entire contents of */home/tim/data* are read into *practice*, beginning below the line with the cursor.

To read in the same file and place it after line 185, you would enter:

    :185r /home/tim/data

Here are other ways to read in a file:

:$r /home/tim/data
:   Place the read-in file at the end of the current file.

:0r /home/tim/data
:   Place the read-in file at the very beginning of the current file.

:/pattern/r /home/tim/data
:   Place the read-in file in the current file, after the line containing *pattern*.

Editing Multiple Files

ex commands enable you to switch between multiple files. The advantage to editing multiple files is speed. If you are sharing the system with other users, it takes time to exit and reenter *vi* for each file you want to edit. Staying in the same editing session and traveling between files is not only faster for access, but you also save abbreviations and command sequences that you have defined (see Chapter 7, *Advanced Editing*), and you keep yank buffers so that you can copy text from one file to another.

Invoking vi on Multiple Files

When you first invoke *vi*, you can name more than one file to edit, and then use *ex* commands to travel between the files. For example:

```
$ vi file1 file2
```

edits *file1* first. After you have finished editing the first file, the *ex* command :w writes (saves) *file1* and :n calls in the next file (*file2*).

Suppose you want to edit two files, *practice* and *note*.

Keystrokes	Results
vi practice note	

```
With a screen editor you can scroll the
the page, move the cursor, delete lines,
insert characters, and more, while seeing
```

Open the two files *practice* and *note*. The first-named file, *practice*, appears on your screen. Perform any edits.

:w

```
"practice" 6 lines, 328 characters
```

Save the edited file *practice* with the *ex* command w.
Press RETURN .

:n

```
Dear Mr.
Henshaw:
Thank you for the prompt . . .
```

Call in the next file, *note*, with the *ex* command n.
Press RETURN . Perform any edits.

:x

```
    "note" 23 lines, 1343 characters
```

Save the second file, *note*, and quit the editing session.

Using the Argument List

ex actually lets you do more than just move to the next file in the argument list with :n. The :args command (abbreviated :ar) lists the files named on the command line, with the current file enclosed in brackets.

Keystrokes   **Results**
vi practice note

```
    With a screen editor you can scroll
    the page, move the cursor, delete lines,
    insert charcters, and more, while seeing
```

Open the two files *practice* and *note*. The first-named file, *practice*, appears on your screen.

:args

```
    [practice] note
```

vi displays the argument list in the status line, with brackets around the current filename.

The :rewind (:rew) command resets the current file to be the first file named on the command line. *elvis* and *vim* provide a corresponding :last command to move to the last file on the command line.

Calling in New Files

You don't have to call in multiple files at the beginning of your editing session. You can switch to another file at any time with the *ex* command :e. If you want to edit another file within *vi*, you first need to save your current file (:w), then give the command:

   :e *filename*

Suppose you are editing the file *practice* and want to edit the file *letter*, then return to *practice*.

Keystrokes   **Results**
:w

```
    "practice" 6 lines, 328 characters
```

Save *practice* with w and press RETURN . *practice* is saved and remains on the screen. You can now switch to another file, because your edits are saved.

`:e letter`

```
    "letter" 23 lines, 1344 characters
```

Call in the file *letter* with e and press RETURN . Perform any edits.

vi "remembers" two filenames at a time as the current and alternate filenames. These can be referred to by the symbols % (current filename) and # (alternate filename). # is particularly useful with `:e`, since it allows you to switch easily back and forth between two files. In the example given just above, you could return to the first file, *practice*, by typing the command `:e #`. You could also read the file *practice* into the current file by typing `:r #`.

If you have not first saved the current file, *vi* will not allow you to switch files with `:e` or `:n` unless you tell it imperatively to do so by adding an exclamation point after the command.

For example, if after making some edits to *letter*, you wanted to discard the edits and return to *practice*, you could type `:e! #`.

The following command is also useful. It discards your edits and returns to the last saved version of the current file:

`:e!`

In contrast to the # symbol, % is useful mainly when writing out the contents of the current buffer to a new file. For example, a few pages earlier, in the section "Renaming the Buffer," we showed how to save a second version of the file *practice* with the command:

`:w practice.new`

Since % stands for the current filename, that line could also have been typed:

`:w %.new`

Switching Files from vi

CTRL **^** Since switching back to the previous file is something that tends to happen a lot, you don't have to move to the *ex* command line to do it. The *vi* command ^^ (the "control" key with the caret key) will do this for you. Using this command is the same as typing `:e #`. As with the `:e` command, if the current buffer has not been saved, *vi* will not let you switch back to the previous file.

Edits Between Files

When you give a yank buffer a one-letter name, you have a convenient way to move text from one file to another. Named buffers are not cleared when a new file is loaded into the *vi* buffer with the :e command. Thus, by yanking or deleting text from one file (into multiple named buffers if necessary), calling in a new file with :e, and putting the named buffer(s) into the new file, you can transfer material between files.

The following example illustrates how to transfer text from one file to another.

Keystrokes   **Results**
"f4yy

```
With a screen editor you can scroll
the page, move the cursor, delete lines,
insert characters, and more, while seeing
the results of the edits as you make them
```

Yank four lines into buffer f.

:w

```
"practice" 6 lines, 238 characters
```

Save the file.

:e letter

```
Dear Mr.
Henshaw:
I thought that you would
be interested to know that:
Yours truly,
```

Enter the file *letter* with :e. Move the cursor to where the copied text will be placed.

"fp

```
Dear Mr.
Henshaw:
I thought that you would
be interested to know that:
With a screen editor you can scroll
the page, move the cursor, delete lines,
insert characters, and more, while seeing
the results of the edits as you make them
Yours truly,
```

Place yanked text from named buffer f below the cursor.

Another way to move text from one file to another is to use the *ex* commands :ya (yank) and :pu (put). These commands work the same way as the equivalent *vi* commands y and p, but they are used with *ex*'s line-addressing capability and named buffers.

For example:

```
:160,224ya  a
```

would yank (copy) lines 160 through 224 into buffer **a**. Next you would move with **:e** to the file where you want to put these lines. Place the cursor on the line where you want to put the yanked lines. Then type:

```
:pu a
```

to put the contents of buffer **a** after the current line.

6

Global Replacement

Sometimes, halfway through a document or at the end of a draft, you may recognize inconsistencies in the way that you refer to certain things. Or, in a manual, some product whose name appears throughout your file is suddenly renamed (marketing!). Often enough it happens that you have to go back and change what you've already written, and you need to make the changes in several places.

The way to make these changes is with a powerful change command called global replacement. With one command you can automatically replace a word (or a string of characters) wherever it occurs in the file.

In a global replacement, the *ex* editor checks each line of a file for a given pattern of characters. On all lines where the pattern is found, *ex* replaces the pattern with a *new string* of characters. For right now, we'll treat the search pattern as if it were a simple string; later in the chapter we'll look at the powerful pattern-matching language known as *regular expressions*.

Global replacement really uses two *ex* commands: `:g` (global) and `:s` (substitute). Since the syntax of global replacement commands can get fairly complex, let's look at it in stages.

The substitute command has the syntax:

```
:s/old/new/
```

This changes the *first* occurrence of the pattern *old* to *new* on the current line. The / (slash) is the delimiter between the various parts of the command. (The slash is optional when it is the last character on the line.)

A substitute command with the syntax:

    :s/*old*/*new*/g

changes *every* occurrence of *old* to *new* on the current line, not just the first occurrence. The :s command allows options following the substitution string. The g
option in the syntax above stands for *global*. (The g option affects each pattern on
a line; don't confuse it with the :g command, which affects each line of a file.)

By prefixing the :s command with addresses, you can extend its range to more
than one line. For example, this line will change every occurrence of *old* to *new*
from line 50 to line 100:

    :50,100s/*old*/*new*/g

This command will change every occurrence of *old* to *new* within the entire file:

    :1,$s/*old*/*new*/g

You can also use % instead of 1,$ to specify every line in a file. Thus the last
command could also be given like this:

    :%s/*old*/*new*/g

Global replacement is much faster than finding each instance of a string and
replacing it individually. Because the command can be used to make many different kinds of changes, and because it is so powerful, we will first illustrate simple
replacements and then build up to complex, context-sensitive replacements.

Confirming Substitutions

It makes sense to be overly careful when using a search and replace command. It
sometimes happens that what you get is not what you expect. You can undo any
search and replacement command by entering u, provided that the command was
the most recent edit you made. But you don't always catch undesired changes
until it is too late to undo them. Another way to protect your edited file is to save
the file with :w before performing a global replacement. Then at least you can
quit the file without saving your edits and go back to where you were before the
change was made. You can also read the previous version of the buffer back in
with :e!.

It's wise to be cautious and know exactly what is going to be changed in your file.
If you'd like to see what the search turns up and confirm each replacement before
it is made, add the c option (for confirm) at the end of the substitute command:

    :1,30s/his/the/gc

It will display the entire line where the string has been located, and the string will be marked by a series of carets (`^^^^`):

```
copyists at his school
         ^^^ _
```

If you want to make the replacement, you must enter **y** (for yes) and press RETURN . If you don't want to make a change, simply press RETURN .*

```
this can be used for invitations, signs, and menus.
  ^^^ _
```

The combination of the *vi* commands n (repeat last search) and dot (**.**) (repeat last command) is also an extraordinarily useful and quick way to page through a file and make repetitive changes that you may not want to make globally. So, for example, if your editor has told you that you're using *which* when you should be using *that*, you can spot-check every occurrence of *which*, changing only those that are incorrect:

/which	Search for *which*.
cwthat ESC	Change to *that*.
n	Repeat search.
n	Repeat search, skip a change.
.	Repeat change (if appropriate).

.

.

.

Context-Sensitive Replacement

The simplest global replacements substitute one word (or a phrase) for another. If you have typed a file with several misspellings (*editer* for *editor*), you can do the global replacement:

```
:%s/editer/editor/g
```

This substitutes *editor* for every occurrence of *editer* throughout the file.

There is a second, slightly more complex syntax for global replacement. This syntax lets you search for a pattern, and then, once you find the line with the pattern, make a substitution on a string different from the pattern. You can think of this as context-sensitive replacement.

---

* *elvis* 2.0 doesn't support this feature. In the other clones, the actual appearance and prompt differ, but the effect is still the same, allowing you to choose whether or not to do the substitution in each case.

The syntax is as follows:

```
:g/pattern/s/old/new/g
```

The first **g** tells the command to operate on all lines of a file. *pattern* identifies the lines on which a substitution is to take place. On those lines containing *pattern*, *ex* is to substitute (**s**) for *old* the characters in *new*. The last **g** indicates that the substitution is to occur globally *on that line*.

For example, in this book, the SGML directives **<keycap>** and **</keycap>** place a box around ESC to show the ESCAPE key. You want ESC to be all in caps, but you don't want to change any instances of *Escape* that might be in the text. To change instances of *Esc* to *ESC* only when *Esc* is on a line that contains the **<keycap>** directive, you could enter:

```
:g/<keycap>/s/Esc/ESC/g
```

If the pattern being used to find the line is the same as the one you want to change, you don't have to repeat it. The command:

```
:g/string/s//new/g
```

would search for lines containing *string* and substitute for that same *string*.

Note that:

```
:g/editer/s//editor/g
```

has the same effect as:

```
:%s/editer/editor/g
```

You can save some typing by using the second form. It is also possible to combine the **:g** command with **:d**, **:mo**, **:co** and other *ex* commands besides **:s**. As we'll show, you can thus make global deletions, moves, and copies.

Pattern-Matching Rules

In making global replacements, UNIX editors such as *vi* allow you to search not just for fixed strings of characters, but also for variable patterns of words, referred to as *regular expressions*.

When you specify a literal string of characters, the search might turn up other occurrences that you didn't want to match. The problem with searching for words in a file is that a word can be used in different ways. Regular expressions help you conduct a search for words in context. Note that regular expressions can be used with the *vi* search commands **/** and **?** as well as in the *ex* **:g** and **:s** commands.

For the most part, the same regular expressions work with other UNIX programs such as *grep*, *sed*, and *awk*.*

Regular expressions are made up by combining normal characters with a number of special characters called *metacharacters*.† The metacharacters and their uses are listed below.

Metacharacters Used in Search Patterns

.   Matches any *single* character except a newline. Remember that spaces are treated as characters. For example, `p.p` matches character strings such as *pep*, *pip*, and *pcp*.

*   Matches zero or more (as many as there are) of the single character that immediately precedes it. For example, `bugs*` will match *bugs* (one *s*) or *bug* (no *s*'s).

       The `*` can follow a metacharacter. For example, since `.` (dot) means any character, `.*` means "match any number of any character."

       Here's a specific example of this. The command `:s/End.*/End/` removes all characters after *End* (it replaces the remainder of the line with nothing).

^   When used at the start of a regular expression, requires that the following regular expression be found at the beginning of the line; for example, `^Part` matches *Part* when it occurs at the beginning of a line, and `^...` matches the first three characters of a line. When not at the beginning of a regular expression, `^` stands for itself.

$ When used at the end of a regular expression, requires that the preceding regular expression be found at the end of the line; for example, `here:$` matches only when `here:` occurs at the end of a line. When not at the end of a regular expression, $ stands for itself.

\   Treats the following special character as an ordinary character. For example, `\.` matches an actual period instead of "any single character," and `\*` matches an actual asterisk instead of "any number of a character." The \ (backslash) prevents the interpretation of a special character. This prevention is called "escaping the character." (Use `\\` to get a literal backslash.)

---

* Much more information on regular expressions can be found in the two O'Reilly books *sed & awk*, by Dale Dougherty and Arnold Robbins, and *Mastering Regular Expressions*, by Jeffrey E.F. Friedl.

† Technically speaking, we should probably call these *metasequences*, since sometimes two characters together have special meaning, and not just single characters. Nevertheless, the term *metacharacters* is in common use in UNIX literature, so we follow that convention here.

[   ]
> Matches any *one* of the characters enclosed between the brackets. For example, [AB] matches either *A* or *B*, and p[aeiou]t matches *pat, pet, pit, pot,* or *put.* A range of consecutive characters can be specified by separating the first and last characters in the range with a hyphen. For example, [A-Z] will match any uppercase letter from *A* to *Z,* and [0-9] will match any digit from *0* to *9.*
>
> You can include more than one range inside brackets, and you can specify a mix of ranges and separate characters. For example, [:;A-Za-z()] will match four different punctuation marks, plus all letters.
>
> Most metacharacters lose their special meaning inside brackets, so you don't need to escape them if you want to use them as ordinary characters. Within brackets, the three metacharacters you still need to escape are \ -]. The hyphen (-) acquires meaning as a range specifier; to use an actual hyphen, you can also place it as the first character inside the brackets.
>
> A caret (^) has special meaning only when it is the first character inside the brackets, but in this case the meaning differs from that of the normal ^ metacharacter. As the first character within brackets, a ^ reverses their sense: the brackets will match any one character *not* in the list. For example, [^a-z] matches any character that is not a lowercase letter.

\(\)
> Saves the pattern enclosed between \(and \) into a special holding space or "hold buffer." Up to nine patterns can be saved in this way on a single line. For example, the pattern:
>
> ```
> \(That\) or \(this\)
> ```
>
> saves *That* in hold buffer number 1 and saves *this* in hold buffer number 2. The patterns held can be "replayed" in substitutions by the sequences \1 to \9. For example, to rephrase *That or this* to read *this or That,* you could enter:
>
> ```
> :%s/\(That\) or \(this\)/\2 or \1/
> ```
>
> You can also use the \n notation within a search or substitute string:
>
> ```
> :s/\(abcd\)\1/alphabet-soup/
> ```
>
> changes *abcdabcd* into *alphabet-soup.*[*]

---

[*] This works with *vi, nvi,* and *vim,* but not with *elvis* 2.0, *vile* 7.4, or *vile* 8.0.

\<   \>

    Matches characters at the beginning (\<) or at the end (\>) of a word. The end or beginning of a word is determined either by a punctuation mark or by a space. For example, the expression \<ac will match only words that begin with *ac*, such as *action*. The expression ac\> will match only words that end with *ac*, such as *maniac*. Neither expression will match *react*. Note that unlike \ (. . . \), these do not have to be used in matched pairs.

~   Matches whatever regular expression was used in the *last* search. For example, if you searched for *The*, you could search for *Then* with /~n. Note that you can use this pattern only in a regular search (with /).* It won't work as the pattern in a substitute command. It does, however, have a similar meaning in the replacement portion of a substitute command.

Several of the clones support optional, extended regular expression syntaxes. See the section "Extended Regular Expressions" in Chapter 8 for more information.

POSIX Bracket Expressions

We have just described the use of brackets for matching any one of the enclosed characters, such as [a-z]. The POSIX standard introduced additional facilities for matching characters that are not in the English alphabet. For example, the French è is an alphabetic character, but the typical character class [a-z] would not match it. Additionally, the standard provides for sequences of characters that should be treated as a single unit when matching and collating (sorting) string data.

POSIX also formalizes the terminology. Groups of characters within brackets are called a "bracket expression" in the POSIX standard. Within bracket expressions, beside literal characters such as *a*, *!*, and so on, you can have additional components. These are:

- *Character classes.* A POSIX character class consists of keywords bracketed by [: and :]. The keywords describe different classes of characters such as alphabetic characters, control characters, and so on (see Table 6-1).

- *Collating symbols.* A collating symbol is a multi-character sequence that should be treated as a unit. It consists of the characters bracketed by [. and .].

---

* This is a rather flaky feature of the original *vi*. After using it, the saved search pattern is set to the *new* text typed after the ~, *not* the combined new pattern, as one might expect. Also, none of the clones behaves this way. So, while this feature exists, it has little to recommend its use.

- *Equivalence classes.* An equivalence class lists a set of characters that should be considered equivalent, such as e and è. It consists of a named element from the locale, bracketed by [= and =].

All three of these constructs must appear inside the square brackets of a bracket expression. For example [[:alpha:]!] matches any single alphabetic character or the exclamation point, [[.ch.]] matches the collating element *ch*, but does not match just the letter *c* or the letter *h*. In a French locale, [[=e=]] might match any of *e*, *è*, or *é*. Classes and matching characters are shown in Table 6-1.

Table 6-1: POSIX Character Classes

Class	Matching Characters
[:alnum:]	Alphanumeric characters
[:alpha:]	Alphabetic characters
[:blank:]	Space and tab characters
[:cntrl:]	Control characters
[:digit:]	Numeric characters
[:graph:]	Printable and visible (non-space) characters
[:lower:]	Lowercase characters
[:print:]	Printable characters (includes whitespace)
[:punct:]	Punctuation characters
[:space:]	Whitespace characters
[:upper:]	Uppercase characters
[:xdigit:]	Hexadecimal digits

You will have to do some research to determine if you have this facility in your version of *vi*. You may need to use a special option to enable POSIX compliance, have a particular environment variable set, or use a version of *vi* that is in an unusual directory.

vi on HP-UX 9.x (and newer) systems support POSIX bracket expressions, as does */usr/xpg4/bin/vi*, on Solaris (but not */usr/bin/vi*). This facility is also available in *nvi*, and in *elvis* 2.1. As commercial UNIX vendors become standards-compliant, expect to see this feature become more widespread.

Metacharacters Used in Replacement Strings

When you make global replacements, the regular expressions above carry their special meaning only within the search portion (the first part) of the command.

For example, when you type this:

```
:%s/1\.  Start/2.  Next, start with $100/
```

note that the replacement string treats the characters . and $ literally, without your having to escape them. By the same token, let's say you enter:

```
:%s/[ABC]/[abc]/g
```

If you're hoping to replace *A* with *a*, *B* with *b*, and *C* with *c*, you'll be surprised. Since brackets behave like ordinary characters in a replacement string, this command will change every occurrence of *A*, *B*, or *C* to the five-character string *[abc]*.

To solve problems like this, you need a way to specify variable replacement strings. Fortunately, there are additional metacharacters that have special meaning in a *replacement* string.

\n   Is replaced with text matched by the *n*th pattern previously saved by \(and \), where *n* is a number from 1 to 9, and previously saved patterns (kept in hold buffers) are counted from the left on the line. See the explanation for \(and \) earlier in this chapter.

\   Treats the following special character as an ordinary character. Backslashes are metacharacters in replacement strings as well as in search patterns. To specify a real backslash, type two in a row (\ \).

&   Is replaced with the entire text matched by the search pattern when used in a replacement string. This is useful when you want to avoid retyping text:

```
:%s/Yazstremski/&, Carl/
```

The replacement will say *Yazstremski, Carl*. The & can also replace a variable pattern (as specified by a regular expression). For example, to surround each line from 1 to 10 with parentheses, type:

```
:1,10s/.*/(&)/
```

The search pattern matches the whole line, and the & "replays" the line, followed by your text.

~   Has a similar meaning as when it is used in a search pattern; the string found is replaced with the replacement text specified in the last substitute command. This is useful for repeating an edit. For example, you could say `:s/thier/their/` on one line and repeat the change on another with `:s/thier/~/`. The search pattern doesn't need to be the same, though.

For example, you could say `:s/his/their/` on one line and repeat the replacement on another with `:s/her/~/`.*

`\u` *or* `\l`

Causes the next character in the replacement string to be changed to upper-case or lowercase, respectively. For example, to change *yes, doctor* into *Yes, Doctor*, you could say:

```
:%s/yes, doctor/\uyes, \udoctor/
```

This is a pointless example, though, since it's easier just to type the replacement string with initial caps in the first place. As with any regular expression, `\u` and `\l` are most useful with a variable string. Take, for example, the command we used earlier:

```
:%s/\(That\) or \(this\)/\2 or \1/
```

The result is *this or That,* but we need to adjust the cases. We'll use `\u` to uppercase the first letter in *this* (currently saved in hold buffer 2); we'll use `\l` to lowercase the first letter in *That* (currently saved in hold buffer 1):

```
:s/\(That\) or \(this\)/\u\2 or \l\1/
```

The result is *This or that.* (Don't confuse the number one with the lowercase l; the one comes after.)

`\U` *or* `\L` *and* `\e` *or* `\E`

`\U` and `\L` are similar to `\u` or `\l`, but all following characters are converted to uppercase or lowercase until the end of the replacement string or until `\e` or `\E` is reached. If there is no `\e` or `\E`, all characters of the replacement text are affected by the `\U` or `\L`. For example, to uppercase *Fortran*, you could say:

```
:%s/Fortran/\UFortran/
```

or, using the & character to repeat the search string:

```
:%s/Fortran/\U&/
```

All pattern searches are case-sensitive. That is, a search for *the* will not find *The.* You can get around this by specifying both uppercase and lowercase in the pattern:

```
/[Tt]he
```

You can also instruct *vi* to ignore case by typing `:set ic`. See Chapter 7, *Advanced Editing,* for additional details.

---

* Modern versions of the *ed* editor use % as the sole character in the replacement text to mean "the replacement text of the last substitute command."

More Substitution Tricks

You should know some additional important facts about the substitute command:

1. A simple `:s` is the same as `:s//~/`. In other words, repeat the last substitution. This can save enormous amounts of time and typing when you are working your way through a document making the same change repeatedly, but you don't want to use a global substitution.

2. If you think of the `&` as meaning "the same thing" (as in what was just matched), this command is relatively mnemonic. You can follow the `&` with a `g`, to make the substitution globally on the line, and even use it with a line range:

    > `:%&g`   *repeat the last substitution everywhere*

3. The `&` key can be used as a *vi* command to perform the `:&` command, i.e., to repeat the last substitution. This can save even more typing than `:s` `RETURN` ; one keystroke versus three.

4. The `:~` command is similar to the `:&` command, but with a subtle difference. The search pattern used is the last regular expression used in *any* command, not necessarily the one used in the last substitute command.

    For example,* in the sequence:

        :s/red/blue/
        :/green
        :~

    The `:~` is equivalent to `:s/green/blue/`.

5. Besides the `/` character, you may use any non-alphanumeric, non-whitespace character as your delimiter, except backslash, double-quote, and the vertical bar (`\`, `"`, and `|`). This is particularly handy when you have to make a change to a pathname.

        :%s;/user1/tim;/home/tim;g

6. When the `edcompatible` option is enabled, *vi* remembers the flags (`g` for global and `c` for confirmation) used on the last substitute, and applies them to the next one.

    This is most useful when you are moving through a file and you wish to make global substitutions. You can make the first change:

        :s/old/new/g
        :set edcompatible

---

* Thanks to Keith Bostic, in the *nvi* documentation, for this example.

After that, subsequent substitute commands will be global.

Despite the name, no known version of UNIX *ed* actually works this way.

Pattern-Matching Examples

Unless you are already familiar with regular expressions, the discussion of special characters above probably looks forbiddingly complex. A few more examples should make things clearer. In the examples that follow, a square (□) is used to mark a space; it is not a special character.

Let's work through how you might use some special characters in a replacement. Suppose that you have a long file and that you want to substitute the word *child* with the word *children* throughout that file. You first save the edited buffer with :w, then try the global replacement:

```
:%s/child/children/g
```

When you continue editing, you notice occurrences of words such as *childrenish*. You have unintentionally matched the word *childish*. Returning to the last saved buffer with :e!, you now try:

```
:%s/child□/children□/g
```

(Note that there is a space after *child*.) But this command misses the occurrences *child.*, *child,*, *child:* and so on. After some thought, you remember that brackets allow you to specify one character from among a list, so you realize a solution:

```
:%s/child[□,.;:!?]/children[□,.;:!?]/g
```

This searches for *child* followed by either a space (indicated by □) or any one of the punctuation characters , . ; : ! ?. You expect to replace this with *children* followed by the corresponding space or punctuation mark, but you've ended up with a bunch of punctuation marks after every occurrence of *children*. You need to save the space and punctuation marks inside a \(and \). Then you can "replay" them with a \1. Here's the next attempt:

```
:%s/child\([□,.;:!?]\)/children\1/g
```

When the search matches a character inside the \(and \), the \1 on the right-hand side restores the same character. The syntax may seem awfully complicated, but this command sequence can save you a lot of work! *Any time you spend learning regular expression syntax will be repaid a thousandfold!*

The command is still not perfect, though. You've noticed that occurrences of *Fairchild* have been changed, so you need a way to match *child* when it isn't part of another word.

As it turns out, *vi* (but not all other programs that use regular expressions) has a special syntax for saying "only if the pattern is a complete word." The character sequence \< requires the pattern to match at the beginning of a word, whereas \> requires the pattern to match at the end of a word. Using both will restrict the match to a whole word. So, in the task given above, \<child\> will find all instances of the word *child*, whether followed by punctuation or spaces. Here's the substitution command you should use:

```
:%s/\<child\>/children/g
```

Search for General Class of Words

Suppose your subroutine names begin with the prefixes: *mgi, mgr,* and *mga*.

```
mgibox routine,
mgrbox routine,
mgabox routine,
```

If you want to save the prefixes, but want to change the name *box* to *square,* either of the following replacement commands will do the trick. The first example illustrates how \ (and \) can be used to save whatever pattern was actually matched. The second example shows how you can search for one pattern but change another:

```
:g/mg\([ira]\)box/s//mg\1square/g
```

```
mgisquare routine,
mgrsquare routine,
mgasquare routine,
```

> The global replacement keeps track of whether an *i, r* or *a* is saved. In that way, *box* is changed to *square* only when *box* is part of the routine's name.

```
:g/mg[ira]box/s/box/square/g
```

```
mgisquare routine,
mgrsquare routine,
mgasquare routine,
```

> This has the same effect as the previous command, but it is a little less safe since it could change other instances of *box* on the same line, not just those within the routine names.

Block Move by Patterns

You can also move blocks of text delimited by patterns. For example, assume you have a 150-page reference manual. Each page is organized into three paragraphs with the same three headings: SYNTAX, DESCRIPTION, and PARAMETERS. A sample of one reference page follows:

```
.Rh 0 "Get status of named file" "STAT"
.Rh "SYNTAX"
.nf
integer*4 stat, retval
integer*4 status(11)
character*123 filename
...
retval = stat (filename, status)
.fi
.Rh "DESCRIPTION"
Writes the fields of a system data structure into the
status array.
These fields contain (among other
things) information about the file's location, access
privileges, owner, and time of last modification.
.Rh "PARAMETERS"
.IP "\fBfilename\fR" 15n
A character string variable or constant containing
the UNIX pathname for the file whose status you want
to retrieve.
You can give the ...
```

Suppose that it is decided to move DESCRIPTION above the SYNTAX paragraph. With pattern matching, you can move blocks of text on all 150 pages with one command!

```
:g /SYNTAX/.,/DESCRIPTION/-1 move /PARAMETERS/-1
```

This command works as follows. First, *ex* finds and marks each line that matches the first pattern (i.e., that contains the word *SYNTAX*). Second, for each marked line, it sets . (dot, the current line) to that line, and executes the command. Using the **move** command, the command moves the block of lines from the current line (dot) to the line before the one containing the word *DESCRIPTION* (/DESCRIP-TION/-1) to just before the line containing *PARAMETERS* (/PARAMETERS/-1).

Note that *ex* can place text only below the line specified. To tell *ex* to place text above a line, you first subtract one with -1, and then *ex* places your text below the previous line. In a case like this, one command saves literally hours of work. (This is a real-life example—we once used a pattern match like this to rearrange a reference manual containing hundreds of pages.)

Block definition by patterns can be used equally well with other *ex* commands. For example, if you wanted to delete all DESCRIPTION paragraphs in the reference chapter, you could enter:

```
:g/DESCRIPTION/,/PARAMETERS/-1d
```

This very powerful kind of change is implicit in *ex*'s line addressing syntax, but it is not readily apparent even to experienced users. For this reason, whenever you are faced with a complex, repetitive editing task, take the time to analyze the problem and find out if you can apply pattern-matching tools to get the job done.

More Examples

Since the best way to learn pattern matching is by example, here is a list of pattern-matching examples, with explanations. Study the syntax carefully, so that you understand the principles at work. You should then be able to adapt these examples to your own situation.

1. Put *troff* italicization codes around the word *RETURN*:

   ```
   :%s/RETURN/\\fI&\\fP/g
   ```

   Notice that two backslashes (\\) are needed in the replacement, because the backslash in the *troff* italicization code will be interpreted as a special character. (\ fI alone would be interpreted as *fI*; you must type \\ fI to get \ *fI*.)

2. Modify a list of pathnames in a file:

   ```
   :%s/\/home\/tim/\/home\/linda/g
   ```

   A slash (used as a delimiter in the global replacement sequence) must be escaped with a backslash when it is part of the pattern or replacement; use \ / to get /. An alternate way to achieve this same effect is to use a different character as the pattern delimiter. For example, you could make the above replacement using colons as delimiters. (The delimiter colons and the *ex* command colon are separate entities.) Thus:

   ```
   :%s:/home/tim:/home/linda:g
   ```

   This is much more readable.

3. Put HTML italicization codes around the word *RETURN*:

   ```
   :%s:RETURN:<I>&</I>:g
   ```

   Notice here the use of & to represent the text that was actually matched, and, as just described, the use of colons as delimiters instead of slashes.

4. Change all periods to semicolons in lines 1 to 10:

    ```
    :1,10s/\./;/g
    ```

    A dot has special meaning in regular expression syntax and must be escaped with a backslash (\ .).

5. Change all occurrences of the word *help* (or *Help*) to *HELP*:

    ```
    :%s/[Hh]elp/HELP/g
    ```

    or:

    ```
    :%s/[Hh]elp/\U&/g
    ```

    The \U changes the pattern that follows to all uppercase. The pattern that follows is the repeated search pattern, which is either *help* or *Help*.

6. Replace *one or more* spaces with a single space:

    ```
    :%s/□□*/□/g
    ```

    Make sure you understand how the asterisk works as a special character. An asterisk following any character (or following any regular expression that matches a single character, such as . or [a-z]) matches *zero or more* instances of that character. Therefore, you must specify *two* spaces followed by an asterisk to match one or more spaces (one space, plus zero or more spaces).

7. Replace one or more spaces following a colon with two spaces:

    ```
    :%s/:□□*/:□□/g
    ```

8. Replace one or more spaces following a period *or* a colon with two spaces:

    ```
    :%s/\([:.]\)□□*/\1□□/g
    ```

    Either of the two characters within brackets can be matched. This character is saved into a hold buffer, using \(and \), and restored on the right-hand side by the \1. Note that within brackets a special character such as a dot does not need to be escaped.

9. Standardize various uses of a word or heading:

    ```
    :%s/^Note[□:s]*/Notes:□/g
    ```

    The brackets enclose three characters: a space, a colon, and the letter *s*. Therefore, the pattern Note[□s:] will match *Note□*, *Notes* or *Note:*. An asterisk is added to the pattern so that it also matches *Note* (with zero spaces after it) and *Notes:* (the already correct spelling). Without the asterisk, *Note* would be missed entirely and *Notes:* would be incorrectly changed to *Notes:□:*.

10. Delete all blank lines:

    `:g/^$/d`

    What you are actually matching here is the beginning of the line (`^`) followed by the end of the line (`$`), with nothing in between.

11. Delete all blank lines, plus any lines that contain only whitespace:

    `:g/^[□tab]*$/d`

    (In the line above, a tab is shown as *tab*.) A line may appear to be blank, but may in fact contain spaces or tabs. The previous example will not delete such a line. This example, like the one above it, searches for the beginning and end of the line. But instead of having nothing in between, the pattern tries to find any number of spaces or tabs. If no spaces or tabs are matched, the line is blank. To delete lines that contain whitespace but that *aren't* empty, you would have to match lines with *at least* one space or tab:

    `:g/^[□tab][□tab]*$/d`

12. Delete all leading spaces on every line:

    `:%s/^□□*\(.*\)/\1/`

    Use `^□□*` to search for one or more spaces at the beginning of each line; then use `\(.*\)` to save the rest of the line into the first hold buffer. Restore the line without leading spaces, using `\1`.

13. Delete all spaces at the end of every line:

    `:%s/\(.*\)□□*$/\1/`

    For each line, use `\(.*\)` to save all the text on the line, but only up until one or more spaces at the end of the line. Restore the saved text without the spaces.

    The substitutions in this example and the previous one will happen only once on any given line, so the g option doesn't need to follow the replacement string.

14. Insert a `>□□` at the start of every line in a file:

    `:%s/^/>□□/`

    What we're really doing here is "replacing" the start of the line with `>□□`. Of course, the start of the line (being a logical construct, not an actual character) isn't really replaced!

    This command is useful when replying to mail or USENET news postings. Frequently, it is desirable to include part of the original message in your reply.

By convention, the inclusion is distinguished from your reply by setting off the included text with a right angle bracket and a couple of spaces at the start of the line. This can be done easily as shown above. (Typically, only part of the original message will be included. Unneeded text can be deleted either before or after the above replacement.) Advanced mail systems do this automatically. However, if you're using *vi* to edit your mail, you can do it with this command.

15. Add a period to the end of the next six lines:

    ```
    :.,+5s/$/./
    ```

    The line address indicates the current line plus five lines. The $ indicates the end of line. As in the previous example, the $ is a logical construct. You aren't really replacing the end of the line.

16. Reverse the order of all hyphen-separated items in a list:

    ```
    :%s/\(.*\)□-□\(.*\)/\2□-□\1/
    ```

    Use \(.*\) to save text on the line into the first hold buffer, but only until you find □-□. Then use \(.*\) to save the rest of the line into the second hold buffer. Restore the saved portions of the line, reversing the order of the two hold buffers. The effect of this command on several items is shown below.

    ```
    more - display files
    ```

    becomes:

    ```
    display files - more
    ```

    and:

    ```
    lp - print files
    ```

    becomes:

    ```
    print files - lp
    ```

17. Change every word in a file to uppercase:

    ```
    :%s/.*/\U&/
    ```

    or:

    ```
    :%s/./\U&/g
    ```

    The \U flag at the start of the replacement string tells *vi* to change the replacement to uppercase. The & character replays the text matched by the search pattern as the replacement. These two commands are equivalent; however, the first form is considerably faster, since it results in only one substitution per line (.* matches the entire line, once per line), whereas the second form results in repeated substitutions on each line (. matches only a single character, with the replacement repeated on account of the trailing **g**).

18. Reverse the order of lines in a file:*

    ```
    :g/.*/mo0
    ```

    The search pattern matches all lines (a line contains zero or more characters). Each line is moved, one by one, to the top of the file (that is, moved after imaginary line 0). As each matched line is placed at the top, it pushes the previously moved lines down, one by one, until the last line is on top. Since all lines have a beginning, the same result can be achieved more succinctly:

    ```
    :g/^/mo0
    ```

19. In a database, on all lines not marked *Paid in full,* append the phrase *Overdue*:

    ```
    :g!/Paid□in□full/s/$/Overdue/
    ```

    or the equivalent:

    ```
    :v/Paid□in□full/s/$/Overdue/
    ```

    To affect all lines *except* those matching your pattern, add a **!** to the **g** command, or simply use the **v** command.

20. For any line that doesn't begin with a number, move the line to the end of the file:

    ```
    :g!/^[0-9]/m$
    ```

    or:

    ```
    :g/^[^0-9]/m$
    ```

    As the first character within brackets, a caret negates the sense, so the two commands have the same effect. The first one says, "Don't match lines that begin with a number," and the second one says, "Match lines that don't begin with a number."

21. Change manually numbered section heads (e.g., 1.1, 1.2, etc.) to a *troff* macro (e.g., .Ah for an A-level heading):

    ```
    :%s/^[1-9]\.[1-9]/.Ah/
    ```

    The search string matches a digit other than zero, followed by a period, followed by another non-zero digit. Notice that the period doesn't need to be escaped in the replacement (though a \ would have no effect, either). The command above won't find chapter numbers containing two or more digits.

---

* From an article by Walter Zintz in *UNIX World,* May 1990.

To do so, modify the command like this:

```
:%s/^[1-9][0-9]*\.[1-9]/.Ah/
```

Now it will match chapters 10 to 99 (digits 1 to 9, followed by a digit), 100 to 999 (digits 1 to 9, followed by two digits), etc. The command still finds chapters 1 to 9 (digits 1 to 9, followed by no digit).

22. Remove numbering from section headings in a document. You want to change the sample lines:

```
2.1 Introduction
10.3.8 New Functions
```

into the lines:

```
Introduction
New Functions
```

Here's the command to do this:

```
:%s/^[1-9][0-9]*\.[1-9][0-9.]*□//
```

The search pattern resembles the one in the previous example, but now the numbers vary in length. At a minimum, the headings contain *number, period, number,* so you start with the search pattern from the previous example:

```
[1-9][0-9]*\.[1-9]
```

But in this example, the heading may continue with any number of digits or periods:

```
[0-9.]*
```

23. Change the word *Fortran* to the phrase *FORTRAN (acronym of FORmula TRANslation):*

```
:%s/\(For\)\(tran\)/\U\1\2\E□(acronym□of□\U\1\Emula□\U\2\Eslation)/g
```

First, since we notice that the words *FORmula* and *TRANslation* use portions of the original word, we decide to save the search pattern in two pieces: `\(For\)` and `\(tran\)`. The first time we restore it, we use both pieces together, converting all characters to uppercase: `\U\1\2`. Next, we undo the uppercase with `\E`; otherwise the remaining replacement text would all be uppercase. The replacement continues with actual typed words, then we restore the first hold buffer. This buffer still contains *For,* so again we convert to uppercase first: `\U\1`. Immediately after, we lowercase the rest of the word: `\Emula`. Finally, we restore the second hold buffer. This contains *tran,* so we precede the "replay" with uppercase, follow it with lowercase, and type out the rest of the word: `\U\2\Eslation`).

A Final Look at Pattern Matching

We conclude this chapter by presenting sample tasks that involve complex pattern-matching concepts. Rather than solve the problems right away, we'll work toward the solutions step by step.

Deleting an Unknown Block of Text

Suppose you have a few lines with this general form:

```
the best of times; the worst of times:  moving
The coolest of times; the worst of times:  moving
```

The lines that you're concerned with always end with *moving*, but you never know what the first two words might be. You want to change any line that ends with *moving* to read:

```
The greatest of times; the worst of times:  moving
```

Since the changes must occur on certain lines, you need to specify a context-sensitive global replacement. Using `:g/moving$/` will match lines that end with *moving*. Next, you realize that your search pattern could be any number of any character, so the metacharacters `.*` come to mind. But these will match the whole line unless you somehow restrict the match. Here's your first attempt:

```
:g/moving$/s/.*of/The□greatest□of/
```

This search string, you decide, will match from the beginning of the line to the first *of.* Since you needed to specify the word *of* to restrict the search, you simply repeat it in the replacement. Here's the resulting line:

```
The greatest of times:  moving
```

Something went wrong. The replacement gobbled the line up to the second *of* instead of the first. Here's why. When given a choice, the action of "match any number of any character" will match as much text as possible. In this case, since the word *of* appears twice, your search string finds:

```
the best of times; the worst of
```

rather than:

```
the best of
```

Your search pattern needs to be more restrictive:

```
:g/moving$/s/.*of times;/The greatest of times;/
```

Now the `.*` will match all characters up to the instance of the phrase *of times;.* Since there's only one instance, it has to be the first.

There are cases, though, when it is inconvenient, or even incorrect, to use the `.*` metacharacters. For example, you might find yourself typing many words to restrict your search pattern, or you might be unable to restrict the pattern by specific words (if the text in the lines varies widely). The next section presents such a case.

Switching Items in a Database

Suppose you want to switch the order of all last names and first names in a (text) database. The lines look like this:

```
Name: Feld, Ray; Areas: PC, UNIX; Phone: 123-4567
Name: Joy, Susan S.; Areas: Graphics; Phone: 999-3333
```

The name of each field ends with a colon, and each field is separated by a semicolon. Using the top line as an example, you want to change *Feld, Ray* to *Ray Feld*. We'll present some commands that look promising but don't work. After each command, we show you the line the way it looked before the change and after the change.

```
:%s/: \(.*\), \(.*\);/: \2 \1;/
```

Name: **Feld, Ray; Areas: PC,** *UNIX*; Phone: 123-4567   *Before*
Name: *UNIX* **Feld, Ray; Areas: PC**; Phone: 123-4567   *After*

We've highlighted the contents of the first hold buffer in **bold** and the contents of the second hold buffer in *italic*. Note that the first hold buffer contains more than you want. Since it was not sufficiently restricted by the pattern that follows it, the hold buffer was able to save up to the second comma. Now you try to restrict the contents of the first hold buffer:

```
:%s/: \(....\), \(.*\);/: \2 \1;/
```

Name: **Feld**, *Ray; Areas: PC, UNIX*; Phone: 123-4567   *Before*
Name: *Ray; Areas: PC, UNIX* **Feld**; Phone: 123-4567   *After*

Here you've managed to save the last name in the first hold buffer, but now the second hold buffer will save anything up to the last semicolon on the line. Now you restrict the second hold buffer, too:

```
:%s/: \(....\), \(...\);/: \2 \1;/
```

Name: **Feld**, *Ray*; Areas: PC, UNIX; Phone: 123-4567   *Before*
Name: *Ray* **Feld**; Areas: PC, UNIX; Phone: 123-4567   *After*

This gives you what you want, but only in the specific case of a four-letter last name and a three-letter first name. (The previous attempt included the same mistake.) Why not just return to the first attempt, but this time be more selective about the end of the search pattern?

```
:%s/: \(.*\), \(.*\); Area/: \2 \1; Area/
```

Name: **Feld**, *Ray*; Areas: PC, UNIX; Phone: 123-4567   *Before*
Name: *Ray* **Feld**; Areas: PC, UNIX; Phone: 123-4567   *After*

This works, but we'll continue the discussion by introducing an additional concern. Suppose that the *Area* field isn't always present or isn't always the second field. The above command won't work on such lines.

We introduce this problem to make a point. Whenever you rethink a pattern match, it's usually better to work toward refining the variables (the metacharacters), rather than using specific text to restrict patterns. The more variables you use in your patterns, the more powerful your commands will be.

In the current example, think again about the patterns you want to switch. Each word starts with an uppercase letter and is followed by any number of lowercase letters, so you can match the names like this:

```
[A-Z][a-z]*
```

A last name might also have more than one uppercase letter (*McFly*, for example), so you'd want to search for this possibility in the second and succeeding letters:

```
[A-Z][A-Za-z]*
```

It doesn't hurt to use this for the first name, too (you never know when *McGeorge Bundy* will turn up). Your command now becomes:

```
:%s/: \([A-Z][A-Za-z]*\), \([A-Z][A-Za-z]*\);/: \2 \1;/
```

Quite forbidding, isn't it? It still doesn't cover the case of a name like *Joy, Susan S.* Since the first-name field might include a middle initial, you need to add a space and a period within the second pair of brackets. But enough is enough. Sometimes, specifying exactly what you want is more difficult than specifying what you *don't* want. In your sample database, the last names end with a comma, so a last-name field can be thought of as a string of characters that are *not* commas:

```
[^,]*
```

This pattern matches characters up until the first comma. Similarly, the first-name field is a string of characters that are *not* semicolons:

```
[^;]*
```

Putting these more efficient patterns back into your previous command, you get:

```
:%s/: \([^,]*\), \([^;]*\);/: \2 \1;/
```

The same command could also be entered as a context-sensitive replacement. If all lines begin with *Name*, you can say:

```
:g/^Name/s/: \([^,]*\), \([^;]*\);/: \2 \1;/
```

You can also add an asterisk after the first space, in order to match a colon that has extra spaces (or no spaces) after it:

```
:g/^Name/s/: *\([^,]*\), \([^;]*\);/: \2 \1;/
```

Using :g to Repeat a Command

As we've usually seen the `:g` command used, it selects lines that are typically then edited by subsequent commands on the same line—for example, we select lines with g, and then make substitutions on them, or select them and delete them:

```
:g/mg[ira]box/s/box/square/g
:g/^$/d
```

However, in his two-part tutorial in *UNIX World*,* Walter Zintz makes an interesting point about the g command. This command selects lines—but the associated editing commands need not actually affect the lines that are selected.

Instead, he demonstrates a technique by which you can repeat *ex* commands some arbitrary number of times. For example, suppose you want to place ten copies of lines 12 through 17 of your file at the end of your current file. You could type:

```
:1,10g/^/ 12,17t$
```

This is a very unexpected use of g, but it works! The g command selects line 1, executes the specified t command, then goes on to line 2, to execute the next copy command. When line 10 is reached, *ex* will have made ten copies.

Collecting Lines

Here's another advanced g example, again building on suggestions provided in Zintz's article. Suppose you're editing a document that consists of several parts. Part 2 of this file is shown below, using ellipses to show omitted text and displaying line numbers for reference:

```
301    Part 2
302    Capability Reference
303    .LP
304    Chapter 7
```

---

* Part 1, "*vi* Tips for Power Users," appears in the April 1990 issue of *UNIX World*. Part 2, "Using *vi* to Automate Complex Edits," appears in the May 1990 issue. The examples presented are from Part 2.

```
305  Introduction to the Capabilities
306  This and the next three chapters ...

400  ... and a complete index at the end.
401  .LP
402  Chapter 8
403  Screen Dimensions
404  Before you can do anything useful
405  on the screen, you need to know ...

555  .LP
556  Chapter 9
557  Editing the Screen
558  This chapter discusses ...

821  .LP
822  Part 3:
823  Advanced Features
824  .LP
825  Chapter 10
```

The chapter numbers appear on one line, their titles appear on the line below, and the chapter text (highlighted for emphasis) begins on the line below that. The first thing you'd like to do is copy the beginning line of each chapter, sending it to an already existing file called *begin*.

Here's the command that does this:

```
:g /^Chapter/ .+2w >> begin
```

You must be at the top of your file before issuing this command. First you search for *Chapter* at the start of a line, but then you want to run the command on the beginning line of each chapter—the second line below *Chapter*. Because a line beginning with *Chapter* is now selected as the current line, the line address .+2 will indicate the second line below it. The equivalent line addresses +2 or ++ work as well. You want to write these lines to an existing file named *begin*, so you issue the w command with the append operator >>.

Suppose you want to send the beginnings of chapters that are only within Part 2. You need to restrict the lines selected by g, so you change your command to this:

```
:/^Part 2/,/^Part 3/g /^Chapter/ .+2w >> begin
```

Here, the g command selects the lines that begin with *Chapter*, but it searches only that portion of the file from a line starting with *Part 2* through a line starting with *Part 3*. If you issue the above command, the last lines of the file *begin* will read as follows:

```
This and the next three chapters ...
Before you can do anything useful
This chapter discusses ...
```

These are the lines that begin Chapters 7, 8, and 9.

In addition to the lines you've just sent, you'd like to copy chapter titles to the end of the document, in preparation for making a table of contents. You can use the vertical bar to tack a second command after your first command, like so:

```
:/^Part 2/,/^Part 3/g /^Chapter/ .+2w >> begin | +t$
```

Remember that with any subsequent command, line addresses are relative to the previous command. The first command has marked lines (within Part 2) that start with *Chapter*, and the chapter titles appear on a line below such lines. Therefore, to access chapter titles in the second command, the line address is + (or the equivalents +1 or .+1). Then use t$ to copy the chapter titles to the end of the file.

As these examples illustrate, thought and experimentation may lead you to some unusual editing solutions. Don't be afraid to try things! Just be sure to back up your file first!

7

Advanced Editing

This chapter introduces you to some of the more advanced capabilities of the *vi* and *ex* editors. You should be reasonably familiar with the material presented in the earlier chapters of this book before you start working with the concepts presented in this chapter.

This chapter is divided into five parts. The first part discusses a number of ways to set options that allow you to customize your editing environment. You'll learn how to use the `set` command and how to create a number of different editing environments using *.exrc* files.

The second part discusses how you can execute UNIX commands from within *vi*, and how you can use *vi* to filter text through UNIX commands.

The third part discusses various ways to save long sequences of commands by reducing them to abbreviations, or even to commands that use only one keystroke (this is called *mapping* keys). It also includes a section on @-functions, which allow you to store command sequences in a buffer.

The fourth part discusses the use of *ex* scripts from the UNIX command line or from within shell scripts. Scripting provides a powerful way to make repetitive edits.

The fifth part discusses some features of *vi* that are especially useful to programmers. *vi* has options that control line indentation and an option to display invisible characters (specifically tabs and newlines). There are search commands that are useful with program code blocks or with C functions.

Customizing vi

You have seen that *vi* operates differently on various terminals. (For instance, on "dumb" terminals, *vi* inserts @ symbols in place of deleted lines; on intelligent terminals, *vi* redraws the screen with each edit.) On modern UNIX systems, *vi* gets operating instructions about your terminal type from the *terminfo* terminal database. (On older systems, *vi* uses the original *termcap* database.)*

There are also a number of options that you can set from within *vi* that affect how it operates. For example, you can set a right margin that will cause *vi* to wrap lines automatically, so you don't need to hit RETURN .

You can change options from within *vi* by using the *ex* command :set. In addition, whenever *vi* is started up, it reads a file in your home directory called *.exrc* for further operating instructions. By placing :set commands in this file, you can modify the way *vi* acts whenever you use it.

You can also set up *.exrc* files in local directories to initialize various options that you want to use in different environments. For example, you might define one set of options for editing English text, but another set for editing source programs. The *.exrc* file in your home directory will be executed first, then the one in your current directory.

Finally, any commands stored in the shell variable EXINIT will be executed by *vi* on startup. The settings in EXINIT take precedence over those in the home directory *.exrc* file.

The :set Command

There are two types of options that can be changed with the :set command: toggle options, which are either on or off, and options that take a numeric or string value (such as the location of a margin or the name of a file).

Toggle options may be on or off by default. To turn a toggle option on, the command is:

    :set *option*

To turn a toggle option off, the command is:

    :set no*option*

---

* The location of these two databases varies from vendor to vendor. Try the commands man terminfo and man termcap to get more information about your specific system.

For example, to specify that pattern searches should ignore case, type:

```
:set ic
```

If you want *vi* to return to being case-sensitive in searches, give the command:

```
:set noic
```

Some options have a value assigned to them. For example, the `window` option sets the number of lines shown in the screen's "window." You set values for these options with an equal sign (=):

```
:set window=20
```

During a *vi* session, you can check which options *vi* is using. The command:

```
:set all
```

displays the complete list of options, including options that you have set and defaults that *vi* has "chosen." The display should look something like this:*

autoindent	nomodelines	noshowmode
autoprint	nonumber	noslowopen
noautowrite	nonovice	tabstop=8
beautify	nooptimize	taglength=0
directory=/var/tmp	paragraphs=IPLPPPQPP LIpplpipnpbp	tags=tags /usr/lib/tags
noedcompatible	prompt	tagstack
errorbells	noreadonly	term=vt102
noexrc	redraw	noterse
flash	remap	timeout
hardtabs=8	report=3	ttytype=vt102
noignorecase	scroll=11	warn
nolisp	sections=NHSHH HUuhsh+c	window=23
nolist	shell=/bin/ksh	wrapscan
magic	shiftwidth=8	wrapmargin=0
nomesg	showmatch	nowriteany

You can find out the current value of any individual option by name, using the command:

```
:set option?
```

The command:

```
:set
```

shows options that you have specifically changed, or set, either in your *.exrc* file or during the current session.

---

* The result of `:set all` depends very much on the version of *vi* you have. This is typical of UNIX *vi*; what comes out of the various clones will be different.

For example, the display might look like this:

```
number sect=AhBhChDh window=20 wrapmargin=10
```

The .exrc File

The *.exrc* file that controls your own *vi* environment is in your home directory (the directory you are in when you first log on). You can modify the *.exrc* file with the *vi* editor, just as you can any other text file.

If you don't yet have an *.exrc* file, simply use *vi* to create one. Enter into this file the set, ab, and map commands that you want to have in effect whenever you use *vi* or *ex*. (ab and map are discussed later in this chapter.) A sample *.exrc* file might look like this:

```
set nowrapscan wrapmargin=7
set sections=SeAhBhChDh nomesg
map q :w^M:n^M
map v dwElp
ab ORA O'Reilly & Associates, Inc.
```

Since the file is actually read by *ex* before it enters visual mode (*vi*), commands in *.exrc* need not have a preceding colon.

Alternate Environments

In addition to reading the *.exrc* file in your home directory, you can allow *vi* to read a file called *.exrc* in the current directory. This allows you to set options that are appropriate to a particular project.

For example, you might want to have one set of options in a directory mainly used for programming:

```
set number autoindent sw=4 terse
set tags=/usr/lib/tags
```

and another set of options in a directory used for text editing:

```
set wrapmargin=15 ignorecase
```

Note that you can set certain options in the *.exrc* file in your home directory and unset them in a local directory.

You can also define alternate *vi* environments by saving option settings in a file other than *.exrc* and reading in that file with the :so command. (so is short for source.)

For example:

```
:so .progoptions
```

Local *.exrc* files are also useful for defining abbreviations and key mappings (described later in this chapter). When we write a book or manual, we save all abbreviations to be used in that book in an *.exrc* file in the directory in which the book is being created.

In all modern versions of *vi*, you have to first set the **exrc** option in your home directory's *.exrc* file before *vi* will read the *.exrc* file in the current directory:

```
set exrc
```

This mechanism prevents other people from placing, in your working directory, an *.exrc* file whose commands might jeopardize the security of your system.*

Some Useful Options

As you can see when you type `:set all`, there are an awful lot of options that can be set. Many of them are used internally by *vi* and aren't usually changed. Others are important in certain cases, but not in others (for example, **noredraw** and **window** can be useful on a dialup line at a low baud rate). The table in the section "Solaris 2.6 vi Options" in Appendix C contains a brief description of each option. We recommend that you take some time to play with setting options—if an option looks interesting, try setting it (or unsetting it) and watch what happens while you edit. You may find some surprisingly useful tools.

As discussed earlier in this book, one option, **wrapmargin**, is essential for editing non-program text. **wrapmargin** specifies the size of the right margin that will be used to autowrap text as you type. (This saves manually typing carriage returns.) A typical value is 7 to 15:

```
:set wrapmargin=10
```

Three other options control how *vi* acts when conducting a search. Normally, a search differentiates between uppercase and lowercase (*foo* does not match *Foo*), wraps around to the beginning of the file (meaning that you can begin your search anywhere in the file and still find all occurrences), and recognizes wildcard

---

* The original versions of *vi* automatically read both files, if they existed. The **exrc** option closes a potential security hole.

characters when pattern matching. The default settings that control these options are `noignorecase`, `wrapscan`, and `magic`, respectively. To change any of these defaults, you would set the opposite toggle options: `ignorecase`, `nowrapscan`, and `nomagic`.

Options that may be of particular interest to programmers include: `autoindent`, `showmatch`, `tabstop`, `shiftwidth`, `number`, and `list`, as well as their opposite toggle options.

Finally, consider using the `autowrite` option. When set, *vi* will automatically write out the contents of a changed buffer when you issue the `:n` (next) command to move to the next file to be edited, and before running a shell command with `:!`.

Executing UNIX Commands

You can display or read in the results of any UNIX command while you are editing in *vi*. An exclamation mark (`!`) tells *ex* to create a shell and to regard what follows as a UNIX command:

```
:!command
```

So if you are editing and you want to check the time or date without exiting *vi*, you can enter:

```
:!date
```

The time and date will appear on your screen; press RETURN to continue editing at the same place in your file.

If you want to give several UNIX commands in a row without returning to *vi* editing in between, you can create a shell with the *ex* command:

```
:sh
```

When you want to exit the shell and return to *vi*, press CTRL-D .

You can combine `:read` with a call to UNIX, to read the results of a UNIX command into your file. As a very simple example:

```
:r !date
```

will read in the system's date information into the text of your file. By preceding the `:r` command with a line address, you can read the result of the command in at any desired point in your file. By default, it will appear after the current line.

Suppose you are editing a file and want to read in four phone numbers from a file called *phone*, but in alphabetical order. *phone* reads:

```
    Willing, Sue  333-4444
    Walsh, Linda  555-6666
    Quercia, Valerie  777-8888
    Dougherty, Nancy  999-0000
```

The command:

```
    :r !sort phone
```

reads in the contents of *phone* after they have been passed through the *sort* filter:

```
    Dougherty, Nancy  999-0000
    Quercia, Valerie  777-8888
    Walsh, Linda  555-6666
    Willing, Sue  333-4444
```

Suppose you are editing a file and want to insert text from another file in the directory, but you can't remember the new file's name. You *could* perform this task the long way: exit your file, give the `ls` command, note the correct filename, reenter your file, and search for your place.

Or you could do the task in fewer steps:

Keystrokes   **Results**

`:!ls`

```
    file1       file2       letter
    newfile     practice
```

Display a list of files in the current directory. Note the correct filename. Press [RETURN] to continue editing.

`:r newfile`

```
    "newfile" 35 lines, 949 characters
```

Read in the new file.

Filtering Text Through a Command

You can also send a block of text as standard input to a UNIX command. The output from this command replaces the block of text in the buffer. You can filter text through a command from either *ex* or *vi*. The main difference between the two methods is that you indicate the block of text with line addresses in *ex* and with text objects (movement commands) in *vi*.

Filtering text with ex

The first example demonstrates how to filter text with *ex*. Assume that the list of names in the preceding example, instead of being contained in a separate file called *phone*, is already contained in the current file on lines 96 through 99. You simply type the addresses of the lines you want to filter, followed by an exclamation mark and the UNIX command to be executed. For example, the command:

```
:96,99!sort
```

will pass lines 96 through 99 through the *sort* filter and replace those lines with the output of *sort*.

Filtering text with vi

In *vi*, text is filtered through a UNIX command by typing an exclamation mark followed by any of *vi*'s movement keystrokes that indicate a block of text, and then by the UNIX command line to be executed. For example:

```
!)command
```

will pass the next sentence through *command*.

There are a few unusual features about how *vi* acts when you use this feature:

- The exclamation mark doesn't appear on your screen right away. When you type the keystroke(s) for the text object you want to filter, the exclamation mark appears at the bottom of the screen, *but the character you type to reference the object does not.*

- Text blocks must be more than one line, so you can use only the keystrokes that would move more than one line (G, { }, ( ), [[ ]], +, -). To repeat the effect, a number may precede either the exclamation mark or the text object. (For example, both !10+ and 10!+ would indicate the next ten lines.) Objects such as w do not work unless enough of them are specified so as to exceed a single line. You can also use a slash (/) followed by a *pattern* and a carriage return to specify the object. This takes the text up to the pattern as input to the command.

- Entire lines are affected. For example, if your cursor is in the middle of a line and you issue a command to go to the end of the next sentence, the entire lines containing the beginning and end of the sentence will be changed, not just the sentence itself.*

- There is a special text object that can be used only with this command syntax: you can specify the current line by entering a second exclamation mark:

```
!!command
```

Remember that either the entire sequence or the text object can be preceded by a number to repeat the effect. For instance, to change lines 96 through 99

---

* Of course, there's always an exception. In this example, *vim* 5.0 changes only the current line.

as in the above example, you could position the cursor on line 96 and enter either:

```
4!!sort
```

or:

```
!4!sort
```

As another example, assume you have a portion of text in a file that you want to change from lowercase to uppercase letters. You could process that portion with the `tr` command to change the case. In this example, the second sentence is the block of text that will be filtered through the command.

```
One sentence before.
With a screen editor you can scroll the
page move the cursor, delete lines, insert
characters, and more, while seeing the results
of your edits as you make them.
One sentence after.
```

Keystrokes   **Results**

`!)`

```
One sentence after.
~
~
~
!_
```

An exclamation mark appears on the last line to prompt you for the UNIX command. The) indicates that a sentence is the unit of text to be filtered.

`tr '[a-z]' '[A-Z]'`

```
One sentence before.
WITH A SCREEN EDITOR YOU CAN SCROLL THE
PAGE MOVE THE CURSOR, DELETE LINES, INSERT
CHARACTERS, AND MORE, WHILE SEEING THE RESULTS
OF YOUR EDITS AS YOU MAKE THEM.
One sentence after.
```

Enter the UNIX command and press RETURN . The input is replaced by the output.

To repeat the previous command, the syntax is:

```
! object !
```

It is sometimes useful to send sections of a coded document to *nroff* to be replaced by formatted output. (Or when editing electronic mail, you might use the *fmt* program to "beautify" your text before sending the message.) Remember that the "original" input is replaced by the output. Fortunately, if there is a mistake, such as an error message being sent instead of the expected output, you can undo the command and restore the lines.

Saving Commands

Often you type the same long phrases over and over in a file. *vi* and *ex* have a number of different ways of saving long sequences of commands, both in command mode and in insert mode. When you call up one of these saved sequences to execute it, all you do is type a few characters (or even only one), and the entire sequence is executed as if you had entered the whole sequence of commands one by one.

Word Abbreviation

You can define abbreviations that *vi* will automatically expand into the full text whenever you type the abbreviation in insert mode. To define an abbreviation, use the *ex* command:

```
:ab abbr phrase
```

abbr is an abbreviation for the specified *phrase*. The sequence of characters that make up the abbreviation will be expanded in insert mode only if you type it as a full word; *abbr* will not be expanded within a word.

Suppose in the file *practice* you want to enter text that contains a frequently recurring phrase such as a difficult product or company name. The command:

```
:ab imrc International Materials Research Center
```

abbreviates *International Materials Research Center* to the initials *imrc*. Now whenever you type *imrc* in insert mode, *imrc* expands to the full text.

Keystrokes   **Results**
ithe imrc

> the International Materials Research Center

Abbreviations expand as soon as you press a non-alphanumeric character (e.g., punctuation), a space, a carriage return, or ESC (returning to command mode). When you are choosing abbreviations, choose combinations of characters that don't ordinarily occur while you are typing text. If you create an abbreviation that ends up expanding in places where you don't want it to, you can disable the abbreviation by typing:

```
:unab abbr
```

To list your currently defined abbreviations, type:

```
:ab
```

The characters that compose your abbreviation cannot also appear at the end of your phrase. For example, if you issue the command:

```
:ab PG This movie is rated PG
```

you'll get the message "No tail recursion," and the abbreviation won't be set. The message means that you have tried to define something that will expand itself repeatedly, creating an infinite loop. If you issue the command:

```
:ab PG the PG rating system
```

you may or may not produce an infinite loop, but in either case you won't get a warning message. For example, when the above command was tested on a System V version of UNIX, the expansion worked. Circa 1990 on a Berkeley version, the abbreviation expanded repeatedly, like this:

```
the the the the the ...
```

until a memory error occurred and *vi* quit.

When tested, we obtained the following results on these *vi* versions:

Solaris 2.6 vi
> The tail recursive version is not allowed, while the version with the name in the middle of the expansion only expands once.

nvi 1.79
> Both versions exceed an internal expansion limit, the expansion stops, and *nvi* produces an error message.

elvis 2.0
> The tail recursive version runs infinitely until the editor is interrupted. The version with the name in the middle eventually stops expanding, but without any error message.

vim 5.0 and 5.1
> Both forms are detected and only expand once.

vile 7.4 and 8.0
> Both forms are detected and only expand once.

We recommend that you avoid repeating your abbreviation as part of the defined phrase.

Using the map Command

While you're editing, you may find that you are using a command sequence frequently, or you may occasionally use a very complex command sequence. To save yourself keystrokes, or the time that it takes to remember the sequence, you can assign the sequence to an unused key by using the `map` command.

The `map` command acts a lot like `ab` except that you define a macro for *vi*'s command mode instead of for insert mode.

`:map x sequence`
> Define character *x* as a *sequence* of editing commands.

`:unmap x`
> Disable the *sequence* defined for *x*.

`:map`
> List the characters that are currently mapped.

Before you can start creating your own maps, you need to know the keys not used in command mode that are available for user-defined commands:

Letters
> g K q V v

Control keys
> ^A ^K ^O ^W ^X

Symbols
> _ * \ =

The = is used by *vi* if Lisp mode is set, and to do text formatting by several of the clones. In many modern versions of *vi*, the _ is equivalent to the ^ command, and *elvis* and *vim* have a "visual mode" that uses the v, V, and ^V keys. The moral is to test your version carefully.

Depending on your terminal, you may also be able to associate map sequences with special function keys.

With maps you can create simple or complex command sequences. As a simple example, you could define a command to reverse the order of words. In *vi*, with the cursor as shown:

```
you can the scroll page
```

the sequence to put *the* after *scroll* would be `dwelp`: delete word, `dw`; move to the end of next word, `e`; move one space to the right, `l`; put the deleted word there, `p`. Saving this sequence:

```
:map v dwelp
```

enables you to reverse the order of two words at any time in the editing session with the single keystroke `v`.

Protecting Keys from Interpretation by ex

Note that when defining a map, you cannot simply type certain keys, such as RETURN , ESC , BACKSPACE , and DELETE as part of the command to be mapped, because these keys already have meaning within *ex*. If you want to include one of these keys as part of the command sequence, you must escape the normal meaning by preceding the key with CTRL-V . The keystroke ^V appears in the map as the ^ character. Characters following the ^V also do not appear as you expect. For example, a carriage return appears as ^M, escape as ^[, backspace as ^H, and so on.

On the other hand, if you want to use a control character as the character to be mapped, in most cases all you have to do is hold down the CTRL key and press the letter key at the same time. So, for example, all you need to do in order to map ^A is to type:

```
:map CTRL-A sequence
```

There are, however, three control characters that must be escaped with a ^V. They are ^T, ^W, and ^X. So, for example, if you want to map ^T, you must type:

```
:map CTRL-V CTRL-T sequence
```

The use of CTRL-V applies to any *ex* command, not just a map command. This means that you can type a carriage return in an abbreviation or a substitution command. For example, the abbreviation:

```
:ab 123 one^Mtwo^Mthree
```

expands to this:

```
one
two
three
```

(Here we show the sequence CTRL-V RETURN as ^M, the way it would appear on your screen.)

You can also globally add lines at certain locations. The command:

```
:g/^Section/s//As you recall, in^M&/
```

inserts, before all lines beginning with the word *Section*, a phrase on a separate line. The & restores the search pattern.

Unfortunately, one character always has special meaning in *ex* commands, even if you try to quote it with CTRL-V . Recall that the vertical bar (|) has special meaning as a separator of multiple *ex* commands. You cannot use a vertical bar in insert mode maps.

Now that you've seen how to use CTRL-V to protect certain keys inside *ex* commands, you're ready to define some powerful map sequences.

Complex Mapping Example

Assume that you have a glossary with entries like this:

```
map - an ex command which allows you to associate
a complex command sequence with a single key.
```

You would like to convert this glossary list to *troff* format, so that it looks like this:

```
.IP "map" 10 n
An ex command...
```

The best way to define a complex map is to do the edit once manually, writing down each keystroke that you have to type. Then recreate these keystrokes as a map. You want to:

1. Insert the MS macro for an indented paragraph at the beginning of the line. Insert the first quotation mark as well (I.IP ").

2. Press ESC to terminate insert mode.

3. Move to the end of the first word (e) and add a second quotation mark, followed by a space and the size of the indent (a" 10n).

4. Press RETURN to insert a new line.

5. Press ESC to terminate insert mode.

6. Remove the hyphen and two surrounding spaces (3x) and capitalize the next word (˜).

That will be quite an editing chore if you have to repeat it more than just a few times.

With `:map` you can save the entire sequence so that it can be re-executed with a single keystroke:

```
:map g I.IP "^[ea" 10n^M^[3x~
```

Note that you have to "quote" both the ESC and RETURN characters with CTRL-V . `^[` is the sequence that appears when you type CTRL-V followed by ESC . `^M` is the sequence shown when you type CTRL-V RETURN .

Now, simply typing g will perform the entire series of edits. At a slow baud rate you can actually see the edits happening individually. At a fast baud rate it will seem to happen by magic.

Don't be discouraged if your first attempt at key mapping fails. A small error in defining the map can give very different results from the ones you expect. Type u to undo the edit, and try again.

More Examples of Mapping Keys

These examples will give you an idea of the clever shortcuts possible when defining keyboard maps:

1. Add text whenever you move to the end of a word:

   ```
   :map e ea
   ```

   Most of the time, the only reason you want to move to the end of a word is to add text. This map sequence puts you in insert mode automatically. Note that the mapped key, e, has meaning in *vi*. You're allowed to map a key that is already used by *vi*, but the key's normal function will be unavailable as long as the map is in effect. This isn't so bad in this case, since the E command is often identical to e.

2. Transpose two words:

   ```
   :map K dwElp
   ```

   We discussed this sequence earlier in the chapter, but now you need to use E (assume here, and in the remaining examples, that the e command is mapped to ea). Remember that the cursor begins on the first of the two words. Unfortunately, because of the l command, this sequence (and the earlier version) doesn't work if the two words are at the end of a line: during the sequence, the cursor ends up at the end of the line, and l cannot move further right. Here's a better solution:

   ```
   :map K dwwP
   ```

   You could also use W instead of w.

3. Save a file and edit the next one in a series:

   ```
   :map q :w^M:n^M
   ```

   Notice that you can map keys to *ex* commands, but be sure to finish each *ex* command with a carriage return. This sequence makes it easy to move from one file to the next and is useful when you've opened many short files with one *vi* command. Mapping the letter q helps you remember that the sequence is similar to a "quit."

4. Put *troff* emboldening codes around a word:

   ```
   :map v i\fB^[e\fP^[
   ```

   This sequence assumes that the cursor is at the beginning of the word. First, you enter insert mode, then you type the code for the bold font. In map commands, you don't need to type two backslashes to produce one backslash. Next, you return to command mode by typing a "quoted" ESC . Finally, you append the closing *troff* code at the end of the word, and you return to command mode. Notice that when we appended to the end of the word, we didn't need to use ea, since this sequence is itself mapped to the single letter e. This shows you that map sequences are allowed to contain other mapped commands. (The ability to use nested map sequences is controlled by *vi's* remap option, which is normally enabled.)

5. Put *troff* emboldening codes around a word, even when the cursor is not at the beginning of the word:

   ```
   :map V lbi\fB^[e\fP^[
   ```

   This sequence is the same as the previous one, except that it uses lb to handle the additional task of positioning the cursor at the beginning of the word. The cursor might be in the middle of the word, so you want to move to the beginning with the b command. But if the cursor were already at the beginning of the word, the b command would move the cursor to the previous word instead. To guard against that case, type an l before moving back with b, so that the cursor never starts on the first letter of the word. You can define variations of this sequence by replacing the b with B and the e with Ea. In all cases, though, the l command prevents this sequence from working if the cursor is at the end of a line. (You could append a space to get around this.)

6. Repeatedly find and remove parentheses from around a word or phrase: *

   ```
   :map = xf)xn
   ```

---

* From the article by Walter Zintz, in *UNIX World*, April 1990.

This sequence assumes that you first found an open parenthesis, by typing / (followed by RETURN .

If you choose to remove the parentheses, then use the map command: delete the open parenthesis with **x**, find the closing one with **f)**, delete it with **x**, and then repeat your search for an open parenthesis with **n**.

If you don't want to remove the parentheses (for example, if they're being used correctly), then don't use the map command: press **n** instead to find the next open parenthesis.

You could also modify the map sequence above to handle matching pairs of quotes.

7. Place C/C++ comments around an entire line:

```
:map g I/* ^[A */^[
```

This sequence inserts **/*** at the line's beginning and appends ***/** at the line's end. You could also map a substitute command to do the same thing:

```
:map g :s;.*;/* & */;^M
```

Here, you match the entire line (with **.***), and when you replay it (with **&**), you surround the line with the comment symbols. Note the use of semicolon delimiters, to avoid having to escape the **/** in the comment.

8. Safely repeat a long insertion:

```
:map ^J :set wm=0^M.:set wm=10^M
```

We mentioned in Chapter 2, *Simple Editing*, that *vi* occasionally has difficulty repeating long insertions of text when **wrapmargin** is set. This map command is a useful workaround. It temporarily turns off the wrapmargin (by setting it to 0), gives the repeat command, and then restores the wrapmargin. Note that a map sequence can combine *ex* and *vi* commands.

In the previous example, even though **^J** is a *vi* command (it moves the cursor down a line), this key is safe to map because it's really the same as the **j** command. There are many keys that either perform the same tasks as other keys or are rarely used. However, you should be familiar with the *vi* commands before you boldly disable their normal use by using them in map definitions.

Mapping Keys for Insert Mode

Normally, maps apply only to command mode—after all, in insert mode, keys stand for themselves and shouldn't be mapped as commands. However, by adding an exclamation mark (!) to the **map** command, you can force it to override the ordinary meaning of a key and produce the map in insert mode. This feature is useful when you find yourself in insert mode but need to escape briefly to command mode, run a command, and then return to insert mode.

For example, suppose you just typed a word but forgot to italicize it (or place quotes around it, etc.). You can define this map:

```
:map! + ^[bi<I>^[ea</I>
```

Now, when you type a + at the end of a word, you will surround the word with HTML italicization codes. The + won't show up in the text.

The sequence above escapes to command mode (`^[`), backs up to insert the first code (`bi<I>`), escapes again (`^[`), and moves ahead to append the second code (`ea</I>`). Since the map sequence begins and ends in insert mode, you can continue entering text after marking the word.

Here's another example. Suppose that you've been typing your text, and you realize that the previous line should have ended with a colon. You can correct that by defining this map sequence:*

```
:map! % ^[kA:^[jA
```

Now, if you type a % anywhere along your current line, you'll append a colon to the end of the previous line. This command escapes to command mode, moves up a line, and appends the colon (`^[kA:`). The command then escapes again, moves down to the line you were on, and leaves you in insert mode (`^[jA`).

Note that we wanted to use uncommon characters (% and +) for the previous map commands. When a character is mapped for insert mode, you can no longer type that character as text.

To reinstate a character for normal typing, use the command:

```
:unmap! x
```

where *x* is the character that was previously mapped for insert mode. (Although *vi* will expand *x* on the command line as you type it, making it look like you are unmapping the expanded text, it will correctly unmap the character.)

Insert-mode mapping is often more appropriate for tying character strings to special keys that you wouldn't otherwise use. It is especially useful with programmable function keys.

---

* From an article by Walter Zintz, in *UNIX World*, April 1990.

Mapping Function Keys

Many terminals have programmable function keys (which are faithfully emulated by today's terminal emulators on bitmapped workstations). You can usually set up these keys to print whatever character or characters you want using a special setup mode on the terminal. However, keys programmed using a terminal's setup mode only work on that terminal; they may also limit the action of programs that want to set up those function keys themselves.

ex allows you to map function keys by number, using the syntax:

```
:map #1 commands
```

for function key number 1, and so on. (It can do this because the editor has access to the entry for that terminal found in either the *terminfo* or the *termcap* database and knows the escape sequence normally put out by the function key.)

As with other keys, maps apply by default to command mode, but by using the `map!` commands as well, you can define two separate values for a function key— one to be used in command mode, the other in insert mode. For example, if you are an HTML user, you might want to put font-switch codes on function keys. For example:

```
:map #1 i<I>^[
:map! #1 <I>
```

If you are in command mode, the first function key will enter insert mode, type in the three characters <I>, and return to command mode. If you are already in insert mode, the key will simply type the three-character HTML code.

If function keys have been redefined in the terminal's setup mode, the `#n` syntax might not work since the function keys no longer put out the expected control or escape sequence as described in its terminal database entry. You will need to examine the *terminfo* source (or *termcap* entry) for your terminal and check the definitions for the function keys. In addition, there are some terminals whose function keys perform only local actions and don't actually send any characters to the computer. Such function keys can't be mapped.

The terminal capabilities `k1`, `k2` through `k0` describe the first ten function keys. The capabilities `11`, `12` through `10` describe the remaining function keys. Using your terminal's setup mode, you can change the control or escape sequence output by the function key to correspond with the *terminfo* or *termcap* entry. (For more information, see *termcap & terminfo*, published by O'Reilly & Associates.)

If the sequence contains ^M, which is a carriage return, press CTRL-M . For instance, in order to have function key 1 available for mapping, the terminal database entry for your terminal must have a definition of k1, such as:

```
k1=^A@^M
```

In turn, the definition:

```
^A@^M
```

must be what is output when you press that key.

To see what the function key puts out, use the *od* (octal dump) command with the -c option (show each character). You will need to press RETURN after the function key, and then CTRL-D to get *od* to print the information. For example:

```
$ od -c
^[[A
^D
0000000 033   [   [   A  \n
0000005
```

Here, the function key sent Escape, two left brackets, and an *A*.

Mapping Other Special Keys

Many keyboards have special keys, such as HOME , END , PAGE UP , and PAGE DOWN that duplicate commands in *vi*. If the terminal's *terminfo* or *term-cap* description is complete, *vi* will be able to recognize these keys. But if it isn't, you can use the **map** command to make them available to *vi*. These keys generally send an escape sequence to the computer—an escape character followed by a string of one or more other characters. In order to trap the escape, you should press ^V before pressing the special key in the map. For example, to map the HOME key on the keyboard of an IBM PC to a reasonable *vi* equivalent, you might define the following map:

```
:map CTRL-V  HOME  1G
```

This appears on your screen as:

```
:map ^[[H 1G
```

Similar map commands display as follows:

:map CTRL-V END G	*displays*	:map ^[[Y G
:map CTRL-V PAGE ^F	*displays*	:map ^[[V ^F
:map CTRL-V PAGE ^B	*displays*	:map ^[[U ^B

You'll probably want to place these maps in your *.exrc* file. Note that if a special key generates a long escape sequence (containing multiple non-printing characters), ^V quotes only the initial escape character, and the map doesn't work. You will have to find the entire escape sequence (perhaps from the terminal manual) and type it in manually, quoting at the appropriate points, rather than simply pressing ^V and then the key.

Mapping Multiple Input Keys

Mapping multiple key strokes is not restricted just to function keys. You can also map sequences of regular keystrokes. This can help make it easier to enter certain kinds of text, such as SGML or HTML.

Here are some `:map` commands, thanks to Jerry Peek, co-author of O'Reilly's *Learning the UNIX Operating System*, which make it easier to enter SGML markup. (The lines beginning with a double quote are comments. This is discussed below in the section "Comments in ex Scripts".)

```
" ADR: need this
:set noremap
" bold:
map! =b </emphasis>^[F<i<emphasis role=bold>
map =B i<emphasis role=bold>^[
map =b a</emphasis>^[
" Move to end of next tag:
map! =e ^[f>a
map =e f>
" footnote (tacks opening tag directly after cursor in text-input mode):
map! =f <footnote>^M<para>^M</para>^M</footnote>^[kO
" Italics ("emphasis"):
map! =i </emphasis>^[F<i<emphasis>
map =I i<emphasis>^[
map =i a</emphasis>^[
" paragraphs:
map! =p ^[jo<para>^M</para>^[O
map =P O<para>^[
map =p o</para>^[
" less-than:
map! *l &lt;
...
```

Using these commands, to enter a footnote you would enter insert mode, and type =f. *vi* would then insert the opening and closing tags, and leave you in insert mode between them:

```
All the world's a stage.<footnote>
<para>
_
</para>
</footnote>
```

Needless to say, these macros proved quite useful during the development of this book.

@-Functions

Named buffers provide yet another way to create "macros"—complex command sequences that you can repeat with only a few keystrokes.

If you type a command line in your text (either a *vi* sequence or an *ex* command *preceded by a colon*), then delete it into a named buffer, you can execute the contents of that buffer with the @ command. For example, open a new line and enter:

```
cwgadfly CTRL-V  ESC
```

This will appear as:

```
cwgadfly^[
```

on your screen. Press ESC again to exit insert mode, then delete the line into buffer g by typing "gdd. Now whenever you place the cursor at the beginning of a word and type @g, that word in your text will be changed to *gadfly*.

Since @ is interpreted as a *vi* command, a dot (.) will repeat the entire sequence, even if the buffer contains an *ex* command. @@ repeats the last @, and u or U can be used to undo the effect of @.

This is a simple example. @-functions are useful because they can be adapted to very specific commands. They are especially useful when you are editing between files, because you can store the commands in their named buffers and access them from any file you edit. @-functions are also useful in combination with the global replacement commands discussed in Chapter 6, *Global Replacement*.

Executing Buffers from ex

You can also execute text saved in a buffer from *ex* mode. In this case, you would enter an *ex* command, delete it into a named buffer, and then use the @ command from the *ex* colon prompt. For example, enter the following text:

```
ORA publishes great books.
ORA is my favorite publisher.
1,$s/ORA/O'Reilly \& Associates/g
```

With your cursor on the last line, delete the command into the g buffer: "gdd. Move your cursor to the first line: kk. Then execute the buffer from the colon command line: :@g RETURN . Your screen should now look like this:

```
O'Reilly & Associates publishes great books.
O'Reilly & Associates is my favorite publisher.
```

Some versions treat * identically to @ when used from the *ex* command line. In addition, if the buffer character supplied after the @ or * command is *, the command will be taken from the default (unnamed) buffer.

Using ex Scripts

Certain *ex* commands you use only within *vi*, such as maps, abbreviations, and so on. If you store these commands in your *.exrc* file, the commands will automatically be executed when you invoke *vi*. Any file that contains commands to execute is called a *script*.

The commands in a typical *.exrc* script are of no use outside *vi*. However, you can save other *ex* commands in a script, and then execute the script on a file or on multiple files. Mostly you'll use substitute commands in these external scripts.

For a writer, a useful application of *ex* scripts is to ensure consistency of terminology—or even of spelling—across a document set. For example, let's assume that you've run the UNIX `spell` command on two files and that the command has printed out the following list of misspellings:

```
$ spell sect1 sect2
chmod
ditroff
myfile ·
thier
writeable
```

As is often the case, `spell` has flagged a few technical terms and special cases it doesn't recognize, but it has also identified two genuine spelling errors.

Because we checked two files at once, we don't know which files the errors occurred in or where they are in the files. Although there are ways to find this out, and the job wouldn't be too hard for only two errors in two files, you can easily imagine how time-consuming the job could grow to be for a poor speller or for a typist proofing many files at once.

To make the job easier, you could write an *ex* script containing the following commands:

```
%s/thier/their/g
%s/writeable/writable/g
wq
```

Assume you've saved these lines in a file named *exscript*. The script could be executed from within *vi* with the command:

```
:so exscript
```

or the script can be applied to a file right from the command line. Then you could edit the files *sect1* and *sect2* as follows:

```
$ ex - sect1 < exscript
$ ex - sect2 < exscript
```

The minus sign following the invocation of *ex* tells it to suppress the normal terminal messages.*

If the script were longer than the one in our simple example, we would already have saved a fair amount of time. However, you might wonder if there isn't some way to avoid repeating the process for each file to be edited. Sure enough, we can write a shell script that includes, but generalizes, the invocation of *ex*, so that it can be used on any number of files.

Looping in a Shell Script

You may know that the shell is a programming language as well as a command-line interpreter. To invoke *ex* on a number of files, we use a simple type of shell script command called the `for` loop. A `for` loop allows you to apply a sequence of commands for each argument given to the script. (The `for` loop is probably the single most useful piece of shell programming for beginners. You'll want to remember it even if you don't write any other shell programs.)

Here's the syntax of a `for` loop:

```
for variable in list
do
        command(s)
done
```

For example:

```
for file in $*
do
        ex - $file < exscript
done
```

(The command doesn't need to be indented; we indented it for clarity.) After we create this shell script, we save it in a file called *correct* and make it executable with the *chmod* command. (If you aren't familiar with the *chmod* command and

---

* According to the POSIX standard, *ex* should use −s instead of − as shown here. Typically, for backwards compatibility, both versions are accepted.

the procedures for adding a command to your UNIX search path, see *Learning the UNIX Operating System*, published by O'Reilly & Associates.) Now type:

```
$ correct sect1 sect2
```

The for loop in *correct* will assign each argument (each file in the list specified by $*, which stands for *all arguments*) to the variable *file* and execute the *ex* script on the contents of that variable.

It may be easier to grasp how the for loop works with an example whose output is more visible. Let's look at a script to rename files:

```
for file in $*
do
        mv $file $file.x
done
```

Assuming this script is in an executable file called *move*, here's what we can do:

```
$ ls
ch01 ch02 ch03 move
$ move ch??
$ ls
ch01.x ch02.x ch03.x move
```

With creativity, you could rewrite the script to rename the files more specifically:

```
for nn in $*
do
        mv ch$nn sect$nn
done
```

With the script written this way, you'd specify numbers instead of filenames on the command line:

```
$ ls
ch01 ch02 ch03 move
$ move 01 02 03
$ ls
sect01 sect02 sect03 move
```

The for loop need not take $* (all arguments) as the list of values to be substituted. You can specify an explicit list as well. For example:

```
for variable in a b c d
```

will assign *variable* to *a*, *b*, *c*, and *d* in turn. Or you can substitute the output of a command. For example:

```
for variable in `grep -l "Alcuin" *`
```

will assign *variable* in turn to the name of each file in which *grep* finds the string *Alcuin*.

If no list is specified:

```
for variable
```

the variable will be assigned to each command-line argument in turn, much as it was in our initial example. This is actually not equivalent to:

```
for variable in $*
```

but to:

```
for variable in "$@"
```

which has a slightly different meaning. The symbol $* expands to $1, $2, $3, etc., but the four-character sequence "$@" expands to "$1", "$2", "$3", etc. Quotation marks prevent further interpretation of special characters.

Let's return to our main point and our original script:

```
for file in $*
do
        ex - $file < exscript
done
```

It may seem a little inelegant to have to use two scripts—the shell script and the *ex* script. And in fact, the shell does provide a way to include an editing script inside a shell script.

Here Documents

In a shell script, the operator << means to take the following lines, up to a specified string, as input to a command. (This is often called a *here document.*) Using this syntax, we could include our editing commands in *correct* like this:

```
for file in $*
do
ex - $file << end-of-script
g/thier/s//their/g
g/writeable/s//writable/g
wq
end-of-script
done
```

The string *end-of-script* is entirely arbitrary—it just needs to be a string that won't otherwise appear in the input and can be used by the shell to recognize when the here document is finished. By convention, many users specify the end of a here document with the string *EOF*, or *E_O_F*, to indicate the end of the file.

There are advantages and disadvantages to each approach shown. If you want to make a one-time series of edits and don't mind rewriting the script each time, the here document provides an effective way to do the job.

However, it's more flexible to write the editing commands in a separate file from the shell script. For example, you could establish the convention that you will always put editing commands in a file called *exscript*. Then you only need to write the *correct* script once. You can store it away in your personal "tools" directory (which you've added to your search path) and use it whenever you like.

Sorting Text Blocks: A Sample ex Script

Suppose you want to alphabetize a file of *troff*-encoded glossary definitions. Each term begins with an .IP macro. In addition, each entry is surrounded by the .KS/.KE macro pair. (This ensures that the term and its definition will print as a block and will not be split across a new page.) The glossary file looks something like this:

```
.KS
.IP "TTY_ARGV" 2n
The command, specified as an argument vector,
that the TTY subwindow executes.
.KE
.KS
.IP "ICON_IMAGE" 2n
Sets or gets the remote image for icon's image.
.KE
.KS
.IP "XV_LABEL" 2n
Specifies a frame's header or an icon's label.
.KE
.KS
.IP "SERVER_SYNC" 2n
Synchronizes with the server once.
Does not set synchronous mode.
.KE
```

You can alphabetize a file by running the lines through the UNIX `sort` command, but you don't really want to sort every line. You want to sort only the glossary terms, moving each definition—untouched—along with its corresponding term. As it turns out, you can treat each text block as a unit by joining the block into one line. Here's the first version of your *ex* script:

```
g/^\.KS/,/^\.KE/j
%!sort
```

Each glossary entry is found between a .KS and .KE macro. j is the *ex* command to join a line (the equivalent in *vi* is J). So, the first command joins every glossary entry into one "line." The second command then sorts the file, producing lines like this:

```
.KS .IP "ICON_IMAGE" 2n Sets or gets ... image.    .KE
.KS .IP "SERVER_SYNC" 2n Synchronizes with ... mode.    .KE
.KS .IP "TTY_ARGV" 2n The command, ... executes.    .KE
.KS .IP "XV_LABEL" 2n Specifies a ... icon's label.    .KE
```

The lines are now sorted by glossary entry; unfortunately, each line also has macros and text mixed in (we've used ellipses [...] to show omitted text). Somehow, you need to insert newlines to "un-join" the lines. You can do this by modifying your *ex* script: mark the joining points of the text blocks *before* you join them, and then replace the markers with newlines. Here's the expanded *ex* script:

```
g/^\.KS/,/^\.KE/-1s/$/@@/
g/^\.KS/,/^\.KE/j
%!sort
%s/@@ /^M/g
```

The first three commands produce lines like this:

```
.KS@@ .IP "ICON_IMAGE" 2nn@@ Sets or gets ... image. @@ .KE
.KS@@ .IP "SERVER_SYNC" 2nn@@ Synchronizes with ... mode. @@ .KE
.KS@@ .IP "TTY_ARGV" 2nn@@ The ... vector, @@ that ... .@@ .KE
.KS@@ .IP "XV_LABEL" 2nn@@ Specifies a ... icon's label. @@ .KE
```

Note the extra space following the @@. The spaces result from the j command, because it converts each newline into a space.

The first command marks the original line breaks with @@. You don't need to mark the end of the block (after the .KE), so the first command uses a -1 to move back up one line at the end of each block. The fourth command restores the line breaks by replacing the markers (plus the extra space) with newlines. Now your file is sorted by blocks.

Comments in ex Scripts

You may want to reuse such a script, adapting it to a new situation. With a complex script like this, it is wise to add comments so that it's easier for someone else (or even yourself!) to reconstruct how it works. In *ex* scripts, anything following a double quote is ignored during execution, so a double quote can mark the beginning of a comment. Comments can go on their own line. They can also go at the end of any command that doesn't interpret a quote as part of the command. (For example, a quote has meaning to map commands and shell escapes, so you can't end such lines with a comment.)

Besides using comments, you can specify a command by its full name, something that would ordinarily be too time consuming from within *vi*. Finally, if you add spaces, the *ex* script above becomes this more readable one:

```
" Mark lines between each KS/KE block
global /^\.KS/,/^\.KE/-1 s /$/@@/
" Now join the blocks into one line
global /^\.KS/,/^\.KE/ join
" Sort each block--now really one line each
%!sort
" Restore the joined lines to original blocks
% s /@@ /^M/g
```

Surprisingly, the `substitute` command does not work in *ex*, even though the full names for the other commands do.

Beyond ex

If this discussion has whetted your appetite for even more editing power, you should be aware that UNIX provides editors even more powerful than *ex*: the *sed* stream editor and the *awk* data manipulation language. There is also the extremely popular Perl programming language. For information on these programs, see the O'Reilly books *sed & awk*, *Learning Perl*, and *Programming Perl*.

Editing Program Source Code

All of the features discussed so far are of interest whether you are editing English text or program source code. However, there are a number of additional features that are of interest chiefly to programmers. These include indentation control, searching for the beginning and end of procedures, and using `ctags`.

The following discussion is adapted from documentation provided by Mortice Kern Systems with their excellent implementation of *vi* for DOS and Windows-based systems, available as a part of the MKS Toolkit or separately as MKS Vi. It is reprinted by permission of Mortice Kern Systems.

Indentation Control

The source code for a program differs from ordinary text in a number of ways. One of the most important of these is the way in which source code uses indentation. Indentation shows the logical structure of the program: the way in which statements are grouped into blocks. *vi* provides automatic indentation control. To use it, issue the command:

```
:set autoindent
```

Now, when you indent a line with spaces or tabs, the following lines will automatically be indented by the same amount. When you press RETURN after typing the first indented line, the cursor goes to the next line and automatically indents the same distance as the previous line.

As a programmer, you will find this saves you quite a bit of work getting the indentation right, especially when you have several levels of indentation.

When you are entering code with autoindent enabled, typing CTRL-T at the start of a line gives you another level of indentation and typing CTRL-D takes one away.

We should point out that CTRL-T and CTRL-D are typed while you are in insert mode, unlike most other commands, which are typed in command mode.

There are two additional variants of the CTRL-D command.*

^ ^D

When you type ^ ^D (^ CTRL-D), *vi* shifts the cursor back to the beginning of the line, but only for the current line. The next line you enter will start at the current auto-indent level. This is particularly useful for entering C preprocessor commands while typing in C/C++ source code.

0 ^D

When you type 0 ^D, *vi* shifts the cursor back to the beginning of the line. In addition, the current auto-indent level is reset to zero; the next line you enter will not be auto-indented.†

Try using the `autoindent` option when you are entering source code. It simplifies the job of getting indentation correct. It can even sometimes help you avoid bugs (e.g., in C source code, where you usually need one closing curly brace (}) for every level of indentation you go backwards).

The << and >> commands are also helpful when indenting source code. By default, >> shifts a line right eight spaces (i.e., adds eight spaces of indentation) and << shifts a line left eight spaces. For example, move the cursor to the beginning of a line and press the > key twice (>>). You will see the line move right. If you now press the < key twice (<<), the line will move back again.

You can shift a number of lines by typing the number followed by >> or <<. For example, move the cursor to the first line of a good-size paragraph and type 5>>. You will shift the first five lines in the paragraph.

---

* These do not work in *elvis* 2.0.

† The *nvi* 1.79 documentation has these two commands switched, but the program actually behaves as described here.

The default shift is eight spaces (right or left). This default can be changed with a command like:

```
:set shiftwidth=4
```

You will find it convenient to have a shiftwidth that is the same size as the width between tab stops.

vi attempts to be smart when doing indenting. Usually, when you see text indented by eight spaces at a time, *vi* will actually insert tab characters into the file, since tabs usually expand to eight spaces. This is the UNIX default; it is most noticeable when you type a tab during normal input, and when files are sent to a printer—UNIX expands them with a tab stop of eight spaces.

If you wish, you can change how *vi* represents tabs on your screen, by changing the `tabstop` option. For example, if you have something that is deeply indented, you might wish to have use a tab stop setting of every four characters, so that the lines will not wrap. The following command will make this change:

```
:set tabstop=4
```

 Changing your tab stops is not recommended. Although *vi* will display the file using an arbitrary tabstop setting, the tab characters in your files will still be expanded using an eight-character tab stop by every other UNIX program. Eight-character tab stops are one of the facts of life on UNIX, and you should just get used to them.

Sometimes indentation won't work the way you expect, because what you believe to be a tab character is actually one or more spaces. Normally, your screen displays both a tab and a space as whitespace, making the two indistinguishable. You can, however, issue the command:

```
:set list
```

This alters your display so that a tab appears as the control character `^I` and an end-of-line appears as a `$`. This way, you can spot a true space, and you can see extra spaces at the end of a line. A temporary equivalent is the `:1` command. For example, the command:

```
:5,20 1
```

displays lines 5 through 20, showing tab characters and end-of-line characters.

A Special Search Command

The characters (, [, { , and < can all be called opening brackets. When the cursor is resting on one of these characters, pressing the % key moves the cursor from the opening bracket forward to the corresponding closing bracket—) ,] , } , or > —keeping in mind the usual rules for nesting brackets.* For example, if you were to move the cursor to the first (in:

```
if ( cos(a[i]) > sin(b[i]+c[i]) )
{
        printf("cos and sin equal!\n");
}
```

and press %, you would see that the cursor jumps to the parenthesis at the end of the line. This is the closing parenthesis that matches the opening one.

Similarly if the cursor is on one of the closing bracket characters, pressing % will move the cursor backwards to the corresponding opening bracket character. For example, move the cursor to the closing brace after the `printf` line above and press %.

vi is even smart enough to find a bracket character for you. If the cursor is not on a bracket character, when you press %, *vi* will search forward on the current line to the first open or close bracket character it finds, and then move to the matching bracket! For instance, with the cursor on the > in the first line of the example above, % will find the open parenthesis, and then move to the close parenthesis.

Not only does this search character help you move forward and backward through a program in long jumps, it lets you check the nesting of brackets and parentheses in source code. For example, if you put the cursor on the first { at the beginning of a C function, pressing % should move you to the } that (you think) ends the function. If it's the wrong one, something has gone wrong somewhere. If there is no matching } in the file, *vi* will beep at you.

Another technique for finding matching brackets is to turn on the following option:

```
:set showmatch
```

Unlike %, setting **showmatch** (or its abbreviation **sm**) helps you while you're in insert mode. When you type a) or a },† the cursor will briefly move back to the matching (or { before returning to your current position. If the match doesn't exist, the terminal beeps. If the match is merely off-screen, *vi* silently keeps going.

---

* Of the versions tested, only *nvi* supported matching < and > with %. *vile* lets you set an option with the sets of pairs of characters that match for %.

† In *elvis*, *vim*, and *vile*, **showmatch** also shows you matching square brackets ([and]).

Using Tags

The source code for a large C or C++ program will usually be spread over several files. Sometimes, it is difficult to keep track of which file contains which function definitions. To simplify matters, a UNIX command called `ctags` can be used together with the `:tag` command of *vi*.

 UNIX versions of `ctags` handle the C language, and often Pascal and Fortran 77. Sometimes they even handle assembly language. Almost universally, however, they do not handle C++. Other versions are available that can generate *tags* files for C++, and for other languages and file types.

The `ctags` command is issued at the UNIX command line. Its purpose is to create an information file that *vi* can use later to determine which files define which functions. By default, this file is called *tags*. From within *vi*, a command of the form:

```
:!ctags file.c
```

will create a file named *tags* in your current directory that contains information on the functions defined in *file.c*. A command like:

```
:!ctags *.c
```

will create a *tags* file describing all the C source files in the directory.

Now suppose your *tags* file contains information on all the source files that make up a C program. Also suppose that you want to look at or edit a function in the program, but do not know where the function is. From within *vi*, the command:

```
:tag name
```

will look at the *tags* file to find out which file contains the definition of the function *name*. It will then read in the file and position the cursor on the line where the name is defined. In this way, you don't have to know which file you have to edit; you only have to decide which function you want to edit.

You can use the tag facility from *vi*'s command mode as well. Place the cursor on the identifier you wish to look up, and then type `^]`. *vi* will perform the tag lookup and move to the file that defines the identifier. Be careful where you place the cursor; *vi* uses the "word" under the cursor starting at the current cursor position, not the entire word containing the cursor.

If you try to use the `:tag` command to read in a new file and you haven't saved your current text since the last time you changed it, *vi* will not let you go to the new file. You must either write out your current file with the `:w` command and then issue `:tag`, or else type:

```
:tag! name
```

to override *vi*'s reluctance to discard edits.

The Solaris 2.6 version of *vi* actually supports tag *stacks*. It appears, however, to be completely undocumented in the Solaris man pages. Because many, if not most, versions of UNIX *vi* don't do tag stacking, we have moved the discussion of this feature to the section "Tag Stacks" in Chapter 8, where tag stacking is introduced.

II

Extensions and Clones

Part II describes various new features that extend the capabilities of *vi* and the availabilities of those features in four *vi* clones. This part contains the following chapters:

- Chapter 8, *vi Clones Feature Summary*
- Chapter 9, *nvi—New vi*
- Chapter 10, *elvis*
- Chapter 11, *vim—vi Improved*
- Chapter 12, *vile—vi Like Emacs*

8

vi Clones Feature Summary

And These Are My Brothers, Darrell, Darrell, and Darrell

There are a number of freely available "clones" of the *vi* editor. Appendix E, *vi and the Internet*, provides a pointer to a web site that lists all known *vi* clones. We have chosen to cover four of the most popular ones. They are:

- Version 1.79 of Keith Bostic's *nvi*

- Version 2.0 of Steve Kirkendall's *elvis*

- Version 5.0 of Bram Moolenaar's *vim*

- Version 7.4 of *vile*, by Kevin Buettner, Tom Dickey, and Paul Fox

The clones were written because the source code for *vi* is not freely available, making it impossible either to port *vi* to a non-UNIX environment or to study the code, and/or because UNIX *vi* (or another clone!) did not provide desired functionality. For example, UNIX *vi* often has limits on the maximum length of a line, and it cannot edit binary files. (The chapters on the various programs present more information about each one's history.)

Each program provides a large number of extensions to UNIX *vi*; often, several of the clones provide the same extensions, although usually not in an identical way. Instead of repeating the treatment of each common feature in each program's chapter, we have centralized the discussion here. You can think of this chapter as presenting "what the clones do," with each clone's chapter presenting "how the clone does it."

This chapter covers the following topics:

Multiwindow editing

This is the ability to split the screen into multiple "windows."* You can edit a different file in each window, or have several views into the same file. This is perhaps the single most important extension over regular *vi*.

GUI interfaces

All of the clones except *nvi* can be compiled to support an X Window interface. If you have a system running X, use of the GUI version may be preferable to splitting the screen of an *xterm* (or other terminal emulator); the GUI versions generally provide such nice features as scrollbars and multiple fonts. The native GUIs of other operating systems may also be supported.

Extended regular expressions

All of the clones make it possible to match text using regular expressions that are similar or identical to those provided by the UNIX *egrep*(1) command.

Enhanced tags

As described in the section "Using Tags" in Chapter 7, *Advanced Editing*, you can use the *ctags* program to build up a searchable database of your files. The clones make it possible to "stack" tags, by saving your current location when you do a tag search. You can then return to that location. Multiple locations can be saved in a Last In First Out (LIFO) order, producing a stack of locations.

Several of the *vi* clone authors and the author of at least one *ctags* clone have gotten together to define a standard form for an enhanced version of the *ctags* format. In particular, it is now easier to use the tags functionality with programs written in C++, which allows overloaded function names.

Improved editing facilities

All of the clones provide the ability to edit the *ex* command line, "infinite undo" capability, arbitrary length lines and eight-bit data, incremental searching, (at least an option) to scroll the screen left to right for long lines instead of wrapping long lines, and mode indicators, as well as other features.

Programming assistance

Several of the editors provide features that allow you to stay within the editor during the typical "edit–compile–debug" cycle of software development.

---

* Note that these are not the windows that you find on X Window-based UNIX workstations, or under MS-Windows or the Apple Macintosh.

Syntax highlighting

    In *elvis*, *vim*, and *vile*, you can arrange to display different parts of a file in different colors and/or fonts. This is particularly useful for editing program source code.

There is one additional feature in the clones that we have chosen *not* to cover: extension languages. As of May 1998, *nvi* has preliminary support for Perl and Tcl integration, *elvis* has its own C-like expression evaluator,* *vim* has a C-like expression evaluator, plus support for Perl, Python, and Tcl integration, and *vile*, which has always had its own built-in extension language, has preliminary support for Perl integration. The extension language integration and support are very recent for all of the programs and will undoubtedly change significantly. For this reason, any discussion of the extension language facilities would be obsolete almost as soon as this book goes to press.

We recommend that you check the online documentation for your clone if you're interested in programming your editor with an extension language.† Extension languages are a feature worth watching; they promise to bring a new dimension of power to *vi* users. The use of well-known programming languages, such as Perl, Python, and Tcl, is an additional advantage, since it is likely that users will already know one or more of them.

Multiwindow Editing

Perhaps the single most important feature that the clones offer over standard *vi* is the ability to edit files in multiple "windows." This makes it possible to easily work on more than one file at the same time, and to "cut and paste" text from one file to another via yanking and putting.‡

There are two fundamental concepts underlying each editor's multiwindow implementation, *buffers* and *windows*.

A buffer holds text to be edited. The text may come from a file, or it may be brand new text to eventually be written to a file. Any given file has only one buffer associated with it.

A window provides a view into a buffer, allowing you to see and modify the text in the buffer. There may be multiple windows associated with the same buffer.

---

* The *elvis* 2.0 documentation mentions that "someday" *elvis* will have a true extension language, most likely Perl, but probably not for version 2.1. Steve Kirkendall doesn't really consider the expression evaluator to be an extension language.

† *emacs* users have been doing this since the beginning; it is one of the reasons that many are rather fanatic about their editor.

‡ In the clones, you need not split the screen to yank and put between files; only the original *vi* discards the cut buffers when switching between files.

Changes made to the buffer in one window are reflected in any other windows open on the same buffer. A buffer may also have no windows associated with it. In this case, you can't do a whole lot with the buffer, although you can open a window on it later. Closing the last window open on a buffer effectively "hides" the file. If the buffer has been modified but not written to disk, the editor may or may not let you close the last window that's open on it.

When you create a new window, the editor splits the current screen. For most of the editors, you create a new window which shows another view on the file you're currently editing. You then switch to the window where you wish to edit the next file, and instruct the editor to start editing the file there. Each editor provides *vi* and *ex* commands to switch back and forth between windows, as well as the ability to change the window size, and hide and restore windows.

In each editor's chapter, we show a sample split screen (editing the same two files), and describe how to split the screen and move between windows.

GUI Interfaces

elvis, *vim*, and *vile* also provide graphical user interface (GUI) versions that can take advantage of a bit-mapped display and mouse. Besides supporting X Windows under UNIX, support for MS-Windows or other windowing systems may also be available. Table 8-1 summarizes the available GUIs for the different clones.

Table 8-1: Available GUIs

Editor	X11	MS-Windows	OS/2	BeOS	Macintosh	Amiga
elvis	✓	✓	✓			
vim	✓	✓	✓	✓	✓	✓
vile	✓	✓	✓			

Extended Regular Expressions

The metacharacters available in *vi*'s search and substitution regular expressions are described in the section "Metacharacters Used in Search Patterns" in Chapter 6, *Global Replacement*. Each of the clones provides some form of extended regular expressions, either as an option or always available. Typically these are the same (or almost the same) as what's provided by *egrep*. Unfortunately, each one's extended flavor is slightly different from the others'.

To give you a feel for what extended regular expressions can do, we present them in the context of *nvi*. Each clone's chapter then describes that editor's extended syntax, without repeating the examples.

nvi extended regular expressions are the Extended Regular Expressions (EREs) as defined by the POSIX standard. In order to enable this feature, use `set extended` either from your *.nexrc* file or from the *ex* colon prompt.

Besides the standard metacharacters described in Chapter 6, and the POSIX bracket expressions mentioned in the section "POSIX Bracket Expressions" in the same chapter, the following metacharacters are available:

| Indicates alternation. For example, `a|b` matches either *a* or *b*. However, this construct is not limited to single characters: `house|home` matches either of the strings *house* or *home*.

`( ... )`

Used for grouping, to allow the application of additional regular expression operators. For example, `house|home` can be shortened (if not simplified) to `ho(use|me)`. The `*` operator can be applied to text in parentheses: `(house|home)*` matches *home*, *homehouse*, *househomehousehouse* and so on.

When `extended` is set, text grouped with parentheses acts like text grouped in `\( ... \)` in regular *vi*; the actual text matched can be retrieved in the replacement part of a substitute command with `\1`, `\2`, etc. In this case, `\(` represents a literal left parenthesis.

+ Matches *one* or more of the preceding regular expressions. This is either a single character, or a group of characters enclosed in parentheses. Note the difference between + and *. The * is allowed to match nothing, but with + there must be at least one match. For example, `ho(use|me)*` matches *ho* as well as *home* and *house*, but `ho(use|me)+` will not match *ho*.

? Matches zero or one occurrence of the preceding regular expression. This indicates "optional" text that is either present or not present. For example, `free?d` will match either *fred* or *freed*, but nothing else.

`{ ... }`

Defines an *interval expression*. Interval expressions describe counted numbers of repetitions. In the description below, *n* and *m* represent integer constants.

`{n}`

Matches exactly *n* repetitions of the previous regular expression. For example, `(home|house){2}` matches *homehome*, *homehouse*, *househome*, and *househouse*, but nothing else.

{n,}

Matches *n* or more repetitions of the previous regular expression. Think of it as "as least *n*" repetitions.

{n,m}

Matches *n* to *m* repetitions. The bounding is important, since it controls how much text would be replaced during a substitute command.*

When `extended` is not set, *nvi* provides the same functionality with \{ and \}.

Enhanced Tags

The "Exuberant *ctags*" program is a *ctags* clone that is considerably more capable than UNIX *ctags*. It produces an extended *tags* file format that makes tag searching and matching a more flexible and capable process. We describe it first, since it is supported by several of the *vi* clones.

This section also describes tag stacks: the ability to save multiple locations visited with the :tag or ^] commands. All of the clones provide tag stacking.

Exuberant ctags

The "Exuberant *ctags*" program was written by Darren Hiebert. Its home page is *http://home.hiwaay.net/~darren/ctags/*. As of this writing, the current version is 2.0.3. The following list of the program's features is adapted from the *README* file in the *ctags* distribution:

- It is capable of generating tags for *all* types of C and C++ language tags, including class names, macro definitions, enum names, enumerators (values inside an enumeration), function (method) definitions, function (method) prototypes/declarations, structure members and class data members, struct names, typedefs, union names and variables.

- It supports both C and C++ code.

- It is very robust in parsing code and is far less easily fooled by code containing #if preprocessor conditional constructs.

- It can be used to print out a human-readable list of selected objects found in source files.

---

* The *, +, and ? operators can be reduced to {0,}, {1,} and {0,1} respectively, but they are much more convenient to use.

- It supports generation of GNU *emacs*-style tag files (*etags*).

- It works on UNIX, QNX, MS-DOS, Windows 95/NT, OS/2, and the Amiga. Some precompiled binaries are available on the web site.

Exuberant *ctags* produces *tags* files in the form described in the next subsection.

The New tags Format

Traditionally, a *tags* file has three tab-separated fields: the tag name (typically an identifier), the source file containing the tag, and an indication of where to find the identifier. This indication is either a simple line number, or a `nomagic` search pattern enclosed either in slashes or in question marks. Furthermore, the *tags* file is always sorted.

This is the format generated by the UNIX *ctags* program. In fact, many versions of *vi* allowed *any* command in the search pattern field (a rather gaping security hole). Furthermore, due to an undocumented implementation quirk, if the line ended with a semicolon and then a double-quote (`;"`), anything following those two characters would be ignored. (The double-quote starts a comment, as it does in *.exrc* files.)

The new format is backwards-compatible with the traditional one. The first three fields are the same: tag, filename, and search pattern. Exuberant *ctags* only generates search patterns, not arbitrary commands. Extended attributes are placed after a separating `;"`. Each attribute is separated from the next by a tab character, and consists of two colon-separated subfields. The first subfield is a keyword describing the attribute, the second is the actual value. Table 8-2 lists the supported keywords.

Table 8-2: Extended ctags Keywords

Keyword	Meaning
kind	The value is a single letter that indicates the lexical type of the tag. It can be `f` for a function, `v` for a variable, and so on. Since the default attribute name is `kind`, a solitary letter can denote the tag's type (e.g., `f` for a function).
file	For tags that are "static", i.e., local to the file. The value should be the name of the file.
	If the value is given as an empty string (just `file:`), it is understood to be the same as the filename field; this special case was added partly for the sake of compactness, and partly to provide an easy way to handle tags files that aren't in the current directory. The value of the filename field is always relative to the directory in which the *tags* file itself resides.
function	For local tags. The value is the name of function in which they're defined.

Table 8-2: Extended ctags Keywords (continued)

Keyword	Meaning
struct	For fields in a `struct`. The value is the name of the structure.
enum	For values in an `enum` data type. The value is the name of the `enum` type.
class	For C++ member functions and variables. The value is the name of the class.
scope	Intended mostly for C++ class member functions. It will usually be `private` for private members or omitted for public members, so users can restrict tag searches to only public members.
arity	For functions. The number of arguments.

If the field does not contain a colon, it is assumed to be of type `kind`. Here are some examples:

```
ARRAYMAXED        awk.h    427;"    d
AVG_CHAIN_MAX     array.c  38;"     d      file:
array.c           array.c  1;"      F
```

ARRAYMAXED is a C `#define` macro defined in *awk.h*. **AVG_CHAIN_MAX** is also a C macro but it is used only in *array.c*. The third line is a bit different: it is a tag for the actual source file! This is generated with the `-i F` option to Exuberant *ctags*, and allows you to give the command `:tag array.c`. More usefully, you can put the cursor over a filename and use the `^]` command to go to that file.

Within the value part of each attribute, the characters backslash, tab, carriage return and newline should be encoded as `\\`, `\t`, `\r`, and `\n`, respectively.

Extended *tags* files may have some number of initial tags that begin with `!_TAG_`. These tags usually sort to the front of the file, and are useful for identifying which program created the file. Here is what Exuberant *ctags* generates:

```
!_TAG_FILE_FORMAT       2                     /extended format; ..../
!_TAG_FILE_SORTED       1                     /0=unsorted, 1=sorted/
!_TAG_PROGRAM_AUTHOR    Darren Hiebert        /darren@hiebert.com/
!_TAG_PROGRAM_NAME      Exuberant Ctags       //
!_TAG_PROGRAM_URL       http://home.hiwaay.net/~darren/ctags   /.../
!_TAG_PROGRAM_VERSION   2.0.3                 /with C++ support/
```

Editors may take advantage of these special tags to implement special features. For example, *vim* pays attention to the `!_TAG_FILE_SORTED` tag and will use a binary search to search the *tags* file instead of a linear search if the file is indeed sorted.

If you use *tags* files, we recommend that you get and install Exuberant *ctags*.

Tag Stacks

The :**tag** *ex* command and the ^] *vi* mode command provide a limited means of finding identifiers, based on the information provided in a *tags* file. Each of the clones extends this ability by maintaining a *stack* of tag locations. Each time you issue the :**tag** *ex* command, or use the ^] *vi* mode command, the editor saves the current location before searching for the specified tag. You may then return to a saved location using (usually) the ^T command or an *ex* command.

Solaris *vi* tag stacking and an example are presented below. The way each clone handles tag stacking is described in each editor's respective chapter.

Solaris vi

Surprisingly enough, the Solaris 2.6 version of *vi* supports tag stacking. Perhaps not so surprisingly, this feature is completely undocumented in the Solaris *ex*(1) and *vi*(1) manual pages. For completeness, we summarize Solaris *vi* tag stacking in Table 8-3, Table 8-4, and Table 8-5. Tag stacking in Solaris *vi* is quite simple.*

Table 8-3: Solaris vi Tag Commands

Command	Function
ta[g][!] *tagstring*	Edit the file containing *tagstring* as defined in the *tags* file. The ! forces *vi* to switch to the new file if the current buffer has been modified but not saved.
po[p][!]	Pop the tag stack by one element.

Table 8-4: Solaris vi Command Mode Tag Commands

Command	Function
^]	Look up the location of the identifier under the cursor in the *tags* file, and move to that location. If tag stacking is enabled, the current location is automatically pushed onto the tag stack.
^T	Return to the previous location in the tag stack, i.e., pop off one element.

Table 8-5: Solaris vi Options for Tag Management

Option	Function
taglength, tl	Controls the number of significant characters in a tag that is to be looked up. The default value of zero indicates that all characters are significant.
tags, tagpath	The value is a list of filenames in which to look for tags. The default value is "tags /usr/lib/tags".

---

* This information was discovered based on experimentation. YMMV (your mileage may vary).

Table 8-5: Solaris vi Options for Tag Management (continued)

Option	Function
tagstack	When set to true, *vi* stacks each location on the tag stack. Use `:set` `notagstack` to disable tag stacking.

To give you a feel for using tag stacks, we present a short example, using Exuberant *ctags* and *vim*.

Suppose you are working with a program that uses the GNU *getopt_long* function, and that you need to understand more about it.

GNU *getopt* consists of three files, *getopt.h*, *getopt.c*, and *getopt1.c*.

First, you create the *tags* file, then you start by editing the main program, found in *main.c*:

```
$ ctags *.[ch]
$ ls
Makefile   getopt.c   getopt.h   getopt1.c   main.c   tags
$ vim main.c
```

Keystrokes   **Results**

/getopt

```
/* option processing. ready, set, go! */
for (optopt = 0, old_optind = 1;
  (c = getopt_long(argc, argv, optlist,
                        optab, NULL)) != EOF;
  optopt = 0, old_optind = optind) {
        if (do_posix)
                opterr = TRUE;
```

Edit *main.c* and move to the call to *getopt_long*.

^]

```
int
getopt_long (argc, argv, options,
            long_options, opt_index)
     int argc;
     char *const *argv;
     const char *options;
     const struct option *long_options;
     int *opt_index;
{
return _getopt_internal (argc, argv, options,
                            long_options,
                            opt_index, 0);
}
"getopt1.c" 189 lines, 4651 characters
```

> Do a tag lookup on *getopt_long*. *vim* moves to
> *getopt1.c*, placing the cursor on the definition of
> *getopt_long*.

It turns out that *getopt_long* is a "wrapper" function for *_getopt_internal*. You place
the cursor on *_getopt_internal* and do another tag search.

Keystrokes   **Results**

`8jf_ ^]`

```
    int
    _getopt_internal (argc, argv, optstring,
                      longopts,longind, long_only)
         int argc;
         char *const *argv;
         const char *optstring;
         const struct option *longopts;
         int *longind;
         int long_only;
    {
      optarg = NULL;
    "getopt.c" 1000 lines, 28705 characters
```

You have now moved to *getopt.c*. To find out more
about `struct option`, move the cursor to *option* and
do another tag search.

`5jfo; ^]`

```
    one.) For long options that have a zero 'flag' field, 'getopt'
    returns the contents of the 'val' field. */

    struct option
    {
    #if defined (__STDC__) && __STDC__
      const char *name;
    #else
      char *name;
    #endif
    "getopt.h" 133 lines, 4691 characters
```

The editor moves to the definition of `struct option` in
getopt.h. You may now look over the comments
explaining how it's used.

`:tags`

```
    # TO tag            FROM line       in file
    1  1 getopt_long         205        main.c
    2  1 _getopt_internal     75        getopt1.c
    3  1 option               68        getopt.c
```

The `:tags` command in *vim* displays the tag stack.

Typing `^T` three times would move you back to *main.c*, where you started. The
tag facilities make it easy to move around as you edit source code.

Improved Facilities

The four clones all provide additional features that make simple text editing easier and more powerful.

Editing the ex command line
> The ability to edit *ex* mode commands as you type them, possibly including a saved history of *ex* commands. Also, the ability to complete filenames and possibly other things, such as commands and options.

No line length limit
> The ability to edit lines of essentially arbitrary length. Also, the ability to edit files containing any 8-bit character.

Infinite undo
> The ability to successively undo all of the changes you've made to a file.

Incremental searching
> The ability to search for text while you are typing the search pattern.

Left/right scrolling
> The ability to let long lines trail off the edge of screen instead of wrapping.

Visual mode
> The ability to select arbitrary contiguous chunks of texts upon which some operation will be done.

Mode indicators
> A visible indication of insert mode versus command mode, as well as indicators of the current line and column.

Command-Line History and Completion

Users of the *csh*, *tcsh*, *ksh*, and *bash* shells have known for years that being able to recall previous commands, edit them slightly, and resubmit them makes them more productive.

This is no less true for editor users than it is for shell users; unfortunately, UNIX *vi* does not have any facility to save and recall *ex* commands.

This lack is remedied in each of the clones. Although each one provides a different way of saving and recalling the command history, each one's mechanism is usable and useful.

In addition to a command history, all of the editors can do some kind of *completion*. This is where you type the beginning of, for example, a filename. You then type a special character (such as tab), and the editor completes the filename for you. All of the editors can do filename completion; some of them can complete other things as well. Details are provided in each editor's chapter.

Arbitrary Length Lines and Binary Data

All four clones can handle lines of any length.* Historic versions of *vi* often had limits of around 1,000 characters per line; longer lines would be truncated.

All four are also 8-bit clean, meaning that they can edit files containing any 8-bit character. It is even possible to edit binary and/or executable files, if necessary. This can be really useful, at times. You may or may not have to tell each editor that a file is binary.

nvi

> Automatically handles binary data. No special command-line or *ex* options are required.

elvis

> Under UNIX, does not treat a binary file differently from any other file. On other systems, it uses the *elvis.brf* file to set the `binary` option, to avoid newline translation issues. (The *elvis.brf* file and `hex` display modes are described in the section "Interesting Features" in Chapter 10.)

vim

> Does not have a limit on the length of a line. When `binary` is not set, *vim* is like *nvi*, and automatically handles binary data. However, when editing a binary file, you should either use the *−b* command-line option or `:set binary`. These set several other *vim* options that make it easier to edit binary files.

vile

> Automatically handles binary data. No special command-line or *ex* options are required.

Finally, there is one tricky detail. Traditional *vi* always writes the file with a final newline appended. When editing a binary file, this might add one character to the file and cause problems. *nvi* and *vim* are compatible with *vi* by default, and add that newline. In *vim* you can set the `binary` option, so this doesn't happen. *elvis* and *vile* never append the extra newline.

Infinite Undo

UNIX *vi* allows you to undo only your last change, or to restore the current line to the state it was in before you started making any changes. All of the clones provide "infinite undo," the ability to keep undoing your changes, all the way back to the state the file was in before you started *any* editing.

---

* Well, up to the maximum value of a C `long`, 2,147,483,647.

Incremental Searching

When *incremental searching* is used, the editor moves the cursor through the file, matching text *as you type* the search pattern. When you finally type RETURN , the search is finished.* If you've never seen it before, it is rather disconcerting at first, but after a while you get used to it.

elvis does not support incremental searching. *nvi* and *vim* enable incremental searching with an option, and *vile* uses two special *vi* mode commands. *vile* can be compiled with incremental searching disabled, but it is enabled by default. Table 8-6 shows the options each editor provides.

Table 8-6: Incremental Searching

Editor	Option	Command	Action
nvi	searchincr		The cursor moves through the file as you type, always being placed on the first character of the text that matches.
vim	incsearch		The cursor moves through the file as you type. *vim* highlights the text that matches what you've typed so far.
vile		^X S, ^X R	The cursor moves through the file as you type, always being placed on the first character of the text that matches. ^X S incrementally searches forward through the file, while ^X R incrementally searches backward.

Left-Right Scrolling

By default, *vi* and most of the clones wrap long lines around the screen. Thus, a single logical line of the file may occupy multiple physical lines on your screen.

There are times when it might be preferable if a long line simply disappeared off the right-hand edge of the screen, instead of wrapping. Moving onto that line and then moving to the right would "scroll" the screen sideways. This feature is available in all of the clones. Typically, a numeric option controls how much to scroll the screen, and a Boolean option controls whether lines wrap or disappear off the edge of the screen. *vile* also has command keys to perform sideways scrolling of the entire screen. Table 8-7 shows how to use horizontal scrolling with each editor.

---

* *emacs* has always had incremental searching.

Table 8-7: Sideways Scrolling

Editor	Scroll Amount	Option	Action
nvi	`sidescroll = 16`	`leftright`	Off by default. When set, long lines simply go off the edge of the screen. The screen scrolls left or right by 16 characters at a time.
elvis	`sidescroll = 8`	`wrap`	Off by default. When set, long lines simply go off the edge of the screen. The screen scrolls left or right by 8 characters at a time.
vim	`sidescroll = 0`	`wrap`	Off by default. When set, long lines simply go off the edge of the screen. With `sidescroll` set to zero, each scroll puts the cursor in the middle of the screen. Otherwise the screen scrolls by the desired number of characters.
vile	`sideways = 0`	`linewrap`	Off by default. When set, long lines wrap. Thus, the default is to have long lines go off the edge of the screen. Long lines are marked at the left and right edges with < and >. With `sideways` set to zero, each scroll moves the screen by ⅓. Otherwise the screen scrolls by the desired number of characters.
		`horizscroll`	On by default. When set, moving the cursor along a long line off-screen shifts the whole screen. When not set, only the current line shifts; this may be desirable on slower displays.

vile has two additional commands, `^X ^R` and `^X ^L`. These two commands scroll the screen right and left, respectively, leaving the cursor in its current location on the line. You cannot scroll so far that the cursor position would go off the screen.

Visual Mode

Typically, operations in *vi* apply to units of text such lines, words, or characters, or to sections of text from the current cursor position to a position specified by a search command. For example, `d/^}` deletes up to the next line that starts with a right brace. *elvis*, *vim*, and *vile* all provide a mechanism to explicitly select a region of text to which an operation will apply. In particular, it is possible to select a rectangular block of text and apply an operation to all the text within the rectangle! See each editor's respective chapter for the details.

Mode Indicators

As you know by now, *vi* has two modes, command mode and insert mode. Usually, you can't tell by looking at the screen which mode you're in. Furthermore, often it's useful to know where in the file you are, without having to use the ^G or *ex* := commands.

Two options address these issues, `showmode` and `ruler`. All four clones agree on the option names and meanings, and even Solaris *vi* has the `showmode` option.

Table 8-8 lists the special features in each editor.

Table 8-8: Position and Mode Indicators

Editor	With ruler, displays	With showmode, displays
nvi	row and column	insert, change, replace, and command mode indicators
elvis	row and column	input and command mode indicators
vim	row and column	insert, replace, and visual mode indicators
vile	row, column, and percent of file	insert, replace, and overwrite mode indicators
vi	N/A	separate mode indicators for open, input, insert, append, change, replace, replace one character, and substitute modes

The GUI versions of *elvis* and *vim* change the cursor shape depending upon the current mode.

Programming Assistance

vi was developed primarily as a programmer's editor. It has features that make things especially easy for the UNIX programmer—someone writing C programs and *troff* documentation. (Real Programmers write Real Documentation in *troff*.) Several of the clones are proud bearers of this tradition, adding a number of features that make them even more usable and capable for the "power user."*

Two features (among many) most deserve discussion:

---

* In contrast to the What You See Is What You Get (WYSIWYG) philosophy, UNIX is the You Asked For It, You Got It operating system. (With thanks to Scott Lee.)

Edit-compile speedup

> *elvis*, *vim*, and *vile* allow you to easily invoke *make*(1), capture the errors from your compiler, and automatically move to the lines containing the errors. You can then fix the errors and re-run *make*, all from within the editor.

Syntax highlighting

> *elvis*, *vim*, and *vile* have the ability to highlight and/or change the color of different syntactic elements in different kinds of files.

Edit-Compile Speedup

Programming often consists of a "compile-test-debug" cycle. You make changes, compile the new code, and then test and debug it. When learning a new language, syntax errors are especially common, and it is frustrating to be constantly stopping and restarting (or suspending and resuming) the editor in between compiles.

elvis, *vim*, and *vile* all provide facilities that allow you to stay within the editor while compiling your program. Furthermore, they capture the compiler's output and use it to automatically go to each line that contains an error.* Consistent use of this ability can save time and improve programmer productivity.

Here is an example, using *elvis*. You are beginning to learn C++, so you start out with the obligatory first program:

Keystrokes

:w hello.C

Results

```
#include <stream.h>

void main()
{
        cout << "hello, world!\n ;
}
```

You enter the program, forgetting the closing quote,
and then write the program to *hello.C.*

:make hello

```
hello.C:5:unterminated string or character
          constant
hello.C:5:possible real start of unterminated
          constant
make: *** [hello] Error 1
Hit <Enter> to continue _
```

You type the :make command to run *make*, which in
turn runs the C++ compiler. (In this case, *g++*.)

---

* Yet another feature that *emacs* users are accustomed to comes to *vi.*

`:errlist`

```
#include <stream.h>

void main()
{
        cout << "hello, world!\n ;
}
line 5: unterminated string or character
        constant
```

The `:errlist` command moves to the line with the error and displays the first compiler error message in the status line.

You can fix the error, resave the file, re-run `:make` and eventually compile your program without errors.

All of the editors have similar facilities. They will all compensate for changes in the file, correctly moving you to subsequent lines with errors. More details are provided in each editor's chapter.

Syntax Highlighting

elvis, vim, and *vile* all provide some form of syntax highlighting. All three also provide syntax coloring, changing the color of different parts of the file on displays that can do so (such as under X11 or the Linux console). See each editor's chapter for more information.

Editor Comparison Summary

Most of the clones support most or all of the features described above. Table 8-9 summarizes what each editor supports. Of course, the table does not tell the full story; the details are provided in each one's individual chapter.

Table 8-9: Feature Summary Chart

Feature	nvi	elvis	vim	vile
Multiwindow editing	✓	✓	✓	✓
GUI		✓	✓	✓
Extended regular expressions	✓	✓	✓	✓
Enhanced tags		✓	✓	✓
Tag stacks	✓	✓	✓	✓
Arbitrary length lines	✓	✓	✓	✓
8-bit data	✓	✓	✓	✓
Infinite undo	✓	✓	✓	✓
Incremental searching	✓		✓	✓

Table 8-9: Feature Summary Chart (continued)

Feature	nvi	elvis	vim	vile
Left-right scrolling	✓	✓	✓	✓
Mode indicators	✓	✓	✓	✓
Visual mode		✓	✓	✓
Edit-Compile Speedup		✓	✓	✓
Syntax Highlighting		✓	✓	✓
Multiple OS support		✓	✓	✓

A Look Ahead

The next four chapters cover *nvi*, *elvis*, *vim*, and *vile*, in that order. Each chapter has the following outline:

1. Who wrote the editor, and why.

2. Important command-line arguments.

3. Online help and other documentation.

4. Initialization—what files and environment variables the program reads, and in what order.

5. Multiwindow editing.

6. GUI interface(s), if any.

7. Extended regular expressions.

8. Improved editing facilities (tag stacks, infinite undo, etc.).

9. Programming assistance (edit-compile speedup, syntax highlighting).

10. Interesting features unique to the program.

11. Where to get the sources, and what operating systems the editor runs on.

    All of the distributions are compressed with *gzip*, GNU zip. If you don't already have it, you can get *gzip* from *ftp://ftp.gnu.org/gnu/gzip/ gzip-1.2.4a.shar*. The *untar.c* program available from the *elvis ftp* site is a very portable, simple program for unpacking *gzip*'ed *tar* files on non-UNIX systems.

Because each of these programs continues to undergo development, we have not attempted an exhaustive treatment of each one's features. Such would quickly become outdated. Instead, we have "hit the highlights," covering the features that you are most likely to need to know about and that are least likely to change as the program evolves. You should supplement this book with each one's online documentation if you need to know how to use every last feature of your editor.

9

nvi — New vi

nvi is short for "new *vi*." It was developed initially at the University of California at Berkeley (UCB), home of the famous BSD (Berkeley Software Distribution) versions of UNIX. It was used for writing this chapter.

Author and History

The original *vi* was developed at UCB in the late 1970s by Bill Joy, then a computer science graduate student, and now a founder and vice president of Sun Microsystems.

Bill Joy first built *ex*, starting with and heavily enhancing the Sixth Edition *ed* editor. The first enhancement was open mode, done with Chuck Haley. Between 1976 and 1979 *ex* evolved into *vi*. Mark Horton then came to Berkeley, added macros "and other features,"* and did much of the work on *vi* to make it work on a large number of terminals and UNIX systems. By 4.1BSD (1981), the editor already had essentially all of the features described in Part I of this book.

---

* From the *nvi* reference manual. Unfortunately, it does not say which features.

Despite all of the changes, *vi*'s core was (and is) the original UNIX *ed* editor. As such, it was code that could not be freely distributed. By the early 1990s, when they were working on 4.4BSD, the BSD developers wanted a version of *vi* that could be freely distributed in source code form.

Keith Bostic of UCB started with *elvis* 1.8,* which was a freely distributable *vi* clone, and began turning it into a "bug for bug compatible" clone of *vi*. *nvi* also complies with the POSIX Command Language and Utilities Standard (IEEE P1003.2) where it makes sense to do so.

Although no longer affiliated with UCB, Keith Bostic continues to maintain, enhance, and distribute *nvi*. The version current at the time of this writing is *nvi* 1.79.

nvi is important because it is the "official" Berkeley version of *vi*. It is part of 4.4BSD-Lite II, and is the *vi* version used on the various popular BSD variants such as NetBSD and FreeBSD.

Important Command-Line Arguments

In a pure BSD environment, *nvi* is installed under the names *ex*, *vi*, and *view*. Typically they are all links to the same executable, and *nvi* looks at how it is invoked to determine its behavior. (UNIX *vi* works this way too.) It allows the Q command from *vi* mode to switch into *ex* mode. The *view* variant is like *vi*, except that the `readonly` option is set initially.

nvi has a number of command-line options. The most useful are described here:

−c *command*
> Execute *command* upon startup. This is the POSIX version of the historical +*command* syntax, but *nvi* is not limited to positioning commands. (The old syntax is also accepted.)

−F Don't copy the entire file when starting to edit. This may be faster, but allows the possibility of someone else changing the file while you're working on it.

−R Start in read-only mode, setting the `readonly` option.

−r Recover specified files, or if no files are listed on the command line, list all the files that can be recovered.

−S Run with the `secure` option set, disallowing access to external programs.†

---

* Although little or no original *elvis* code is left.

† As with anything labelled "secure," blind trust is usually inappropriate. Keith Bostic says, though, that you *can* trust *nvi*'s `secure` option.

-s Enter batch (script) mode. This is only for *ex*, and is intended for running edit-
    ing scripts. Prompts and non-error messages are disabled. This is the POSIX
    version of the historic "–" argument; *nvi* supports both.

-t *tag*
    Start editing at the specified *tag*.

-w *size*
    Set the initial window size to *size* lines.

Online Help and Other Documentation

nvi comes with quite comprehensive printable documentation. In particular, it
comes with *troff* source, formatted ASCII, and formatted PostScript for the following documents:

The vi Reference Manual
    The reference manual for *nvi*. This manual describes all of the *nvi* command
    line options, commands, options, and *ex* commands.

The vi Man Page
    The man page for *nvi*.

The vi Tutorial
    This document is a tutorial introduction to editing with *vi*.

The ex Reference Manual
    The reference manual for *ex*. This manual is the original one for *ex*; it is a bit
    out-of-date with respect to the facilities in *nvi*.

Also included are ASCII files that document some of the *nvi* internals, and provide
a list of features that should be implemented, and files that can be used as an
online tutorial to *vi*.

The actual online help built in to *nvi* is minimal, consisting of two commands,
:exusage and :viusage. These commands provide one-line summaries of each
ex and *vi* command. This is usually sufficient to remind you about how something
works, but not very good for learning about new or obscure features in *nvi*.

You can give a command as an argument to the :exusage and :viusage commands, in which case *nvi* will display the help just for that command. *nvi* prints
one line explaining what the command does, and a one-line summary of the command's usage.

Initialization

If the **-s** or "**–**" options have been specified, then *nvi* will bypass all initializations. Otherwise, *nvi* performs the following steps:

1. Read and execute the file */etc/vi.exrc*. It must be owned either by **root** or by you.

2. Execute the value of the **NEXINIT** environment variable if it exists, otherwise use **EXINIT** if it exists. Only one will be used, not both. Bypass executing *$HOME/.nexrc* or *$HOME/.exrc*.

3. If *$HOME/.nexrc* exists, read and execute it. Otherwise, if *$HOME/.exrc* exists, read and execute it. Only one will be used.

4. If the **exrc** option has been set, then look for and execute either *./.nexrc* if it exists, or *./.exrc*. Only one will be used.

nvi will not execute any file that is writable by anyone other than the file's owner.

The *nvi* documentation suggests putting common initialization actions into your *.exrc* file (i.e., options and commands for UNIX *vi*), and having your *.nexrc* file execute **:source .exrc** before or after the *nvi*-specific initializations.

Multiwindow Editing

To create a new window in *nvi*, you use a capitalized version of one of the *ex* editing commands: **Edit**, **Fg**, **Next**, **Previous**, **Tag** or **Visual**. (As usual, these commands can be abbreviated.) If your cursor is in the top half of the screen, the new window is created on the bottom half, and vice versa. You then switch to another window with CTRL-W :

```
<preface id="VI6-CH-0">
<title>Preface </title>

<para>
Text editing is one of the most common uses of any computer system, and
<command>vi</command> is one of the most useful standard text editors
on your system.
With <command>vi</command> you can create new files, or edit any existing
UNIX text file.
</para>

ch00.sgm: unmodified: line 1
# Makefile for vi book
#
# Arnold Robbins

CHAPTERS = ch00_6.sgm ch00_5.sgm ch00.sgm ch01.sgm ch02.sgm ch03.sgm \
     ch04.sgm ch05.sgm ch06.sgm ch07.sgm ch08.sgm
```

```
APPENDICES = appa.sgm appb.sgm appc.sgm appd.sgm

POSTSCRIPT = ch00_6.ps ch00_5.ps ch00.ps ch01.ps ch02.ps ch03.ps \
        ch04.ps ch05.ps ch06.ps ch07.ps ch08.ps \
```
`Makefile: unmodified: line 1`

This example shows *nvi* editing two files, *ch00.sgm* and *Makefile*. The split screen is the result of typing `nvi ch00.sgm` followed by `:Edit Makefile`. The last line of each window acts as the status line, and is where colon commands are executed for that window. The status lines are highlighted in reverse video.

The windowing *ex* mode commands and what they do are described in Table 9-1.

Table 9-1: nvi Window Management Commands

Command	Function
bg	Hide the current window. It can be recalled with the `fg` and `Fg` commands.
di[splay] b[uffers]	Display all buffers, including named, un-named, and numeric buffers.
di[splay] s[creens]	Display the filenames of all backgrounded windows.
Edit *filename*	Edit *filename* in a new window.
Edit /tmp	Create a new window editing an empty buffer. */tmp* is interpreted specially to create a new temporary file.
fg *filename*	Uncover *filename* into the current window. The previous file moves to the background.
Fg *filename*	Uncover *filename* in a new window. The current window is split, instead of redistributing the screen space among all open windows.
Next	Edit the next file in the argument list in a new window.
Previous	Edit the previous file in the argument list in a new window. (The corresponding `previous` command, which moves back to the previous file, exists in *nvi*; it is not in UNIX *vi*.)
resize ±*nrows*	Increase or decrease the size of the current window by *nrows* rows.
Tag *tagstring*	Edit the file containing *tagstring* in a new window.

The CTRL-W command cycles between windows, top to bottom. The `:q` and `ZZ` commands exit the current window.

You may have multiple windows open on the same file. Changes made in one window are reflected in the other, although changes made in *nvi*'s insert mode are not seen in the other window until after you finalize the change by typing ESC. You will not be prompted to save your changes until you issue a command that would cause *nvi* to leave the last window open upon a file.

GUI Interfaces

nvi does not provide a graphical user interface (GUI) version.

Extended Regular Expressions

Extended regular expressions were introduced in the section "Extended Regular Expressions" in Chapter 8. Here, we just summarize the metacharacters that *nvi* provides. *nvi* also supports the POSIX bracket expressions, `[[:alnum:]]`, and so on.

You use `:set extended` to enable extended regular expression matching.

| Indicates alternation. The left and right sides need not be just single characters.

`( ... )`

Used for grouping, to allow the application of additional regular expression operators.

When `extended` is set, text grouped with parentheses acts like text grouped in `\( ... \)` in regular *vi*; the actual text matched can be retrieved in the replacement part of a substitute command with `\1`, `\2`, etc. In this case, `\(` represents a literal left parenthesis.

+ Matches one or more of the preceding regular expressions. This is either a single character or a group of characters enclosed in parentheses.

? Matches zero or one occurrence of the preceding regular expression.

`{ ... }`

Defines an *interval expression*. Interval expressions describe counted numbers of repetitions. In the description below, *n* and *m* represent integer constants.

`{n}`

Matches exactly *n* repetitions of the previous regular expression.

`{n, }`

Matches *n* or more repetitions of the previous regular expression.

`{n,m}`

Matches *n* to *m* repetitions.

When `extended` is not set, *nvi* provides the same functionality with `\{` and `\}`.

As might be expected, when `extended` is set, you should precede the above metacharacters with a backslash in order to match them literally.

Improvements for Editing

This section describes the features of *nvi* that make simple text editing easier and more powerful.

Command-Line History and Completion

nvi saves your *ex* command lines, and makes it possible to edit them for resubmission.

This facility is controlled with the `cedit` option.

When you type the first character of this string on the colon command line, *nvi* opens a new window on the command history that you can then edit. When you hit RETURN on any given line, *nvi* executes that line. ESC is a good choice for this option. (Use ^V ^[to enter it.)

Because the RETURN key actually executes the command, be careful to use either the j or ↓ keys to move down from one line to the next.

In addition to being able to edit your command line, you can also do filename expansion. This feature is controlled with the `filec` option.

When you type the first character of this string on the colon command line, *nvi* treats the blank delimited word in front of the cursor as if it had an * appended to it and does shell-style filename expansion. ESC is also a good choice for this option.* (Use ^V ^[to enter it.) When this character is the same as for the `cedit` option, the command-line editing is performed only when it is entered as the first character on the colon command line.

It is easiest to set these options in your *.nexrc* file:

```
set cedit=^[
set filec=^[
```

Tag Stacks

Tag stacking is described in the section "Tag Stacks" in Chapter 8. *nvi*'s tag stack is the simplest of the four clones. Table 9-2 and Table 9-3 show the commands it uses.

---

* Although the *nvi* documentation indicates that TAB is another common choice, we could not get that to work. In practice, using ESC for both options works well.

Table 9-2: nvi Tag Commands

Command	Function
di[splay] t[ags]	Display the tag stack.
ta[g][!] *tagstring*	Edit the file containing *tagstring* as defined in the *tags* file. The ! forces *nvi* to switch to the new file if the current buffer has been modified but not saved.
Ta[g][!] *tagstring*	Just like :tag, except that the file is edited in a new window.
tagp[op][!] *tagloc*	Pop to the given tag, or to the most recently used tag if no *tagloc* is supplied. The location may be either a filename of the tag of interest or a number indicating a position in the stack.
tagt[op][!]	Pop to the oldest tag in the stack, clearing the stack in the process.

Table 9-3: nvi Command Mode Tag Commands

Command	Function
^]	Look up the location of the identifier under the cursor in the *tags* file, and move to that location. The current location is automatically pushed onto the tag stack.
^T	Return to the previous location in the tag stack, i.e., pop off one element.

You can set the **tags** option to a list of file names where *nvi* should look for a tag. This provides a simplistic search path mechanism. The default value is `"tags /var/db/libc.tags /sys/kern/tags"`, which on a 4.4BSD system looks in the current directory, and then in the files for the C library and the operating system source code.

The **taglength** option controls how many characters in a tagstring are significant. The default value of zero means to use all the characters.

nvi behaves like *vi*; it uses the "word" under the cursor starting at the current cursor position. If your cursor is on the *i* in *main*, *nvi* will search for the identifier *in*, not *main*.

nvi relies on the traditional *tags* file format. Unfortunately, this format is very limited. In particular, it has no concept of programming language *scope*, which allows the same identifier to be used in different contexts to mean different things. The problem is exacerbated by C++, which explicitly allows function name *overloading*, i.e., the use of the same name for different functions.

nvi gets around the *tags* file limitations by using a different mechanism entirely: the *cscope* program. *cscope* is a proprietary but relatively inexpensive program available from the Bell Labs Software Toolchest. It reads C source files and builds a database describing the program. *nvi* provides commands that query the database and allow you to process the results. Because *cscope* is not universally available, we do not cover its use here. Details of the *nvi* commands are provided in the *nvi* documentation.

The extended *tags* file format produced by Exuberant *ctags* does not produce any errors with *nvi* 1.79; however, *nvi* does not take advantage of this format either.

Infinite Undo

In *vi*, the dot (.) command generally acts as the "do again" command; it repeats the last editing action you performed, be it a deletion, insertion, or replacement.

nvi generalizes the dot command into a full "redo" command, applying it even if the last command was u for "undo."

Thus, to begin a series of "undo" commands, first type a u. Then, for each . (dot) that you type, *nvi* will continue to undo changes, moving the file progressively closer to its original state.

Eventually, you will reach the initial state of your file. At that point, typing . will just ring the bell (or flash the screen). You can now begin redoing by typing u to "undo the undos" and then using . to reapply successive changes.

nvi does not allow you to provide a count to either the u or the . command.

Arbitrary Length Lines and Binary Data

nvi can edit files with arbitrary length lines and with an arbitrary number of lines.

nvi automatically handles binary data. No special command-line options or *ex* options are required. You use ^X followed by one or two hexadecimal digits to enter any 8-bit character into your file.

Incremental Searching

As mentioned in the section "Incremental Searching", you enable incremental searching in *nvi* using `:set searchincr`.

The cursor moves through the file as you type, always being placed on the first character of the text that matches.

Left-Right Scrolling

As mentioned in the section "Left-Right Scrolling" in Chapter 8, you enable left-right scrolling in *nvi* using `:set leftright`. The value of `sidescroll` controls the number of characters by which *nvi* shifts the screen when scrolling left to right.

Programming Assistance

nvi does not provide specific programming assistance facilities.

Interesting Features

nvi is the most minimal of the clones, without a large number of additional features that have not yet been covered. Yet it does have several important features worthy of mention.

Internationalization support
> Most of the informational and warning messages in *nvi* can be replaced with translations into a different language, using a facility known as a "message catalog." *nvi* implements this facility itself, using a straightforward mechanism documented in the file *catalog/README* in the *nvi* distribution. Message catalogs are provided for Dutch, English, French, German, Russian, Spanish, and Swedish.

Arbitrary buffer names
> Historically, *vi* buffer names are limited to the 26 characters of the alphabet. *nvi* allows you to use any character as a buffer name.

Special interpretation of `/tmp`
> For any *ex* command that needs a filename argument, if you use the special name `/tmp`, *nvi* will replace it with the name of a unique temporary file.

Sources and Supported Operating Systems

nvi can be obtained from *http://www.bostic.com/vi*. This is a web page from which you can download the current version, and also ask to be added to a mailing list that is notified about new versions of *nvi* and/or new features.

The source code for *nvi* is freely distributable. The licensing terms are described in the *LICENSE* file in the distribution, and they permit distribution in source and binary form.

nvi builds and runs under UNIX. It also can be built to run under LynxOS 2.4.0, and possibly later versions. It may build and run on other POSIX compliant systems as well, but the documentation does not contain a specific list of known operating systems.

Compiling *nvi* is straightforward. Retrieve the distribution via *ftp*. Uncompress and untar it, run the *configure* program, and then run *make*.

```
$ gzip -d < nvi.tar.gz | tar -xvpf -
...
$ cd nvi-1.79; ./configure
...
$ make
...
```

nvi should configure and build with no problems. Use *make install* to install it.

Should you need to report a bug or problem in *nvi*, the person to contact is Keith Bostic, at *bostic@bostic.com*.

10

elvis

elvis was written and is maintained by Steve Kirkendall. An earlier version became the basis for *nvi*. This chapter was written using *elvis*.

Author and History

With our thanks for his help, we'll let Steve Kirkendall give the history in his own words:

> I started writing *elvis* 1.0 after an early clone called *stevie* crashed on me, causing me to lose a few hours' work and totally destroying my confidence in that program. Also, *stevie* stored the edit buffer in RAM which simply wasn't practical in Minix. So I started writing my own clone, which stored its edit buffer in a file. And even if my editor crashed, the edited text could still be retrieved from that file.

> *elvis* 2.x is almost completely separate from 1.x. I wrote this, my second *vi* clone, because my first one inherited too many limitations from the real *vi*, and from Minix. The biggest change is the support for multiple edit buffers and multiple windows, neither of which could be retrofitted into 1.x very easily. I also wanted to shed the line-length limitation, and have online help written in HTML.

As to the name "elvis," Steve says that at least part of the reason he chose the name was to see how many people would ask him why he chose the name!* It is also common for *vi* clones to have the letters "vi" somewhere in their names.

Important Command-Line Arguments

elvis is not typically installed as *vi*, though it can be. If invoked as *ex*, it operates as a line editor and allows the Q command from *vi* mode to switch into *ex* mode.

elvis has a number of command-line options. The most useful are described here:

−a Load each file named on the command line into a separate window.

−r Perform recovery after a crash.

−R Start editing each file in read-only mode.

−i Start editing in input mode instead of in command mode. This may be easier for novice users.

−s Set the `safer` option for the whole session, not just execution of *.exrc* files. This adds a certain amount of security, but should not necessarily be trusted blindly. In *elvis* 2.1, this option is renamed −S, and (following the POSIX standard) −s provides *ex* scripting.

−f *filename*
  Use *filename* for the session file instead of the default name. Session files are discussed below.

−G *gui*
  Use the given interface. The default is the *termcap* interface. Other choices include *x11, win32, curses, open,* and *quit.* Not all the interfaces may be compiled into your version of *elvis.*

−c *command*
  Execute *command* upon start-up. This is the POSIX version of the historical +*command* syntax. (The old syntax is also accepted.)

−t *tag*
  Start editing at the specified *tag.*

−V Output more verbose status information. Useful for diagnosing problems with initialization files.

−? Print a summary of the possible options.

---

* ☺ In around eight years, I was only number four! A.R.

Online Help and Other Documentation

elvis is very interesting in this department. The online help is comprehensive, and written entirely in HTML. This makes is easy to view in your favorite Web browser. *elvis* also has an HTML display mode (discussed below), making it easy and pleasant to view the online help from within *elvis* itself.

When viewing HTML files, you use the tag commands (^] and ^T) to go to different topics and then return, making it easy to browse the help files. We applaud this innovation in online help.

Of course, *elvis* also comes with UNIX *man* pages.

Initialization

This section describes *elvis*'s session files and itemizes the steps it takes during initialization.

The Session File

elvis is intended to eventually meet COSE (Common Open System Environment) standards. These require that programs be able to save their state and return to that saved state at a later time.

To be able to do this, *elvis* maintains all its state in a session file. Normally *elvis* creates the session file when it starts, and removes it when it exits, but if *elvis* crashes, a left-over session file can be used to implement recovery of the edited files.

Initialization Steps

elvis performs the following initialization steps. Interestingly, much of the customization for *elvis* is moved out of editor options and into initialization files.

1. Initialize all hardcoded options.

2. Select an interface from those compiled into *elvis*. *elvis* will choose the "best" of the ones that are compiled in and that can work. For example, the X11 interface is considered to be better than the *termcap* interface, but it may not be usable if X Windows is not currently running.

   The selected interface can process the command line for initialization options that are specific to it.

3. Create the session file if it doesn't exist; otherwise, read it (in preparation for recovery).

4. Initialize the `elvispath` option from the `ELVISPATH` environment variable. Otherwise, give it a default value. `"~/.elvislib:/usr/local/lib/elvis"` is a typical value, but the actual value will depend upon how *elvis* was configured and built.

5. Search `elvispath` for an *ex* script named *elvis.ini* and run it. The default *elvis.ini* file performs the following actions:

    • Chooses a digraph table based on the current operating system. (Digraphs are a way to define the system's extended ASCII character set and how characters from the extended set should be entered.)

    • Sets options based on the program's name (for example, *ex* vs. *vi* mode).

    • Handles system-dependent tweaks, such as setting the colors for X11 and adding menus to the interface.

    • Picks an initialization filename, either *.exrc* for UNIX, or *elvis.rc* for non-UNIX systems. Call this file *f*.

    • If the `EXINIT` environment variable exists, executes its value. Otherwise, `:source` *~/f*, where *f* is the filename chosen previously.

    • If the `exrc` option has been set, then runs the `:safer` command on *f* in the current directory.

    • For X11, sets the normal, bold, and italic fonts, if they have not been set already.

6. Load the pre- and post-read and pre- and post-write command files, if they exist. Also load the *elvis.msg* file. All of these files are described later in this chapter.

7. Load and display the first file named on the command line.

8. If the `-a` option was given, load and display the rest of the files, each in its own window.

Multiwindow Editing

To create a new window in *elvis*, you use the *ex* `:split` command. You then use one of the regular *ex* commands, such as `:e` *filename* or `:n` to edit a new file. This is the simplest method; other, shorter methods are described below. You can switch back and forth between windows with CTRL-W CTRL-W .

```
<preface id="VI6-CH-0">
<title>Preface </title>

<para>
Text editing is one of the most common uses of any computer system, and
<command>vi</command> is one of the most useful standard text editors
```

```
on your system.
With <command>vi</command> you can create new files, or edit any
existing UNIX text file.
```

```
# Makefile for vi book
#
# Arnold Robbins

CHAPTERS = ch00_6.sgm ch00_5.sgm ch00.sgm ch01.sgm ch02.sgm ch03.sgm \
        ch04.sgm ch05.sgm ch06.sgm ch07.sgm ch08.sgm
APPENDICES = appa.sgm appb.sgm appc.sgm appd.sgm

POSTSCRIPT = ch00_6.ps ch00_5.ps ch00.ps ch01.ps ch02.ps ch03.ps \
        ch04.ps ch05.ps ch06.ps ch07.ps ch08.ps \
        appa.ps appb.ps appc.ps appd.ps
```

The split screen is the result of typing `elvis ch00.sgm` followed by `:split Makefile`.

Like *nvi*, *elvis* gives each window its own status line. *elvis* is unique in that it uses a highlighted line of underscores, instead of reverse video, for the status line. *ex* colon commands are carried out on each window's status line.

Table 10-1 describes the windowing *ex* mode commands and what they do.

Table 10-1: elvis Window Management Commands

Command	Function
sp[lit] [file]	Create a new window; load it with *file* if supplied. Otherwise, the new window shows the current file.
new sne[w]	Create a new empty buffer, and then create a new window to show that buffer.
sn[ext] [file...]	Create a new window, showing the next file in the argument list. The current file is not affected.
sN[ext]	Create a new window, showing the *previous* file in the argument list. The current file is not affected.
sre[wind][!]	Create a new window, showing the first file in the argument list. Reset the "current" file to be the first one with respect to the :next command. The current file is not affected.
sl[ast]	Create a new window, showing the last file in the argument list. The current file is not affected.
sta[g][!] tag	Create a new window showing the file where the requested *tag* is found.
sa[ll]	Create a new window for any files named in the argument list that don't already have a window.
wi[ndow] [target]	With no *target*, list all windows. The possible values for *target* are described in Table 10-2.

Table 10-1: elvis Window Management Commands (continued)

Command	Function
close	Close the current window. The buffer that the window was displaying remains intact. If it was modified, the other *elvis* commands that quit will prevent you from quitting until you explicitly save or discard the buffer.
wquit	Write the buffer back to the file and close the window. The file is saved whether or not it has been modified.
qall	Issues a :q command for each window. Buffers without windows are not affected.

Table 10-2 describes the windowing *ex* arguments and their meanings.

Table 10-2: Arguments to the elvis Window command

Argument	Meaning
+	Switch to the next window, like ^w k.
++	Switch to the next window, wrapping like ^w ^w.
-	Switch to the previous window, like ^w j.
--	Switch to the previous window, wrapping.
num	Switch to the window whose windowid=*num*.
buffer-name	Switch to the window editing the named buffer.

elvis provides a number of *vi* mode commands for moving between windows. They are summarized in Table 10-3.

Table 10-3: elvis Window Commands from vi Command Mode

Command	Function
^W c	Hide the buffer and close the window. This is identical to the :close command.
^W d	Toggle the display mode between "normal" and the buffer's usual display mode. This is a per-window option. Display modes are discussed in the section "Display Modes".
^W j	Move down to the next window.
^W k	Move up to the previous window.
^W n	Create a new window, and create a new buffer to be displayed in the window. It is similar to the :snew command.
^W q	Save the buffer and close the window, identical to zz.
^W s	Split the current window, equivalent to :split.

Table 10-3: elvis Window Commands from vi Command Mode (continued)

Command	Function
^W s	Toggle the `wrap` option. This option controls whether long lines wrap, or whether the whole screen scrolls to the right. This is a per-window option. This option is discussed in the section "Left-Right Scrolling" later in this chapter.
^W]	Create a new window, then look up the tag underneath the cursor. It is similar to the `:stag` command.
[count] ^W ^W	Move to next window, or to the *count*th window.
^W +	Increase the size of the current window (*termcap* interface only).
^W –	Reduce the size of the current window (*termcap* interface only).
^W \	Make the current window as large as possible (*termcap* interface only).

GUI Interfaces

The screen shots and explanation for this section were supplied by Steve Kirkendall. We thank him.

elvis's X11 interface provides a scrollbar and mouse support, and allows you to select which fonts to use. There is no way to change fonts after *elvis* has created the first window. The fonts must all be monospace fonts, typically some variation of a Courier or "fixed" font.

elvis 2.0's X11 interface supports multiple fonts and colors, a blinking cursor that changes shape to indicate your editing mode (insert vs. command), a scrollbar, and mouse actions. The mouse can be used for selecting text, cutting and pasting between applications, and performing tag searches.

elvis 2.1 adds a configurable toolbar, dialogue windows, a status bar, and the `-client` flag. It also works better on monochrome X terminals.

Because *elvis* 2.1 has a significantly improved X11 interface over 2.0, and because it should be released by the time this book is published, details in the rest of this section apply to it. A number of features, several command-line options, and the ability to configure *elvis* via X resources are all missing from Version 2.0.

The Basic Window

The basic *elvis* window is shown in Figure 10-1.

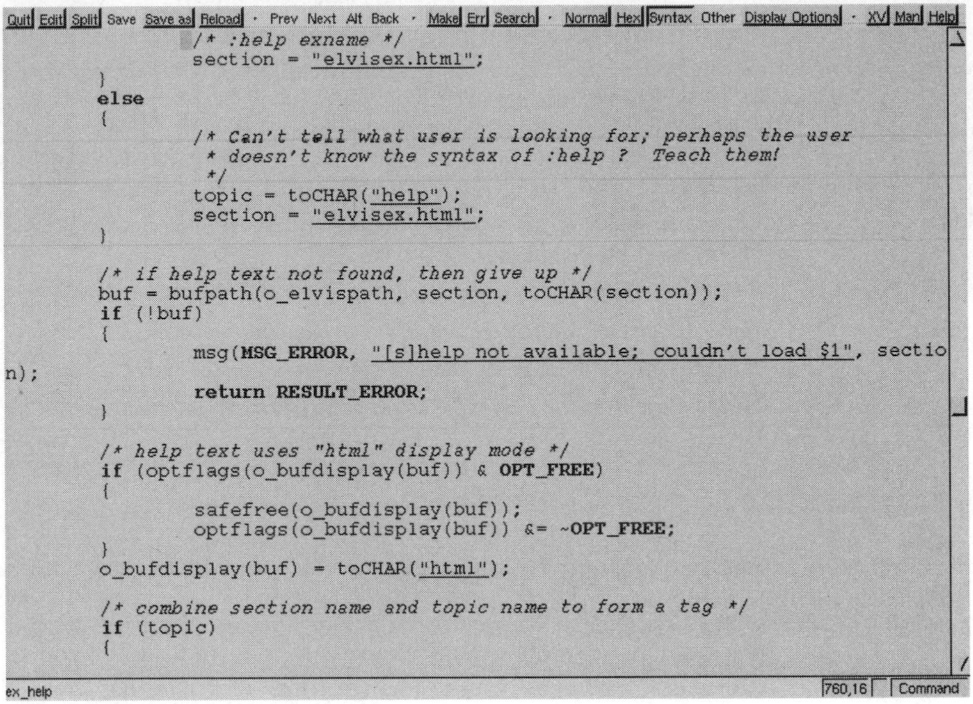
Quit Edit Split Save Save as Reload · Prev Next Alt Back · Make Err Search · Normal Hex Syntax Other Display Options · XV Man Help
/* :help exname */
section = "elvisex.html";
}
else
{
/* Can't tell what user is looking for; perhaps the user
* doesn't know the syntax of :help ? Teach them!
*/
topic = toCHAR("help");
section = "elvisex.html";
}
/* if help text not found, then give up */
buf = bufpath(o_elvispath, section, toCHAR(section));
if (!buf)
{
msg(MSG_ERROR, "[s]help not available; couldn't load $1", sectio
n);
return RESULT_ERROR;
}
/* help text uses "html" display mode */
if (optflags(o_bufdisplay(buf)) & OPT_FREE)
{
safefree(o_bufdisplay(buf));
optflags(o_bufdisplay(buf)) &= ~OPT_FREE;
}
o_bufdisplay(buf) = toCHAR("html");
/* combine section name and topic name to form a tag */
if (topic)
{
ex_help
760,16
Command
Figure 10-1: The elvis GUI window

elvis provides a separate text search pop-up dialogue box, which is shown in Figure 10-2.

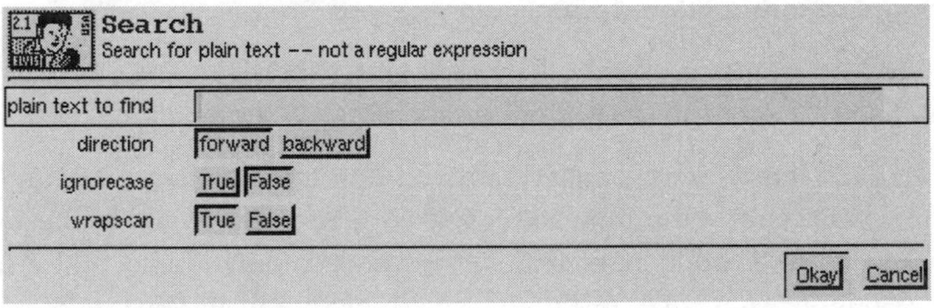
Search
Search for plain text -- not a regular expression
plain text to find
direction
forward
backward
ignorecase
True
False
wrapscan
True
False
Okay
Cancel
Figure 10-2: The elvis search dialogue

The look and feel are intended to resemble Motif, but *elvis* doesn't actually use the Motif libraries.

Command-line options let you choose the four different fonts that *elvis* uses, normal, italic, bold, and "control," which is the font for the toolbar text and button labels. You may also specify foreground and background colors, the initial window geometry, and whether *elvis* should start out iconified.

The new `-client` option causes *elvis* to look for an already running *elvis* process, and send it a message requesting it to start editing the files named on the command line. Doing it this way allows you to share yanked text and other information between the files *elvis* is currently editing and the new files.

Besides the toolbar, there is also a status bar that displays status messages and any available information about toolbar buttons.

Mouse Behavior

The mouse behavior tries to strike a balance between *xterm*(1) and what makes sense for an editor. To do this correctly, *elvis* distinguishes between clicking and dragging.

Dragging the mouse always selects text. Dragging with button 1 pressed (usually the left button) selects characters, dragging with button 2 (the middle button) selects a rectangular area, and dragging with button 3 (usually the right button) selects whole lines. These operations correspond to *elvis'* v, ^V, and V commands, respectively. (These commands are described later in this chapter.) When you release the button at the end of the drag, the selected text is immediately copied into an X11 cut buffer, so you can paste it into another application such as *xterm*. The text remains selected, so you can apply an operator command to it.

Clicking button 1 cancels any pending selection, and moves the cursor to the clicked-on character. Clicking button 3 moves the cursor without canceling the pending selection; you use this to extend a pending selection.

Clicking button 2 "pastes" text from the X11 cut buffer (like *xterm*). If you're entering an *ex* command line, the text will be pasted into the command line as though you had typed it. If you're in visual command mode or input mode, the text will be pasted into your edit buffer. When pasting, it doesn't matter where you click in the window; *elvis* always inserts the text at the position of the text cursor.

Double-clicking button 1 simulates a ^] keystroke, causing *elvis* to perform tag lookup on the clicked-on word. If *elvis* happens to be displaying an HTML document, then tag lookup pursues hypertext links, so you can double-click on any underlined text to view the topic that describes that text. Double-clicking button 3 simulates a ^T keystroke, taking you back to where you did the last tag lookup.

The Toolbar

The X11 interface supports a user-configurable toolbar. By default, the toolbar is enabled unless your `~/.exrc` file has a `set notoolbar` command.

The default toolbar already has some buttons defined. You use the `:gui` command to reconfigure the toolbar.

There are a number of commands. In particular, you can reconfigure the toolbar to suit your tastes, deleting one or all of the existing buttons, adding new ones, and controlling the spacing between buttons or groups of buttons. Here is a simple example:

```
:gui Make:make
:gui Make " Rebuild the program
:gui Quit:q
:gui Quit?!modified
```

These commands add two new buttons. The first line adds a button named "Make," which will execute the `:make` command when pressed. (The `:make` command is described later in this chapter.) The second line adds descriptive text for the "Make" button that shows up in the status line when the button is pressed. In this case, the `"` does not start a comment; rather it is an operator for the `:gui` command.

The second button, named "Quit," is created by the third line. It exits the program. The fourth line changes its behavior. If the condition (`!modified`) is true, the button will behave normally. But if it's false, the button will ignore any mouse clicks, and it will also be displayed as being "flat," instead of having the normal 3-D appearance. Thus, if the current file is modified, you won't be able to use the "Quit" button to exit.

You can create pop-up dialogues that appear when a toolbar button is pressed. The dialogue can set the value(s) of pre-defined variables (options) that can then be tested from the *ex* command associated with the button. There are 26 pre-defined variables, named `a-z`, that are set aside for user "programs" of this sort to use. This example associates a dialogue with a new button named "Split":

```
:gui Split"Create a new window, showing a given file
:gui Split;"File to load:" (file) f = filename
:gui Split:split (f)
```

The first command associates descriptive text with the "Split" button. The second command creates the pop-up dialogue: its prompt is *File to load:* and it will set the `filename` option. The `(file)` indicates that any string may be entered, but that the TAB key may be used for filename completion. The `f = filename` copies

the value of `filename` into `f`. Finally, the third command actually executes the
`:split` command on the value of `f`, which will be the new filename supplied by
the user.

The facility is quite flexible; see the online help for the full details.

Options

A large number of options control the X11 interface. You typically set these in
your *.exrc* file. There are options and abbreviations for setting the various fonts,
enabling and configuring the toolbar, status bar, scrollbars, and the cursor. Other
options control the cursor's behavior when you switch windows with ^W ^W and
whether the cursor goes back to the original *xterm* when *elvis* exits.

The online documentation describes all of the X11-related *ex* options. Here, we
describe some of the more interesting ones:

`autoiconify`
> Normally, when the ^W ^W command switches focus to an iconified window,
> that window is de-iconified. When `autoiconify` is true, *elvis* will iconify
> the old window, so that the number of open *elvis* windows remains constant.

`blinktime`
> The value is a number between 1 and 10 that indicates for how many tenths
> of a second the cursor should be visible and then invisible. A value of 0 dis-
> ables blinking.

`firstx`, `firsty`, `stagger`
> `firstx` and `firsty` control the position of the first window that *elvis* cre-
> ates. If not set, the `-geometry` option or the window manager controls
> placement. If `stagger` is set to a non-zero value, any new windows are cre-
> ated that many pixels down and to the right of the current window. Setting it
> to zero lets the window manager to do the placement.

`outlinemono`
> When set, *elvis* provides a white outline around characters when using a
> monochrome X display. This makes text easier to read. The value can range
> from 0 for no outline to 3 for the heaviest; the default is 2. This option has no
> effect on color displays.

`stopshell`
> Stores a command which runs an interactive shell, for the `:shell` and `:stop`
> *ex* commands, and the ^Z visual command. The default value is `xterm &`,
> which starts an interactive terminal emulator in another window.

`xscrollbar`
  Values `left` and `right` place the scrollbar on the indicated side of the window, while `none` disables the scrollbar. The default is `right`.

elvis 2.1 adds the ability to be configured via X resources. The resource values can be overridden by command-line flags, or by explicit `:set` or `:color` commands in the initialization scripts. *elvis*'s resources are listed in Table 10-4.

Table 10-4: elvis X Resources

Resource Class (Name is lowercase of class)	Type	Default Value
Elvis.Toolbar	Boolean	true
Elvis.Statusbar	Boolean	true
Elvis.Font	Font	fixed
Elvis.Geometry	Geometry	80x34
Elvis.Foreground	Color	black
Elvis.Background	Color	gray90
Elvis.MultiClickTimeout	Timeout	3
Elvis.Control.Font	Font	variable
Elvis.Cursor.Foreground	Color	red
Elvis.Cursor.Selected	Color	red
Elvis.Cursor.BlinkTime	Timeout	3
Elvis.Tool.Foreground	Color	black
Elvis.Tool.Background	Color	gray75
Elvis.Scrollbar.Foreground	Color	gray75
Elvis.Scrollbar.Background	Color	gray60
Elvis.Scrollbar.Width	Number	11
Elvis.Scrollbar.Repeat	Timeout	4
Elvis.Scrollbar.Position	Edge	right

The "Timeout" type gives a time value, in tenths of a second. The "Edge" type gives a scrollbar position, one of `left`, `right`, or `none`.

For example, if your X resource database contains the line `elvis.font: 10x20`, the default text font would be `10x20`. This value would be used if the `normalfont` option was unset.

Extended Regular Expressions

Extended regular expressions were introduced in the section "Extended Regular Expressions" in Chapter 8. The additional metacharacters available in *elvis* are:

\+ Matches one or more of the preceding regular expressions.

\? Matches zero or one of the preceding regular expressions.

\@ Matches the word under the cursor.

\= Indicates where to put the cursor when the text is matched. For instance, hel\=lo would put the cursor on the second *l* in the next occurrence of *hello*.

\{...\}
     Describes an interval expression, such as x\{1,3\} to match *x*, *xx*, or *xxx*.

POSIX bracket expressions (character classes, etc.) are not available,* nor is alternation with the | character or grouping with parentheses.

Improved Editing Facilities

This section describes the features of *elvis* that make simple text editing easier and more powerful.

Command-Line History and Completion

Everything you type on the *ex* command line is saved in a buffer named `Elvis ex history`. This is accessible like any other *elvis* buffer, but is not directly useful when just viewed in a window.

In order to access the history, you use the arrow keys on your terminal to display previous commands and to edit them. Use ↑ and ↓ to page through the list, and ← and → to move around on a command line. You can insert characters by typing and erase them by backspacing over them. Much as when editing in a regular *vi* buffer, the backspace does remove the characters, but the line is not updated as you type, so be careful!

When entering text into the `Elvis ex history` buffer (i.e., on the colon command line), the TAB key can be used for filename expansion. The preceding word is assumed to be a partial filename, and *elvis* searches for all matching files. If there are multiple matches, it fills in as many characters of the name as possible, and then beeps; or, if no additional characters are implied by the matching filenames, *elvis* lists all matching names and redisplays the command line. If there is a

---

* Well, in *elvis* 2.0 they're there, they just don't work. This is fixed in *elvis* 2.1.

single match, *elvis* completes the name and appends a tab character. If there are no matches, *elvis* simply inserts a tab character.

To get a real tab character, precede it with a ^V. You can also disable filename completion entirely by setting the `Elvis ex history` buffer's `inputtab` option to `tab`, via the following command:

```
:(Elvis ex history)set inputtab=tab
```

Tag Stacks

Tag stacking is described in the section "Tag Stacks" in Chapter 8. In *elvis*, tag stacking is very straightforward, as shown in Table 10-5 and Table 10-6.

Table 10-5: elvis Tag Commands

Command	Function
ta[g][!] [*tagstring*]	Edit the file containing *tagstring* as defined in the *tags* file. The ! forces *elvis* to switch to the new file if the current buffer has been modified but not saved.
stac[k]	Display the current tag stack.
po[p][!]	Pop a cursor position off the stack, restoring the cursor to its previous position.

Table 10-6: elvis Command Mode Tag Commands

Command	Function
^]	Look up the location of the identifier under the cursor in the *tags* file, and move to that location. The current location is automatically pushed onto the tag stack.
^T	Return to the previous location in the tag stack, i.e., pop off one element.

Unlike traditional *vi*, when you type ^], *elvis* looks up the entire word containing the cursor, not just the part of the word from the cursor location forward.

In HTML mode (discussed in the section "Display Modes"), the commands all work the same except that `:tag` expects to be given a URL instead of a tag name. URLs don't depend on having a *tags* file, so the *tags* file is ignored when in HTML mode. *elvis* 2.0 doesn't support any network protocols,* so its URLs can only consist of a file name and/or an HTML `#label`.

Several `:set` options affect how *elvis* works with tags, as described in Table 10-7.

---

* This is no longer true in *elvis* 2.1; see the section "elvis Futures" for details.

Table 10-7: elvis Options for Tag Management

Option	Function
`taglength, tl`	Control the number of significant characters in a tag that is to be looked up. The default value of zero indicates that all characters are significant.
`tags, tagpath`	The value is a list of directory and/or filenames in which to look for *tags* files. *elvis* looks for a file named *tags* in any entry that is a directory. Entries in the list are colon-separated (or semicolon on DOS/Windows), in order to allow spaces in directory names. The default value is just `"tags"`, which looks for a file named *tags* in the current directory. This can be overridden by setting the `TAGPATH` environment variable.
`tagstack`	When set to true, *elvis* stacks each location on the tag stack. Use `:set notagstack` to disable tag stacking.

Version 2.1 of *elvis* (in beta test as of this writing) supports the extended *tags* file format described earlier. *elvis* comes with its own version of *ctags*. The version in *elvis* 2.1 generates the enhanced format described earlier. Here is an example of the special `!_TAG_` lines it produces:

```
!_TAG_FILE_FORMAT       2       /supported features/
!_TAG_FILE_SORTED       1       /0=unsorted, 1=sorted/
!_TAG_PROGRAM_AUTHOR    Steve Kirkendall        /kirkenda@cs.pdx.edu/
!_TAG_PROGRAM_NAME      Elvis Ctags     //
!_TAG_PROGRAM_URL       ftp://ftp.cs.pdx.edu/pub/elvis/README.html   //
!_TAG_PROGRAM_VERSION   2.1     //
```

Finally, in *elvis*, each window has its own tag stack.

Infinite Undo

With *elvis*, before being able to undo and redo multiple levels of changes, you must first set the `undolevels` option to the number of levels of "undo" that *elvis* should allow. A negative value disallows *any* undoing (which is not terribly useful). The *elvis* documentation warns that each level of undo uses around 6K bytes of the session file (the file that describes your editing session), and thus can eat up disk space rather quickly. It recommends not setting `undolevels` any higher than 100 and "probably much lower."

Once you've set `undolevels` to a non-zero value, you enter text as normal. Then each successive u command undoes one change. To redo (undo the undo), you use the (rather mnemonic) CTRL-R command.

In *elvis*, the default value of `undolevels` is zero, which causes *elvis* to mimic UNIX *vi*. The option applies per buffer being edited; see the section "Initialization Steps" for a description of how to set it for every file that you edit.

Once `undolevels` has been set, a count to either the u or ^R commands undoes or redoes the given number of changes.

Arbitrary Length Lines and Binary Data

elvis can edit files with arbitrary length lines, and with an arbitrary number of lines.

Under UNIX, *elvis* does not treat a binary file differently from any other file. On other systems, it uses the *elvis.brf* file to set the `binary` option. This avoids newline translation issues. You can enter eight-bit text by typing ^X followed by two hexadecimal digits. Using the `hex` display mode is an excellent way to edit binary files. (The *elvis.brf* file and the `hex` display mode are described in the section "Interesting Features".)

Left-Right Scrolling

As mentioned in the section "Incremental Searching" in Chapter 8, you enable left-right scrolling in *elvis* using `:set nowrap`. The value of `sidescroll` controls the number of characters by which *elvis* shifts the screen when scrolling left to right. The ^W S command toggles the value of this option.

Visual Mode

elvis allows you to select regions one character at a time, one line at a time, or rectangularly, using the commands shown in Table 10-8.

Table 10-8: elvis Block Mode Command Characters

Command	Function
v	Start region selection, character at a time mode.
V	Start region selection, line at a time mode.
^v	Start region selection, rectangular mode.

elvis highlights (using reverse video) the text as you are selecting. To make your selection, simply use the normal motion keys. The screen below shows a rectangular region:

```
The 6th edition of <citetitle>Learning the vi Editor</citetitle>
brings the book into the late 1990&rsquo;s.
In particular, besides the &ldquo;original&rdquo; version of
<command>vi</command> that comes as a standard part of every UNIX
system, there are now a number of freely available &ldquo;clones&rdquo;
or work-alike editors.
```

elvis only permits a few operations on selected areas of text. Some operations work only on whole lines, even if you've selected a region that does not contain whole lines (see Table 10-9).

Table 10-9: elvis Block Mode Operations

Command	Operation
c, d, y	Change, delete, or yank text. Only d works exactly on rectangles.
<, >, !	Shift text left or right, filter text. These operate on the whole lines containing the marked region.

After using the d command to delete the region, the screen now looks like this:

```
The 6th edition of <citetitle>Learning the vi Editor</citetitle>
brings the 90&rsquo;s.
In particulo;original&rdquo; version of
<command>vi as a standard part of every
system, there are n available &ldquo;clones&rdquo;
or work-alike editors.
```

Programming Assistance

elvis' programming assistance capabilities are described in this section.

Edit-Compile Speedup

elvis provides commands that make it easier to stay within the editor while work-ing on a program. You can recompile a single file, rebuild your entire program, and work through compiler errors one at a time. The *elvis* commands are summa-rized in Table 10-10.

Table 10-10: elvis Program Development Commands

Command	Option	Function
cc[!] [*args*]	ccprg	Run the C compiler. Useful for recompiling an individual file.
mak[e][!] [*args*]	makeprg	Recompile everything that needs recompiling (usually via make(1)).
er[rlist][!] [*file*]		Move to the next error's location.

The cc command recompiles an individual source file. You run it from the colon command line. For example, if you are editing the file *hello.c*, and you type :cc, *elvis* will compile *hello.c* for you.

If you supply additional arguments to the `:cc` command, those arguments will be passed on to the C compiler. In this case, you need to supply *all* the arguments, including the filename.

The `:cc` command works by executing the text of the `ccprg` option. The default value is `"cc ($1?$1:$2)"`. *elvis* sets $2 to the name of the current source file, and $1 to the arguments you give to the `:cc` command. The value of `ccprg` thus uses your arguments if they are present; otherwise, it just passes the current file's name to the system `cc` command. (You can, of course, change `ccprg` to suit your taste.)

Similarly, the `:make` command is intended to recompile everything that needs recompiling. It does this by executing the contents of the `makeprg` option, which by default is `"make $1"`. Thus, you could type `:make hello` to make just the *hello* program, or just `:make` to make everything.

elvis captures the output of the compile or *make*, and looks for things that look like filenames and line numbers. When it finds likely candidates, it treats them as such, and moves to the location of the first error. The `:errlist` command moves to each successive error location, in turn. *elvis* displays the error message text in the status line as you move to each location.

If you supply a *filename* argument to `:errlist`, *elvis* will load a fresh batch of error messages from that file, and move to the location of the first error.

The *vi* mode command * (asterisk) is equivalent to `:errlist`. This is more convenient to use when you have a lot of errors to step through.

Finally, one really nice feature is that *elvis* compensates for changes in the file. As you add or delete lines, *elvis* keeps track, so that when you go to the next error, you end up on the correct line, which is not necessarily the one with the same absolute line number as in the compiler's error message.

Syntax Highlighting

To cause *elvis* to do syntax highlighting, use the `:display syntax` command. This is a per-window command. (The other *elvis* display modes are described in the section "Display Modes".) *elvis* displays text in up to six different fonts: *normal, bold, italic, underlined, emphasized,* and *fixed.* (These can be abbreviated to a single letter.) The syntax display modes use the following options to associate fonts with various parts of the syntax:

- `commentfont`: The font (*normal, italic,* etc.) to use for programming language comments

- `functionfont`: The font to use for identifiers that are function names

- `keywordfont`: The font to use for programming language keywords

- `prepfont`: The font to use for C and C++ preprocessor directives

- `stringfont`: The font to use for string constants (such as `"Don't panic!"` in Awk)

- `variablefont`: The font to use for variables, fields, and so on

- `otherfont`: The font to use for things that don't fall into the other categories but that should not be displayed in the normal font (e.g., type names defined with the C `typedef` keyword)

The description of each language's comments, functions, keywords, etc., is stored in the *elvis.syn* file. This file comes with a number of specifications in it already. As an example, here is the syntax specification for Awk:

```
# Awk.  This is actually for Thompson Automation's AWK compiler, which is
# somewhat beefier than the standard AWK interpreter.
language tawk awk
extension .awk
keyword BEGIN BEGINFILE END ENDFILE INIT break continue do else for function
keyword global if in local next return while
comment #
function (
string "
regexp /
useregexp (,~
other allcaps
```

The format is mostly self-explanatory, and is fully documented in the *elvis* online documentation.

The reason *elvis* associates fonts with different parts of a file's syntax is its ability to print files as they're shown on the screen (see the discussion of the `:lpr` command in the section "Display Modes").

In addition to specifying the font to use for each kind of item, you can associate a color with each kind of font (*normal*, *italic*, and so on). This is done with the `:color` command.

On a non-bitmapped display such as the Linux console, all of the fonts map into the one used by the console driver. This makes it rather difficult to distinguish *normal* from *italic*, for example. However, on some displays (such as the Linux console), you can still change the color of the different fonts. If you have a Linux system with *elvis*, use it to edit a convenient C source file, and then issue the following commands:

```
:display syntax
:color normal white
:color bold yellow
:color emphasized green
:color italic cyan
:color fixed red
```

Your screen will change to highlight C keywords in yellow, comments in light blue, preprocessor directives in green, and character and string constants in red. We regret that we can't reproduce the effect here in print. ☺

In *elvis*, the syntax colors are per-window attributes. You can change the color for the italic font in one window, and it will not affect the color for the italic font in another window. This is true even if both windows are showing the same file.

Syntax coloring makes program editing much more interesting and lively. But you have to be careful in your choice of colors!

Interesting Features

elvis has a number of interesting features:

Internationalization support
> Like *nvi*, *elvis* also has a home-grown method for allowing translations of messages into different languages. The *elvis.msg* file is searched for along the `elvispath` and loaded into a buffer named `Elvis messages`.
>
> Messages have the form "*terse message*: *long message*." Before printing a message, *elvis* looks up the terse form, and if there is a corresponding long form, that message is used. Otherwise, the terse message is used.

Display modes
> This is perhaps the most interesting of *elvis'* features. For certain kinds of files, *elvis* formats the file content on the screen, giving a surprisingly good approximation of a WYSIWYG effect. *elvis* can also use the same formatting for printing the buffer to several kinds of printers. Display modes get their own subsection, below.

Pre- and post-operation command files
> *elvis* loads four files (if they exist), that allow you to customize its behavior before and after reading and writing a file. This feature also gets its own subsection, below.

Open mode
> *elvis* is the only one of the clones that actually implements *vi*'s open mode. (Think of open mode as like *vi*, but with only a one-line window. The "advantage" to open mode is that it can be used on terminals that don't have cursor motion capabilities.)

Security

The :safer command sets the safer option for execution of non-home-directory *.exrc* files, or any other untrusted files. When safer is set, "certain commands are disabled, wildcard expansion in filenames is disabled, and certain options are locked (including the safer option itself)". The *elvis* documentation is no more specific than this; don't blindly trust *elvis* to provide complete security for you.

Built-in calculator

elvis extends the *ex* command language with a built-in calculator (sometimes referred to as an expression evaluator in the documentation). It understands C expression syntax, and is most used in the :if, :calc, and :eval commands. See the online help for the details, as well as the sample initialization files in the *elvis* distribution for examples.

Macro debugger (2.1)

elvis 2.1 has a debugger for *vi* macros (the :map command). This can be useful when writing complicated input or command maps.

Display Modes

elvis has several display modes. Depending on the kind of file, *elvis* produces a formatted version of the file, producing a WYSIWYG effect. The display modes are outlined in Table 10-11.

Table 10-11: elvis Display Modes

Mode	Display Appearance
normal	No formatting, displays your text as it exists in the file.
syntax	Like normal, but with syntax coloring turned on.
hex	An interactive hex dump, reminiscent of mainframe hex dumps. This is good for editing binary files.
html	A simple Web page formatter. The tag commands can be used to follow links and return.
man	Simple man page formatter. Like the output of nroff –man.

The :normal command will switch the display from one of the formatted views to normal mode. Use :display *mode* to switch back. As a shortcut, the ^W d command will toggle the display modes for the window.

Of the available modes, html and man are the most WYSIWYG in nature. The online documentation clearly defines the subset of both markup languages that *elvis* understands.

elvis uses the `html` mode for displaying its online help, which is written in HTML and has *many* cross-referencing links within it.

The example below shows *elvis* editing one of the HTML help files. The screen is split. Both windows show the same buffer; the bottom window is using the `html` display mode, while the top is using the `normal` display mode:

```
<html><head>
<title>Elvis 2.0 Sessions</title>
</head><body>

<h1>10. SESSIONS, INITIALIZATION, AND RECOVERY</h1>

This section of the manual describes the life-cycle of an
edit session. We begin with the definition of an
<a href="#SESSION">edit session</a> and
what that means to elvis.
This is followed by sections discussing
<a href="#INIT">initialization</a>
and <a href="#RECOVER">recovery after a crash.</a>
```

10.0 SESSIONS, INITIALIZATION, AND RECOVERY

> This section of the manual describes the life-cycle of an
> edit session. We begin with the definition of an **edit
> session** and what that means to elvis. This is
> followed by sections discussing **initialization** and
> **recovery after a crash.**

10.1 Sessions

The `man` mode is also interesting, since normally you have to format and print a man page to be sure you've done a decent job of laying it out. The following quote from the online help seems appropriate.

> Troff source was never designed to be interactively edited, and although I did the best I could, attempting to edit in `man` mode is still a disorienting experience. I suggest you get in the habit of using `normal` mode when making changes, and `man` mode to preview the effect of those changes. The `^W d` command makes switching between modes a pretty easy thing to do.

As an interesting adjunct, both the `html` and `man` modes also work with the `:color` command described in the section "Syntax Highlighting". This is particularly nice with `man` mode. For example, by default on a Linux console, only bold text (.B) is distinguishable from normal text. But with syntax coloring on, both bold and italic (.I) text become distinct. The mode commands are summarized in Table 10-12.

Table 10-12: elvis Display Mode Commands

Command	Function
di[splay] [*mode* [*lang*]]	Change the display mode to *mode*. Use *lang* for syntax mode.
no[rmal]	Same as :display normal, but much easier to type.

Associated with each window is the **bufdisplay** option, which should be set to one of the supported display modes. The standard *elvis.arf* file (see the next subsection) will look at the extension of the buffer's filename and attempt to set the display to a more interesting mode than **normal**.

Finally, *elvis* can also apply its WYSIWYG formatting to printing the contents of a buffer. The :**lpr** command formats a line range (or the whole buffer, by default) for printing. You can print to a file or down a pipe to a command. By default, *elvis* prints to a pipe that executes the system print spooling command.

The :**lpr** command is controlled by several options, described in Table 10-13.

Table 10-13: elvis Options for Print Management

Option	Function
lptype, lp	The printer type.
lpconvert, lpcvt	If set, convert Latin-8 extended ASCII to PC-8 extended ASCII.
lpcrlf, lpc	The printer needs CR-LF to end each line.
lpout, lpo	The file or command to print to.
lpcolumns, lpcols	The printer's width.
lpwrap, lpw	Simulate line wrapping.
lplines, lprows	The length of the printer's page.
lpformfeed, lpff	Send a form-feed after the last page.
lppaper, lpp	The size of the paper (letter, a4, etc.). This only matters for PostScript printers.

Most of the options are self-explanatory. *elvis* supports several printer types, as described in Table 10-14.

Table 10-14: Values for the lptype Option

Name	Printer Type
ps	PostScript, one logical page per sheet of paper.
ps2	PostScript, two logical pages per sheet of paper.
epson	Most dot-matrix printers, no graphic characters supported.
pana	Panasonic dot-matrix printers.

Table 10-14: Values for the `lptype` *Option (continued)*

Name	Printer Type
ibm	Dot-matrix printers with IBM graphic characters.
hp	Hewlett-Packard printers, and most non-PostScript laser printers.
cr	Line printers, overtyping is done with carriage-return.
bs	Overtyping is done via backspace characters. This setting is the closest to traditional UNIX *nroff.*
dumb	Plain ASCII, no font control.

If you have a PostScript printer, by all means use an `lptype` of `ps` or `ps2`. Use the latter to save paper, which is particularly handy when printing drafts.

Pre- and Post-Operation Control Files

elvis gives you the ability to control its actions at four points when reading and writing files: before and after reading a file, and before and after writing a file. It does this by executing the contents of four *ex* scripts at those respective points. These scripts are searched for using the directories listed in the `elvispath` option.

elvis.brf

> This file is executed Before Reading a File. The default version looks at the file's extension, and attempts to guess whether or not the file is binary. If it is, the `binary` option is turned on, to prevent *elvis* from converting newlines (which may be actual CR-LF pairs in the file) into linefeeds internally.

elvis.arf

> This file is executed After Reading a File. The default version examines the file's extension in order to turn on syntax highlighting.

elvis.bwf

> This file is executed Before Writing a File, in particular, before completely replacing an original file with the contents of the buffer. The default version implements copying the original file to a file with a *.bak* extension. You must set the `backup` option for this to work.

elvis.awf

> This file is executed After Writing a File. There is no default file for this, although it might be a good place to add hooks into a source code control system.

The use of command files to control these actions is quite powerful. It allows you to easily tailor *elvis'* behavior to suit your needs; in other editors these kinds of features are much more hardwired into the code.

elvis Futures

At the time of this writing, *elvis* 2.1 is in late beta-test, and it will probably be released by the time this book hits the bookstore. Steve Kirkendall has graciously supplied the following list of changes and new features that will be in *elvis* 2.1:

- Under Windows 95 and Windows/NT, there is now a graphical version of *elvis*. This is in addition to the text-mode port that was included in 2.0.

- A text-mode OS/2 port has been added.

- In X Windows, there is now a status bar and a configurable toolbar. The toolbar can invoke configurable dialogue windows. Also, many of the X features take their defaults from the standard X resource database. New command-line flags include -mono, -fork, and -client.

- The DOS version offers mouse support, similar to that of X Windows.

- *elvis* 2.1 supports the enhanced tags format described at length in the section "Exuberant ctags" in Chapter 8.

  elvis 2.1 does some innovative things with tags. When reading overloaded tags, it tries to guess which one you're looking for, and presents the most likely one first. If you reject it (by hitting ^] again, or typing :tag again), then it presents you with the next most likely match, and so on. It also notes the attributes of the tags that you reject or accept, and uses those to improve its guessing heuristic for later searches.

  The :tag command's syntax has been extended to allow you to search for tags by features other than just the tag name. This is powerful, but too complex to describe here [in Steve Kirkendall's email message]. There's a whole chapter in the manual [online help] that describes the use of tags.

  There is also a :browse command which finds all matching tags at once, and builds an HTML table from them. From this table, you can follow hypertext links to any matching tags you want.

  Finally, *elvis* 2.1 has a new tagprg option which, if set, discards the built-in tag searching algorithm and instead runs an external program to perform the search.

- The visual % command has been extended to recognize #if, #else, and #endif directives if you're using the syntax display mode.

- A new tex display mode has been added. It is not programmable, but is still somewhat useful.

- The ^W d command is a little smarter in 2.1 than it was in 2.0. Now it will toggle between syntax and any of the fancy formatting display modes (html, man, tex) if that's appropriate. This makes editing web pages a little more convenient.

- *elvis* can fetch files via HTTP or FTP. It can also write via FTP. Simply give a URL wherever *elvis* expects a filename. To access your own account on an FTP site (instead of the anonymous account), the directory name portion of the URL must begin with /~—*elvis* will read your ~/.netrc file to find the right name and password. The html display mode makes good use of these features! (By the way, the network functions work in Windows and OS/2, too.)

- For the sake of POSIX compliance, the command-line flags have changed. -s used to set the safer flag for extra security, but now it causes *elvis* to read a script from stdin and execute it. [This matches *nvi*. A.R.] Use an uppercase -S to set safer now.

- A new -o *filename* flag has been added so you can redirect the startup messages out to a file, instead of stdout/stderr. This is of critical importance to Windows 95 and Windows NT users because Windows discards anything written to stdout/stderr, which made WinElvis configuration problems almost impossible to diagnose. With -o *filename* you can send the diagnostic info to a file and view it later.

- A new :alias command has been added, for defining *ex* macros. It is intended to resemble the *csh* alias command.

- *elvis* 2.0 implemented the POSIX named character classes (in regular expressions) incorrectly. *elvis* 2.1 fixes that. For example, you can search for a C identifier via /\<[[:alpha:]_][[:alnum:]_]*.

Sources and Supported Operating Systems

The official WWW location for *elvis* is *ftp://ftp.cs.pdx.edu/pub/elvis/README.html*. From there, you can download the *elvis* distribution or get it directly using *ftp* from *ftp://ftp.cs.pdx.edu/pub/elvis/elvis-2.0.tgz*.

The source code for *elvis* is freely distributable. The licensing terms are described in the *COPYING* file in the distribution, and they permit distribution in source and binary form. *elvis* 2.1 will be distributed under the terms of *perl's* Artisitc License.

elvis works under UNIX, MS-DOS, Windows 95, and Windows NT. As of this writing, a port to OS/2 is in progress, but is not yet integrated into the sources (but see the previous section).

Compiling *elvis* is straightforward. Retrieve the distribution via *ftp* or via a web browser. Uncompress and untar it,* run the *configure* program, and then run *make*:

```
$ gzip -d < elvis-2.0.tgz | tar -xvpf -
...
$ cd elvis-2.0; ./configure
...
$ make
...
```

elvis should configure and build with no problems. Use *make install* to install it.

 In *elvis* 2.0, on Linux systems using GCC, you should recompile the file *lp.c* without optimization. Otherwise, at least in our experience, *elvis* tends to core dump when using the `:lpr` command to format and print the contents of an edit buffer.

Should you need to report a bug or problem in *elvis*, the person to contact is Steve Kirkendall, at *kirkenda@cs.pdx.edu.*

---

* The *untar.c* program available from the *elvis ftp* site is a very portable, simple program for unpacking *gzip*'ed *tar* files on non-UNIX systems.

11

vim — vi Improved

vim stands for "Vi Improved." It was written by Bram Moolenaar, who continues to maintain it. Today, *vim* is perhaps the most widely used *vi* clone, and there exists a separate Internet domain (*vim.org*) dedicated to it. Various versions of *vim* were used for most of the work updating this book; much of the later work was done with Version 5.0. Version 5.1 became current as the updates were finishing; this is mostly a bug fix release.

Author and History

This section is adapted from material supplied by Bram Moolenaar, *vim*'s author. We thank him.

Work on *vim* started when the author bought an Amiga computer. Coming from the UNIX world, he started using a *vi*-like editor called *stevie*. But it was far from perfect. Fortunately, it came with the source code. This is where work on *vim* started. At first it was a matter of making the editor more *vi* compatible and fixing bugs. After a while the program became very usable, and *vim* Version 1.14 was published on Fred Fish disk 591 (a collection of free software for the Amiga).

Other people began to use the program, liked it, and started helping development. A port to UNIX was done, then later to MS-DOS and other systems. *vim* became one of the most widely available *vi* clones. More features were added gradually: multi-level undo, multiwindowing, etc. Some features were unique to *vim*, but many were inspired by other *vi* clones. The goal has always been to provide the best for the user.

Today *vim* is one of the most full-featured of the *vi*-style editors anywhere. The online help is extensive. (It is described in more detail below.)

One of the more obscure features of *vim* is to be able to type from right to left. This is useful for languages like Hebrew and Farsi. This illustrates *vim*'s versatility. In Version 5.0 the *vi* compatibility was also improved, and the performance was further tuned. Being a rock-stable editor, on which professional software developers can rely, is another of *vim*'s design goals. Crashing with *vim* is rare, and when it happens you can recover your changes.

The development on *vim* continues. Plans for *vim* 6.0 include support for folding (being able to hide part of the text, e.g., the body of a function). The group of people helping to add features and port *vim* to more platforms is growing. The quality of the ports to different computer systems is increasing. The MS-Windows version will get dialogues and a file-selector. This opens up the hard-to-learn *vi* commands to a large group of users.

Important Command-Line Arguments

vim looks at how it was invoked to decide how it should behave. If invoked as *ex*, it will operate as a line editor. It also allows the Q command from *vi* mode to switch into *ex* mode. If invoked as *view*, it will start in *vi* mode, but mark each file initially as being read-only.

When invoked as *gvim* or *gview*, *vim* will start the GUI version, under X Windows or in whatever other graphical interface is appropriate. If a leading *r* is prepended to any of the names, *vim* enters "restricted" mode, where certain actions are disabled.

vim has a large number of command-line options. The most useful are described here:

−c *command*

> Execute *command* upon startup. This is the POSIX version of the historical +*command* syntax, but *vim* is not limited to positioning commands. (The old syntax is also accepted.) You can give up to ten −c commands.

-R Start in read-only mode, setting the `readonly` option.

-r Recover specified files, or if no files are listed on the command line, list all the files that can be recovered.

-s Enter batch (script) mode. This is only for *ex*, and is intended for running editing scripts. This is the POSIX version of the historic "−" argument.

-b Start in binary mode. This sets a few options that make it possible to edit a binary file.

-f For the GUI version, stay in the foreground. This should be used by programs that invoke *vim* and wait for it to finish, such as mail handling programs.

-g Start the GUI version of *vim*, if it has been compiled in.

-o *[N]*

Open *N* windows, if given, otherwise open one window for each file argument.

-i *viminfo*

Read the given *viminfo* file for initialization, instead of the default *viminfo* file.

-n Do not create a swap file. Recovery will not be possible, but this is useful for editing files on slow media, such as floppies.

-q *filename*

Treat *filename* as the "quick fix" file. This file should contain a list of error messages that *vim* will use for navigating to the location of each error in your program. Quick fix mode is discussed in the section "Edit-Compile Speedup".

-u *vimrc*

Read the given *vimrc* file for initialization, and skip all other normal initialization steps.

-U *gvimrc*

Read the given *gvimrc* file for GUI initialization, and skip all other normal GUI initialization steps.

-Z Enter restricted mode (same as having a leading *r* in the name). You cannot start shell commands or suspend the editor when this is in effect.

The −i, −n, −u and −U options are discussed in more detail below. There are several more options; the interested reader is referred to the online documentation for the full details.

Online Help and Other Documentation

vim comes with extensive and comprehensive online help. This help is comprised of over 50 ASCII text files, totalling almost 25,500 lines of text!

The online help is hypertextual in nature; you use the tag commands ^] and ^T to follow a reference and to go back to a previous position. If you have a color display, using the help with syntax coloring is particularly pleasant and effective.

The hypertext format is unique to *vim*; however the *doc* directory contains a *Makefile* and *awk* scripts that convert the files into HTML for perusal with a Web browser. (The `html` display mode in *elvis* works just fine. ☺) The point to start from would be *help.html*, generated from *help.txt*, the starting point for the online help.

Also included, of course, is a UNIX man page for *vim*.

To start the help system, give the `:help` command. This splits the screen. With no arguments, *vim* displays the *help.txt* file. With an argument to `:help`, *vim* does its best to find the help on that topic. In our experience, it does an excellent job. (This facility seems to be built on top of the tags mechanism, which has been applied to the text of the help files.)

Initialization

This section describes *vim*'s initialization steps, including those taken for the GUI versions of *vim*.

Initialization for All vim Invocations

vim performs the following initialization steps:

1. Set the `shell` and `term` options from the `SHELL` and `TERM` environment variables, respectively. On MS-DOS and Win32, use `COMSPEC` to set `shell` if `SHELL` is not set.

2. If −u was supplied, execute the given file, and skip the rest of the startup file based initializations. The −s option has the same effect for *ex* mode; only the −u option will be interpreted. Use of −u `NONE` causes *vim* to skip *all* further initializations.

3. Execute the system-wide *vimrc* file. The exact path is set when *vim* is compiled. A typical value is */usr/local/share/vim/vimrc*.

4. Execute instructions in the first place that exists of the following four:

   • The environment variable `VIMINIT`.

   • The user *vimrc* file, *$HOME/.vimrc* under UNIX (or Linux). The location will be different on non-UNIX systems. If *.vimrc* does not exist, *vim* looks for *_vimrc*. On the non-UNIX systems, the order is reversed.

   • The environment variable `EXINIT`.

   • The user *exrc* file, *$HOME/.exrc*. On non-UNIX systems, *_exrc* is tried. However, in this case, *vim* only looks for one or the other, not both.

5. If the `exrc` option has been set, then *vim* looks in the current directory for the first file that exists of the following four. The others are ignored.

   • *.vimrc*

   • *_vimrc*

   • *.exrc*

   • *_exrc*

   On MS-DOS and Win32 systems, the *_xxxrc* files are looked for before the *.xxxrc* files.

6. If they have not yet been set, the `shellpipe` and `shellredir` options are initialized based on the value of the `shell` option. The `shellredir` option is discussed in the section "Edit-Compile Speedup".

7. If −n was given on the command line, `updatecount` is set to zero. (This option controls how often the swap file is updated. The more often, the more the swap file is synchronized with all your changes, but possibly with decreased performance. Zero means never.)

8. If −b was supplied, set the appropriate options for editing binary files.

9. Perform GUI initializations. See the next subsection.

10. If `viminfo` is set, read the file indicated there.

11. If −q was supplied, read the named quick fix file. The quick fix facility is described in the section "Edit-Compile Speedup".

12. Open and fill all windows, as per the −o option. If −q was supplied, go to the first error.

13. Jump to the tag given by the −t option, if supplied. Execute any commands given with −c.

That's a lot of steps. As in other areas, *vim*'s extra facilities also provide extra flexibility and customizability.

As for *nvi*, you can place common initialization actions into your *.exrc* file (i.e., options and commands for UNIX *vi* and/or the other clones), and have your *.vimrc* file execute :`source` `.exrc` before or after the *vim*-specific initializations.

The *viminfo* file is much like the *elvis* session file. It can be used to save a large part of the state of your editing session in between logins. The *viminfo* file stores the following items:

- The command-line history
- The search string history
- Contents of registers
- File marks, pointing to locations in files
- Last search/substitute pattern (for n and &)

vim reads this file at startup, and when exiting, merges its current state with the contents of the file and then rewrites it.

Initialization for the GUI

If running the GUI version of *vim*, usually *vim* will fork a new process in order to run in the background, so that you can continue to give commands to the parent shell. The −f option disables this behavior.

If −U was supplied, *vim* executes the given file and skips the rest of the GUI startup file based initializations. Use of −U NONE causes *vim* to skip *all* further initializations.

Without −U, *vim* reads the system-wide *gvimrc* file (typically */usr/local/share/vim/ gvimrc*) and then the user *gvimrc* file, *$HOME/.gvimrc*.

These files can be used to configure the GUI. In particular, you can set up your own menus at this point.

Multiwindow Editing

There are a large number of *vi* mode commands for manipulating windows, as well as a number of *ex* mode commands that correspond to most of the *vi* mode commands.

As in *elvis*, the :`split` command will create a new window, and then you can use the *ex* command :e `filename` to edit a new file in the new window. Also as in *elvis*, CTRL-W CTRL-W will let you switch back and forth between windows.

```
<preface id="VI6-CH-0">
<title>Preface </title>
```

```
<para>
Text editing is one of the most common uses of any computer system, and
<command>vi</command> is one of the most useful standard text editors
on your system.
With <command>vi</command> you can create new files, or edit any
existing UNIX text
file.
```

```
ch00.sgm
# Makefile for vi book
#
# Arnold Robbins

CHAPTERS = ch00_6.sgm ch00_5.sgm ch00.sgm ch01.sgm ch02.sgm ch03.sgm \
        ch04.sgm ch05.sgm ch06.sgm ch07.sgm ch08.sgm
APPENDICES = appa.sgm appb.sgm appc.sgm appd.sgm

POSTSCRIPT = ch00_6.ps ch00_5.ps ch00.ps ch01.ps ch02.ps ch03.ps \
        ch04.ps ch05.ps ch06.ps ch07.ps ch08.ps \
```

```
Makefile
```

The split screen is the result of typing `vim ch00.sgm` followed by `:split Makefile`.

Unlike *nvi* and *elvis*, all windows share the bottom line of the screen for execution of *ex* commands. However, the status line for each file displays `[+]` if that file has been modified. Options control the use of reverse video versus highlighting for the status line, as well as whether the bottom window even has one. By default, the bottom window has a status line when there's more than one window.

Table 11-1 describes the most important *vim* window management commands.

Table 11-1: vim Window Management Commands

Command	Function
[*N*]sp[lit] [*position*] [*file*]	Splits the current window into two. *N* is the height of the new window. *position* indicates where in the file to position the cursor. If *file* is given, edit it in the new window, instead of the current file.
[*N*]new [*position*] [*file*]	Creates a new window, editing an empty buffer. If *file* is given, edit it instead of the empty buffer. *N* and *position* are the same as for `:split`.
[*N*]sv[iew] [*position*] [*file*]	Same as `:split`, but set the `readonly` option for the buffer.
q[uit][!]	Quit the current window (exit if given in the last window). If this is the last window on a changed buffer, the command fails, unless the `!` is given, in which case the changes are lost. When the `hidden` option is set, the buffer is not freed, even with `!`.

Table 11-1: vim Window Management Commands (continued)

Command	Function
clo[se][!]	Close the current window. Setting the `hidden` option will just hide an unsaved buffer; if not set, the command fails. If supplied, the trailing ! forces the window to be closed, even if it is the last window and the buffer was modified.
hid[e]	Close the current window, if it is not the last one on the screen. The buffer becomes hidden if this was the last window open upon the buffer.
on[ly][!]	Make this window the only one on the screen. Other windows with changes are not closed, unless `hidden` is set or ! is used. In any case, changes are never lost; the other buffers become hidden, but they are not discarded.
res[ize] [±n]	Increase or decrease the current window height by *n*.
res[ize] [n]	Set the current window height to *n* if supplied, otherwise, set it to the largest size possible without hiding the other windows.
qa[ll][!]	Exit *vim*. The ! forces an exit, even if some buffers have been modified but not saved.
wqa[ll][!] xa[ll][!]	Write all changed buffers and exit. The ! forces a write of `readonly` buffers. *vim* will not exit if any buffer cannot be written.
wa[ll][!]	Write all modified buffers that have filenames. The ! forces a write of `readonly` buffers.
[N]sn[ext]	Split the window and move to the next file in the argument list, or to the *N*th file if a count is supplied.
sta[g] [tagname]	Split the window and then run the `:tag` command as appropriate in the new window.

There are many more commands for managing the argument list and the list of open buffers. For example, the `:all` command creates one window for each command line argument. See the *vim* online help for details. We have included just the most useful of the commands in the above table.

As *vim* has the most *ex* commands, so too it has the most *vi* mode commands, as shown in Table 11-2. As with most *vi* commands, you can prefix many of the windowing commands with a count.

Table 11-2: vim Window Commands from vi Mode

Command	Function
^W s ^W S ^W ^S	Same as :split without a *file* argument. ^W ^S may not work on all terminals.
^W n ^W ^N	Same as :new without a *file* argument.
^W ^ ^W ^^	Perform :split #, split the window and edit the alternate file. With a count, edit the *n*th buffer.
^W q ^W ^Q	Same as the :quit command. ^W ^Q may not work on all terminals.
^W c	Same as the :close command.
^W o ^W ^O	Like the :only command.
^W <DOWN> ^W ^J ^W j	Move cursor to *n*th window below the current one. *n* is supplied as a prefix argument.
^W <UP> ^W ^K ^W k	Move cursor to *n*th window above the current one. *n* is supplied as a prefix argument.
^W w ^W ^W	With count, go to *n*th window. Otherwise, move to the window below the current one. If in the bottom window, move to the top one.
^W W	With count, go to *n*th window. Otherwise, move to window above the current one. If in the top window, move to the bottom one.
^W t ^W ^T	Move the cursor to the top window.
^W b ^W ^B	Move the cursor to the bottom window.
^W p ^W ^P	Go to the most recently accessed (previous) window.
^W r ^W ^R	Rotate all the windows downwards. The cursor stays in the same window.
^W R	Rotate all the windows upwards. The cursor stays in the same window.

Table 11-2: vim Window Commands from vi Mode (continued)

Command	Function
`^W x` `^W ^X`	Without count, exchange the current window with the next one. If there is no next window, exchange with the previous window. With count, exchange the current window with the *n*th window (first window is 1). The cursor is put in the other window.
`^W =`	Make all windows the same height.
`^W -`	Decrease current window height. A preceding count indicates by how much.
`^W +`	Increase current window height. A preceding count indicates by how much.
`^W _` `^W ^_`	Set the current window size to the value given in a preceding count. This is like `:resize` with an absolute count. Without a count, the window is made as large as possible.
z*N* RETURN	Set the current window height to *N*.
`^W ]` `^W ^]`	Split the current window. In the new upper window, use the identifier under the cursor as a tag and go to it. A preceding count indicates the new window's height.
`^W f` `^W ^F`	Split the current window, and edit the file name under the cursor in the new window. Rather complicated file searching is done for this command, see `:help ^W_f` for details.
`^W i` `^W ^I`	Open a new window and in it, move the cursor to the first line that matches the keyword under the cursor. The search starts at the beginning of the file, and lines that look like comments are ignored. With a preceding count, go to the *n*th matching line, and don't ignore comments.
`^W d` `^W ^D`	Open a new window, with the cursor on the first macro definition line that contains the keyword under the cursor. The search starts from the beginning of the file. If a count is given, the *count*th matching line is jumped to.

Miscellaneous remarks: The command `^W ^C` does not close the current window, since usually `^C` is the interrupt character, which ends up cancelling the command. If mouse support is enabled and you are using the GUI version of *vim*, you can resize a window by dragging on its status line with the mouse. Finally, *vim* has *many* options that control the behavior of the various commands. In particular, check out the `hidden`, `splitbelow`, `equalalways`, `winheight`, and `cmdheight` options. See the online help for full details.

GUI Interfaces

The screen shot and the explanation for this section were supplied by Bram Moolenaar. We thank him.

The *vim* GUI is available for UNIX, with Athena and Motif interfaces, Windows 95 and Windows NT, and BeOS. GUI versions for the Amiga, VMS, and the Macintosh are being worked on. A screen shot is shown in Figure 11-1.

The main advantage of the GUI version is that all colors can be used, without the configuration problems that many terminal emulators have with color. The picture shows the Motif version. What you can't see in the monochrome picture are the various colors that are used to highlight items in the text. For example, the comments are blue and strings are magenta.

The GUI window contains a menu at the top, one scrollbar for each window at the right, and a scrollbar at the bottom for horizontal scrolling. Not only do the scrollbars make it easy to browse through the file, they also give an indication of the current position in the file.

The cursor is after the /free at the bottom line, which is a search command that is being typed. The cursor is bright green, and is blinking. This makes it easy to spot in between the colored text. The color and the blinking are configurable with the guicursor option. When in insert mode, the cursor changes shape to a vertical bar. In replace mode it becomes a half-height cursor. This makes it very easy to recognize the current mode.

The top window contains a shell script, the middle a *Makefile*, the lower a C program. They are all highlighted automatically when the file is opened. These are three of the about 70 syntaxes that are supported by the distribution (see the section "Syntax Highlighting").

All occurrences of *to* in the text are highlighted with a yellow background. This is the hlsearch option in action. It shows matches of the last used search pattern. This is very useful when you are searching for the places where a variable in your source code is used. All matches are easily spotted, and the n command jumps to each next match.

The reverse video *free* in the top window is the current match for the search pattern that is being typed in the commandline. This shows the incsearch option in action. Each time a character is typed for the pattern, the match will be adjusted. The text is scrolled when necessary, to reveal a match further away. Using this, you can directly see where the search command is taking you, and adjust the pattern until you can see that it gets you where you wanted to go. This is especially useful in noticing typing mistakes in the pattern.

File   Edit   Window   IDE   Syntax   Words L3   Help

```
#! /bin/sh

# Guess values for system-dependent variables and create Makefiles.
# Generated automatically using autoconf version 2.12
# Copyright (C) 1992, 93, 94, 95, 96 Free Software Foundation, Inc.
#
# This configure script is free software; the Free Software Foundation
# gives unlimited permission to copy, distribute and modify it.

# Defaults:
ac_help=
ac_default_prefix=/usr/local
# Any additions from configure.in:
ac_help="$ac_help
  --enable-perlinterp     Include Perl interpreter."
ac_help="$ac_help
```
configure
```
ALL_GUI_PRO   = gui.pro gui_motif.pro gui_athena.pro gui_x11.pro gui_w32.pro gui_a

### our grand parent directory should know who we are...
### only used for "make tar"
VIMVERSION = `eval "basename \`cd ../; pwd\`"`

### Command to create dependencies based on #include "..."
### prototype headers are ignored due to -DPROTO, system
### headers #include <...> are ignored if we use the -MM option, as
### e.g. provided by gcc-cpp.
### Include USE_GUI to get gependency on gui.h
CPP_DEPEND = $(CC) -M$(CPP_MM) $(DEPEND_CFLAGS)

# flags for cproto
#      __inline and __attribute__ are not recognized by cproto
#      maybe the "/usr/bin/cc -E" has to be adjusted for some systems
```
Makefile
```
/* vi:set ts=8 sts=4 sw=4:
 *
 * VIM - Vi IMproved    by Bram Moolenaar
 *
 * Do ":help uganda"  in Vim to read copying and usage conditions.
 * Do ":help credits" in Vim to see a list of people who contributed.
 */

#define EXTERN
#include "vim.h"

#ifdef SPAWNO
# include <spawno.h>              /* special MSDOS swapping library */
#endif

static void mainerr __ARGS((int, char_u *));
```
main.c
```
/free
```

Figure 11-1: The vim GUI window

What you don't see in the picture are the file browser and dialogues, which are used when a command is selected from a menu. This is a new feature in *vim* Version 5.2.* For example, the `File/Save as` menu will pop up a file browser, where you can select the name of the file you want to write. If the file already exists, a dialogue pops up which asks you if you want to overwrite the file or not. This is much nicer than getting the *Use ! to override* error message. A disadvantage is that you have to grab the mouse, and thus move your hand between the keyboard and the mouse. If you don't want this, just don't use the menus. You can disable the menu (and make space for some extra text) by removing the m flag from the `guioptions` option.

One nice specialty of *vim* is that almost everything is configurable. This also includes the menus. If you don't like the menus provided, you can define your own. This works almost like defining a mapping. For example, this adds an `IDE/Make-n` menu, to execute the `:make -n` command:

```
:amenu IDE.Make-n :make -n<CR>
```

To include a dot or space in a menu name, precede it with a backslash. To get the same menu entry, but with a space before the `-n`:

```
:amenu IDE.Make\ -n   :make -n<CR>
```

As you can see, the backslash is not needed in the argument, only in the menu name. All this makes a nice GUI environment, while all the good old *vi* commands still work as in the terminal version.

The online help fully describes all of the GUI options, and how to create your own menus.

Extended Regular Expressions

Of all the clones, *vim* provides the richest set of regular expression matching facilities. Much of the descriptive text in the list below is borrowed from the *vim* documentation:

`\|` Indicates alternation, `house\|home`.

`\+` Matches one or more of the preceding regular expression.

`\=` Matches zero or one of the preceding regular expression.

`\{n,m}`
     Matches *n* to *m* of the preceding regular expression, as much as possible. *n* and *m* are numbers between 0 and 32000; *vim* requires only the left brace to be preceded by a backslash, not the right brace.

---

* Version 5.2 is in beta release as this book goes to press. A.R.

\{n}
>   Matches *n* of the preceding regular expression.

\{n,}
>   Matches at least *n* of the preceding regular expression, as much as possible.

\{,m}
>   Matches 0 to *m* of the preceding regular expression, as much as possible.

\{}
>   Matches 0 or more of the preceding regular expression, as much as possible (same as *).

\{-n,m}
>   Matches *n* to *m* of the preceding regular expression, as few as possible.

\{-n}
>   Matches *n* of the preceding regular expression.

\{-n,}
>   Matches at least *n* of the preceding regular expression, as few as possible.

\{-,m}
>   Matches 0 to *m* of the preceding regular expression, as few as possible.

\i Matches any identifier character, as defined by the `isident` option.

\I Like \i, but excluding digits.

\k Matches any keyword character, as defined by the `iskeyword` option.

\K Like \k, but excluding digits.

\f Matches any filename character, as defined by the `isfname` option.

\F Like \f, but excluding digits.

\p Matches any printable character, as defined by the `isprint` option.

\P Like \p, but excluding digits.

\s Matches a whitespace character (exactly space and tab).

\S Matches anything that isn't a space or a tab.

\b Backspace.

\e Escape.

\r Carriage return.

\t Tab.

\n Reserved for future use. Eventually, it will be used for matching multi-line patterns. See the *vim* documentation for more details.

~   Matches the last given substitute (i.e., replacement) string.

`\(...\)`

    Provides grouping for `*`, `\+`, and `\=`, as well as making matched sub-texts available in the replacement part of a substitute command (`\1`, `\2`, etc.).

`\1` Matches the same string that was matched by the first sub-expression in `\(` and `\)`. For example: `\([a-z]\).\1` matches *ata, ehe, tot*, etc. `\2`, `\3`, and so on may be used to represent the second, third, and so forth subexpressions.

The `isident`, `iskeyword`, `isfname`, and `isprint` options define the characters that appear in identifiers, keywords, and filenames, and that are printable. Use of these options makes regular expression matching very flexible.

Improved Editing Facilities

This section describes the features of *vim* that make simple text editing easier and more powerful.

Command-Line History and Completion

vim keeps a history of your *ex* commands, search strings, and expressions in its extended command language. These are three separate histories. The size of each is controlled by the `history` option; the default is 20. You may wish to increase it in your *.vimrc* file, although *vim* does take steps to maintain only unique commands.

To access the history, use the ↑ cursor key on the colon command line. This will move backwards through the saved commands (most recent first). The ↓ key will move forwards. You can move around on the command line using the ← and → keys. By default, text that you type is inserted into the command line. You can use the INS (Insert) key on your keyboard to toggle this mode, in which case what you type will replace what's on the command line. The BACKSPACE key will erase characters.

You can use the SHIFT or CTRL key in combination with the ← and → keys to move the cursor left or right one word at time. This may or may not work on all keyboards, though. You can use ^B or HOME to move the cursor to the beginning of the command line, and ^E or END to move to the end of the command line. The control key versions should always work.

The behavior of the ESC character can vary. If *vim* is in *vi* compatibility mode, ESC acts likes RETURN and executes the command. When *vi*-compatibility is turned off, ESC will exit the command line without executing anything.

vim also provides completion facilities on the *ex* command line. The `wildchar` option contains the character that you type when you want *vim* to do a completion. The default value is the tab character. You can use completion for all of the following:

Command names
> Available at the start of the command line.

Tag values
> After you've typed `:tag`.

Filenames
> When typing a command that takes a filename argument. When multiple files match a pattern during filename completion, the value of the `suffixes` option sets a priority among them, in order to pick the one *vim* will actually use. (See `:help suffixes` for the details.)

Option values
> When entering a `:set` command. This has two features: when typing the name of the option itself, hitting TAB will complete the option name. You can then type the = sign and hit TAB again, and *vim* will fill in the current value of the variable.

Besides just the TAB key to do an expansion, a number of other control keys provide additional functionality. Table 11-3 describes the commands and what they do.

Table 11-3: vim Command-Line Completion Commands

Command	Function
^D	Lists the names that match the pattern. For filenames, directories will be highlighted.
Value of `wildchar`	(Default: tab) Performs a match, inserting the generated text. For multiple matches, the first match is inserted. Hitting TAB successively cycles among all the matches.
^N	Go to next of multiple `wildchar` matches, if any; otherwise, recall more recent history line.
^P	Go to previous of multiple `wildchar` matches, if any; otherwise, recall older history line.
^A	Insert all names that match the pattern.
^L	If there is exactly one match, insert it; otherwise, expand to the longest common prefix of the multiple matches.

The completion facilities are extensive; see `:help cmdline` for the full details. Besides command-line completion, *vim* also provides insert mode completion.

When typing text, especially in programs, the same words appear quite often. *vim* has commands that search backwards or forwards for a match with a half-finished word. For example, if you were typing this text and had entered *ex*, giving the ^P command would have completed it to *example*. This is a nice way to reduce the number of typed characters and to avoid spelling mistakes.

Completion works not only with words in the text where you are typing, you can also fetch words from much further away. Table 11-4 shows an overview of the relevant commands.

Table 11-4: vim Insert Mode Completion Commands

Command	Function
^N	Complete a word from the current buffer, searching forward (mnemonic: next).
^P	Complete a word from the current buffer, searching backward (mnemonic: previous).
^X ^K	Complete words from a dictionary.
^X ^I	Complete words from included files.
^X ^D	Complete a macro (defined word) from included files.
^X ^]	Complete words from a tags file.
^X ^F	Complete a filename.
^X ^L	Complete a whole line from the current buffer.

See :help ins-completion for more details.

Tag Stacks

Tag stacking is described in the section "Tag Stacks" in Chapter 8. *vim* provides the richest set of facilities for working with tags. Besides just the ability to stack tags, if there are multiple matching tags, you can choose among them. You can also do a tag selection and window splitting operation in one command. See Table 11-5 for a list of *vim* tag commands.

Table 11-5: vim Tag Commands

Command	Function
ta[g][!] [*tagstring*]	Edit the file containing *tagstring* as defined in the *tags* file. The ! forces *vim* to switch to the new file if the current buffer has been modified but not saved. The file may or may not be written out depending upon the setting of the autowrite option.
[*count*]ta[g][!]	Jump to the *count*th newer entry in the tag stack.

Table 11-5: vim Tag Commands (continued)

Command	Function
[*count*]po[p][!]	Pops a cursor position off the stack, restoring the cursor to its previous position. If supplied, go to the *count*th older entry.
tags	Display the contents of the tag stack.
ts[elect][!] [*tagstring*]	List the tags that match *tagstring*, using the information in the tags file(s). If no *tagstring* is given, the last tag name from the tag stack is used.
sts[elect][!] [*tagstring*]	Like :tselect, but splits the window for the selected tag.
[*count*]tn[ext][!]	Jump to the *count*th next matching tag (default 1).
[*count*]tp[revious][!] [*count*]tN[ext][!]	Jump to the *count*th previous matching tag (default 1).
[*count*]tr[ewind][!]	Jump to the first matching tag. With *count*, jump to the *count*th matching tag.
tl[ast][!]	Jump to the last matching tag.

Normally, *vim* shows you which matching tag, out of how many, has been jumped to:

```
tag 1 of >3
```

It uses a greater-than sign (>) to indicate that it has not yet tried all the matches. You can use :tnext or :tlast to try more matches. If this message is not displayed because of some other message, use :0tn to see it.

The output of the :tags command is shown below. The current location is marked with a greater than sign (>):

```
  # TO tag       FROM line in file
  1  1 main            1  harddisk2:text/vim/test
> 2  2 FuncA          58  -current-
  3  1 FuncC         357  harddisk2:text/vim/src/amiga.c
```

The :tselect command lets you pick from more than one matching tag. The "priority" (**pri** field) indicates the quality of the match (global versus static, exact case versus case-independent, etc.); this is described more fully in the *vim* documentation.

```
 nr pri kind tag              file ~
  1 F    f    mch_delay           os_amiga.c
                mch_delay(msec, ignoreinput)
> 2 F    f    mch_delay           os_msdos.c
                mch_delay(msec, ignoreinput)
  3 F    f    mch_delay           os_unix.c
                mch_delay(msec, ignoreinput)
Enter nr of choice (<CR> to abort):
```

The :tag and :tselect commands can be given an argument that starts with /. In that case, this argument is treated as a regular expression. *vim* will find all the tags that match the given regular expression.* For example, :tag /normal will find the macro NORMAL, the function normal_cmd, and so on. Use :tselect /normal and enter the number of the tag you want.

The *vi* command mode commands are described in Table 11-6. Besides using the keyboard, as in the other editors, you can also use the mouse, if mouse support is enabled in your version of *vim*.

Table 11-6: vim Command Mode Tag Commands

Command	Function

^]
  g <LeftMouse>
  CTRL-<LeftMouse>
	Look up the location of the identifier under the cursor in the *tags* file, and move to that location. The current location is automatically pushed onto the tag stack.

^T	Return to the previous location in the tag stack, i.e., pop off one element. A preceding count specifies how many elements to pop off the stack.

The *vim* options that affect tag searching are described in Table 11-7.

Table 11-7: vim Options for Tag Management

Option	Function
taglength, tl	Controls the number of significant characters in a tag that is to be looked up. The default value of zero indicates that all characters are significant.
tags	The value is a list of filenames in which to look for tags. As a special case, if a filename starts with ./, the dot is replaced with the directory part of the current file's pathname, making it possible to use *tags* files in a different directory. The default value is "./tags,tags".
tagrelative	When set to true (the default), and using a *tags* file in another directory, filenames in that *tags* file are considered to be relative to the directory where the *tags* file is.

The *vim* 5.1 distribution comes with Version 2.0.3 of the Exuberant *ctags* program. As of this writing, this is the current version of Exuberant *ctags*.

vim can use *emacs* style *etags* files, but this is only for backwards compatibility; the format is not documented in the *vim* documentation, nor is the use of *etags* files encouraged.

---

* Prior to Version 5.1, *vim* keyed its treatment of the :tag or :tselect argument as a regular expression based on the presence or absence of special characters. The use of / disambiguates the process.

Finally, like *elvis*, *vim* also looks up the entire word containing the cursor, not just the part of the word from the cursor location forward.

Infinite Undo

In *vim*, being able to undo and redo multiple levels of changes is controlled by the `undolevels` option. This option is a number indicating how many levels of "undo" that *vim* should allow. A negative value disallows *any* undoing (which is not terribly useful).

When `undolevels` is set to a non-zero value, you enter text as normal. Then each successive u command undoes one change. To redo (undo the undo), you use the (rather mnemonic) CTRL-R command.

vim is different from *elvis*; it starts out with a default value for `undolevels` of 1,000, which should be close enough to infinite for any given editing session. Also, the option is global, and not per buffer.

Once `undolevels` has been set, a count to either the u or ^R commands undoes or redoes the given number of changes.

vim actually implements undoing and redoing in two different ways. When the `cpoptions` (compatibility options) option contains the letter u, the u command works like in *vi*, and ^R repeats the previous action (like . in *nvi*). When u is absent from `cpoptions`, u undoes one step and ^R redoes one step. This is easier to use, but not *vi*-compatible.

Arbitrary Length Lines and Binary Data

vim does not have a limit on the number or lengths of lines. When editing a binary file, you should either use the -b command-line option or :set binary. These set several other *vim* options that make it easier to edit binary files. To enter 8-bit text, use ^V followed by three decimal digits.

Incremental Searching

As mentioned in the section "Incremental Searching" in Chapter 8, you enable incremental searching in *vim* using :set incsearch.

The cursor moves through the file as you type. *vim* highlights the text that matches what you've typed so far.

You may wish to use this with the `hlsearch` option, which highlights all matches of the most recent search pattern. This option is particularly useful when looking for all uses of a particular variable or function in program source code.

Left-Right Scrolling

As mentioned in the section "Left-Right Scrolling" in Chapter 8, you enable left-right scrolling in *vim* using `:set nowrap`. The value of `sidescroll` controls the number of characters by which *vim* shifts the screen when scrolling left to right. With `sidescroll` set to zero, each scroll puts the cursor in the middle of the screen. Otherwise, the screen scrolls by the desired number of characters.

vim also has several commands that scroll the window sideways, shown in Table 11-8.

Table 11-8: vim Sideways Scrolling Commands

Command	Function
zl	Scroll the window left.
zh	Scroll the window right.
zs	Scroll the window to put the cursor at the left (start) of the screen.
ze	Scroll the window to put the cursor at the right (end) of the screen.

Visual Mode

vim allows you to select regions one character at a time, one line at a time, or rectangularly, using the commands shown in Table 11-9.

Table 11-9: vim Block Mode Command Characters

Command	Function
v	Start region selection, character at a time mode.
V	Start region selection, line at a time mode.
^v	Start region selection, rectangular mode.

vim highlights (using reverse video) the text as you are selecting. To make your selection, simply use the normal motion keys. If `showmode` is set, *vim* will indicate the mode as one of *visual*, *visual line*, or *visual block*. If *vim* is running inside an *xterm*, you can also use the mouse to select text (see `:help mouse-using` for the details). This also works in the GUI versions. The screen below shows a rectangular region:

```
The 6th edition of <citetitle>Learning the vi Editor</citetitle>
brings the book into the late 1990&rsquo;s.
In particular, besides the &ldquo;original&rdquo; version of
<command>vi</command> that comes as a standard part of every UNIX
system, there are now a number of freely available &ldquo;clones&rdquo;
or work-alike editors.
```

After applying the ~ operator, the screen looks like this:

```
The 6th edition of <citetitle>Learning the vi Editor</citetitle>
brings the BOOK INTO THE LATE 1990&rsquo;s.
In particulAR, BESIDES THE &LDQUo;original&rdquo; version of
<command>vi</COMMAND> THAT COMES as a standard part of every UNIX system,
there are nOW A NUMBER OF FREELY available &ldquo;clones&rdquo;
or work-alike editors.
```

vim permits many operations on the selected text. Some operations work only on whole lines, even if you've selected a region that does not contain whole lines.

vim has special commands for increasing the "swept out" area, and it allows you to apply almost any *vi* mode command to the highlighted text, as well as some commands that are unique to visual mode.

When defining the area to be operated on, a number of commands make it easy to treat words, sentences, or blocks of C/C++ code as single objects. These are described in Table 11-10. These commands can be used by themselves to extend the region, or they can be used in conjunction with an operator. For example, daB deletes a brace-enclosed block of text, including the braces.

Table 11-10: vim Block Mode Object Selectors

Command	Selects
aw	A word (with whitespace)
iw	An inner word (without whitespace)
aW	A WORD (with whitespace)
iW	An inner WORD (without whitespace)
as	A sentence (with whitespace)
is	An inner sentence (without whitespace)
ap	A paragraph (with whitespace)
ip	An inner paragraph (without whitespace)
ab	A (...) block (includes parentheses)
ib	An inner (...) block (not including the parentheses)
aB	A {...} block (includes braces)
iB	An inner {...} block (not including the braces)

The terms "word" and "WORD" have the same meaning as for the w and W motion commands.

vim allows you to use many operators on highlighted text. The available operators are summarized in Table 11-11.

Table 11-11: vim Block Mode Operations

Command	Operation
~	Flip the case of the selected text.
o, O	Move to the other end of the highlighted text. o moves from the start of the highlighted area to end, and vice versa. o in block mode moves to the other end of the text on the current line. You can continue sweeping out the area from the new position.
<, >, !	Shift text left or right, filter text. These operate on the whole lines containing the marked region. In the future, for a block, only the block will be shifted.
=	Filters text through the program named by the `equalprg` option. (Typically a simple text formatter such as *fmt.*) This operates on the whole lines containing the marked region.
gq	Formats the lines containing the marked region to be no longer that what's set in `textwidth`. This operates on the whole lines containing the marked region.
:	Start an *ex* command for the highlighted lines. This operates on the whole lines containing the marked region.
c, d, y	Change, delete, or yank text. These work even on rectangular text, although the c command only enters text on the first line in the block.
c, r, s	Change the highlighted text.
C, S, R	If using CTRL-V , the rectangle is deleted and insert mode is entered in the first line. Otherwise, whole lines are replaced.
x	Delete the highlighted text.
X, Y	Delete or yank the whole lines containing the highlighted area.
D	Delete to the end of the line. When using CTRL-V , the highlighted block and the rest of the text to end of each line is deleted. If not using CTRL-V , the whole line is deleted.
J	Join the highlighted lines. This operates on the whole lines containing the marked region.
U	Make uppercase. This command is unique to visual mode.
u	Make lowercase. This command is unique to visual mode.
^]	Use the highlighted text as the tag to find in a tag search.

Programming Assistance

vim has extensive facilities for both the edit–compile–debug cycle and syntax highlighting.

Edit-Compile Speedup

The facilities in *vim* were inspired by the "quick fix" mode of the Manx Aztec C compiler for the Amiga. In fact, the *vim* documentation refers to this feature as "quick fix" mode. The features are quite flexible, allowing you to tailor them to your programming environment (see Table 11-12).

Table 11-12: vim Program Development Commands

Command	Function
mak[e] [*arguments*]	Run *make*, based on the settings of several options as described below, then go to the location of the first error.
cf[ile][!] [*errorfile*]	Read the error file and jump to the first error. With an *errorfile*, use that file for errors and set the errorfile option to it. The ! forces *vim* to move to another buffer if the current one has been modified but not saved.
cl[ist][!]	List the errors that include a filename. With !, list all errors.
[*count*]cn[ext][!]	Display the *count*th next error that includes a filename. If there are no filenames at all, go to the *count*th next error.
[*count*]cN[ext][!] [*count*]cp[revious][!]	Display the *count*th previous error that includes a filename. If there are no filenames at all, go to the *count*th previous error.
clast[!] [*n*]	Display error *n* if supplied. Otherwise, display the last error.
crewind[!] [*n*]	Display error *n* if supplied. Otherwise, display the first error.
cc[!] [*n*]	Displays error *n* if supplied, otherwise redisplays the current error.
cq[uit]	Quit with an error code, so that the compiler will not compile the same file again. This is intended primarily for use with the Amiga compiler.

Like *elvis*, as you move through the errors *vim* also compensates for changes in the file, so that when you go to the next error, you end up on the correct line.

The *vim* options that control the :make command are presented in Table 11-13.

Table 11-13: vim Program Development Options

Option	Value	Function
shell	/bin/sh	The shell to use to execute the command for rebuilding your program.
makeprg	make	The program that will actually handle all the recompilation.

Table 11-13: vim Program Development Options (continued)

Option	Value	Function
shellpipe	2>&1| tee	Whatever is needed to cause the shell to save both standard output and standard error from the compilation in the error file.
makeef	/tmp/vim##.err	The name of a file which will contain the compiler output. The ## causes *vim* to create unique filenames.
errorformat	%f:%l:\ %m	A description of what error messages from the compiler look like. This example value is for GCC, the GNU C compiler.

When you execute :make, *vim* constructs a command by concatenating the various pieces described above. Any arguments you supply are passed to *make* in the appropriate place. It then echoes this command to your screen. For example, if you type :make -k, you might see something like this:

```
:!make -k 2>&1| tee /tmp/vim34215.err
...
```

By using the *tee*(1) program, the output from *make* and the compiler is saved in the error file (*/tmp/vim34215.err*), and also sent to standard output, in this case your screen.

When the *make* finishes, *vim* reads the error file, and goes to the location of the first error. It uses the value of the **errorformat** option to parse the contents of the error file, in order to find file names and line numbers. (The format of this variable is described in full in :help errorformat.) You can then use the :cc command to see the error messages, and the :cnext command to move to the next error.

Syntax Highlighting

Highlighting in *vim* is based primarily on colors. To enable syntax highlighting, put **syntax on** into your *.vimrc* file. This will cause *vim* to read the *syntax.vim* file, which defines the default highlight coloring and then sets things up to use highlighting appropriate to each language.

vim has a very powerful sub-language for defining syntax highlighting. The *syntax.txt* help file in *vim* 5.1 that describes it is over 1,500 lines long. Therefore, we won't attempt to give all the details here. Instead, the sample file below should give you some taste for what *vim* can do. The example consists of portions of the syntax file for Awk:

```
" Vim syntax file
" Language:    awk, nawk, gawk, mawk
" Maintainer:  Antonio Colombo <antonio.colombo@jrc.org>
" Last change: 1997 November 29

" Remove any old syntax stuff hanging around
syn clear

" A bunch of useful Awk keywords
syn keyword awkStatement        break continue delete exit
...

syn keyword awkFunction         atan2 close cos exp int log rand sin \
                                sqrt srand
...

syn keyword awkConditional      if else
syn keyword awkRepeat           while for do

syn keyword awkPatterns         BEGIN END
syn keyword awkVariables        ARGC ARGV FILENAME FNR FS NF NR
...

" Octal format character.
syn match   awkSpecialCharacter contained "\\[0-7]\{1,3\}"
" Hex    format character.
syn match   awkSpecialCharacter contained "\\x[0-9A-Fa-f]\+"

syn match   awkFieldVars        "\$[0-9]\+"

syn match   awkCharClass        contained "\[:[^:\]]*:\]"
syn match   awkRegExp contained "/\^"ms=s+1
syn match   awkRegExp contained "\$/"me=e-1
syn match   awkRegExp contained "[?.*{}|+]"
...

" Numbers, allowing signs (both -, and +)
" Integer number.
syn match   awkNumber           "[+-]\=\<[0-9]\+\>"
" Floating point number.
syn match   awkFloat            "[+-]\=\<[0-9]\+\.[0-9]+\>"
...

syn match   awkComment "#.*" contains=awkTodo

if !exists("did_awk_syntax_inits")
  let did_awk_syntax_inits = 1
  " The default methods for highlighting.  Can be overridden later
  hi link awkConditional        Conditional
  hi link awkFunction           Function
  hi link awkRepeat             Repeat
  hi link awkStatement          Statement
  ...
  hi link awkNumber             Number
```

```
    hi link awkFloat            Float
    ...

    hi link awkComment          Comment
    ...
endif

let b:current_syntax = "awk"
```

The file above uses `syntax keyword` to give names to certain classes of key-words (such as real Awk keywords and built-in functions), and `syntax match` to give names to regular expressions that match certain kinds of objects (such as numbers). Then the `hi link` statements link the named classes of objects to the predefined highlighting conventions.

The *syntax.vim* file predefines the standard conventions, with a number of lines like these:

```
hi Comment      term=bold ctermfg=Cyan guifg=#80a0ff
hi Constant     term=underline ctermfg=Magenta guifg=#ffa0a0
hi Special      term=bold ctermfg=LightRed guifg=Orange
hi Identifier   term=underline ctermfg=DarkCyan guifg=#40ffff
...
```

The first argument defines the class, and the rest define what kind of highlighting to do on what kind of terminal. `term` is for a normal terminal, `cterm` is for a color terminal (in this case, the ForeGround color), and `gui` is for *vim*'s GUI inter-face.

In *vim*, the syntax colors are global attributes. Changing the `Comment` color changes the color for all comments in all windows, no matter what programming language you're editing.

Since the syntax descriptions use attribute linking, you can make language-specific changes. For example, to change the comment color for Awk, you can define attributes for `awkComment`, like this:

```
hi awkComment guifg=Green
```

vim comes with a large number of syntax descriptions for different languages. The coloring for Awk is slightly psychedelic (lots of red and pink), although the color-ing for context diffs is actually rather pleasant, as is the color scheme for UNIX mailbox files. The HTML mode is also pretty interesting. Overall, it's quite a lot of fun to use.

Interesting Features

vim is a *very* featureful editor. We cannot describe everything in full detail here. Instead, we've chosen to discuss several of the most important and unique features that it has.

Automatic file type detection
> *vim* will notice how the lines of a text file end. It sets the `fileformat` variable to one of `dos` (CR-LF), `unix` (LF), or `mac` (CR) to indicate the file's current mode. By default, *vim* will write the file back out in the same format, but if you change the value of `fileformat`, *vim* will use that convention. This is an easy way to convert between Linux (or UNIX) and MS-DOS files, and makes editing DOS files under UNIX or Linux very easy. (In contrast, the other clones all display a `^M` at the end of each line.)

vim is "charityware"
> The licensing terms are described later in this chapter; they are fairly liberal. However, the author encourages users who like *vim* to send a donation to a children's center in Uganda.

Significant C programming extensions
> *vim* has a large set of features for working with C and C++ programs.

The "auto command" facility
> *vim* defines a large number of events, such as before or after reading a file, entering or leaving a window, and so on. For each event, you can set up an "auto command," i.e., a command to be executed when that event occurs.

vim Is Charityware

With *vim*, Bram Moolenaar has taken a different approach from the usual shareware or freeware author. If you use *vim* and you like it, Mr. Moolenaar requests that you send a donation to help orphans in Uganda. We applaud his efforts.

Mr. Moolenaar spent a year as a volunteer at Kibaale Children's Centre (KCC), located in Kibaale, a small town in the south of Uganda, near Tanzania. The KCC works to provide food, medical care, and education for children in this area, which is suffering from AIDS more than in any other part of the world. Because of the high incidence of AIDS, many of the children are orphans.

In order to continue supporting KCC, Mr. Moolenaar is trying to raise funds and organize sponsorship. You can find a much longer explanation in the file *uganda.txt* in the *vim* distribution. This includes directions for sending donations. You can also look at *http://www.vim.org/iccf/*.

C and C++ Programming Features

vim, in the grand tradition of *vi*, is first and foremost a programmer's editor. In particular, it is a C programmer's editor, and happily, C++ programmers can take advantage of it too. There are *lots* of features that make the C programmer's life easier. We describe the most significant ones here.

Smart indenting

All versions of *vi* have the `autoindent` option, which, when set, automatically indents the current line by the same amount as the one next to it. This is handy for C programmers who indent their code, and for anyone else who may need to indicate some kind of structure in their text via indentation.

vim carries this feature further, with two options, `smartindent` and `cindent`. The `cindent` option is the more interesting of the two, and is the topic of this subsection. See Table 11-14 for a list of *vim* indentation and formatting options.

Table 11-14: vim Indentation and Formatting Options

Option	Function
autoindent	Simple-minded indentation, uses that of the previous line.
smartindent	Similar to `autoindent`, but knows a little about C syntax. Deprecated in favor of `cindent`.
cindent	Enables automatic indenting for C programs, and is quite smart. C formatting is affected by the rest of the options in this table.
cinkeys	Input keys that trigger indentation options.
cinoptions	Allows you to tailor your preferred indentation style.
cinwords	Keywords that start an extra indentation on the following line.
formatoptions	Made up of a number of single letter flags that control several behaviors, notably how comments are formatted as you type them.
comments	Describes different formatting options for different kinds of comments, both those with starting and ending delimiters, as in C, and those that start with a single symbol and go to the end of the line, such as in a *Makefile* or shell program.

When set up appropriately, *vim* automatically rearranges the indentation of your C program as you type. For instance, after an `if`, *vim* automatically indents the next line. If the body of the `if` is enclosed in braces, when you type the right brace, *vim* will automatically indent it back one tab stop, to line up underneath the `if`. As another example, with the settings shown below, upon typing the colon that goes with a `case`, *vim* will shift the line with the `case` left one tab stop to line up under the `switch`.

The following *.vimrc* produces, in our opinion, very nicely formatted C code:

```
set nocp incsearch
set cinoptions=:0,p0,t0
set cinwords=if,else,while,do,for,switch,case
set formatoptions=tcqr
set cindent
syntax on
source ~/.exrc
```

The `nocp` option turns off strict *vi* compatibility. The `incsearch` option turns on incremental searching. The settings for `cinoptions`, `cinwords`, and `for-matoptions` differ from the defaults; the result is to produce a fairly strict "K&R" C formatting style. Finally, syntax coloring is turned on, and then the rest of the *vi* options are read in from the user's *.exrc* file.

We recommend that you start up *vim*, set these options as shown, and then spend some time working on a C or C++ program. Five minutes of playing with this facility will give you a better feel for it than whatever static examples we could present on the printed page. We think you'll find the facility really enjoyable to use.

Include file searching

Often, when working with large C programs, it is helpful to be able to see where a particular type name, function, variable or macro is defined. The tag facility can help with this, but doing a tag lookup actually moves you to the found location, which may be more than you need.

vim has a number of commands that search through the current file *and* through included files to find other occurrences of a keyword. We summarize them here.

The *vi* and *ex* commands fall into four categories: those that display the first occurrence of a particular object (in the status line), those that display all occurrences of a particular object, those that jump to the location of the first occurrence, and those that open a new window and jump to the first occurrence. Commands that do all four exist to look for keywords, usually the identifier under the cursor, and to look for macro definitions of the identifier under the cursor.

These commands use the smart syntax facilities (the `comments` variable described earlier) to ignore occurrences of the searched-for identifier inside comments. With a preceding count, they go to the count th occurrence. The search for the identifier starts at the beginning of the file, unless otherwise noted.

See Table 11-15 for a list of the *vim* identifier searching commands.

Table 11-15: vim Identifier Search Commands

Command	Function
[i	Display the first line that contains the keyword under the cursor.
]i	Display the first line that contains the keyword under the cursor, but start the search at the current position in the file. This command is most effective when given a count.
[I	Display all lines that contain the keyword under the cursor. Filenames and line numbers are displayed.
]I	Display all lines that contain the keyword under the cursor, but start from the current position in the file.
[^I	Jump to the first occurrence of the keyword under the cursor. (Note that ^I is a TAB.)
] ^I	Jump to the first occurrence of the keyword under the cursor, but start the search from the current position.
^W i ^W ^I	Open a new window showing the location of the first (or *count*th) occurrence of the identifier under the cursor.
[d	Display the first macro definition for the identifier under the cursor.
]d	Display the first macro definition for the identifier under the cursor, but start the search from the current position.
[D	Display all macro definitions for the identifier under the cursor. Filenames and line numbers are displayed.
]D	Display all macro definitions for the identifier under the cursor, but start the search from the current position.
[^D	Jump to the first macro definition for the identifier under the cursor.
] ^D	Jump to the first macro definition for the identifier under the cursor, but start the search from the current position.
^W d ^W ^D	Open a new window showing the location of the first (or *count*th) macro definition of the identifier under the cursor.

Two options, `define` and `include`, describe the source code lines that define macros and include source files. They have default values appropriate for C, but can be changed to suit your programming language (e.g., the value `^\(#\s*define\|[a-z]*\s*const\s*[a-z]*\)` for `define` could be used to also look for definitions of C++ named constants).

The same facilities are also available as *ex* commands, shown in Table 11-16.

Table 11-16: vim Identifier Search Commands from ex Mode

Command	Function
[*range*]is[earch][!] [*count*] [/]*pattern*[/]	Like [i and]i, but searches in *range* lines. The default is the whole file. The !, if supplied, forces comments to be searched also. Without the /'s, a word search is done. With them, a regular expression search is done.
[*range*]il[ist][!] [/]*pattern*[/]	Like [I and]I, but searches in *range* lines. The default is the whole file.
[*range*]ij[ump][!] [*count*] [/]*pattern*[/]	Like [^I and] ^I, but searches in *range* lines. The default is the whole file.
[*range*]isp[lit][!] [*count*] [/]*pattern*[/]	Like ^W i and ^W ^I, but searches in *range* lines. The default is the whole file.
[*range*]ds[earch][!] [*count*] [/]*pattern*[/]	Like [d and]d, but searches in *range* lines. The default is the whole file.
[*range*]dl[ist][!] [/]*pattern*[/]	Like [D and]D, but searches in *range* lines. The default is the whole file.
[*range*]dj[ump][!] [*count*] [/]*pattern*[/]	Like [^D and] ^D, but searches in *range* lines. The default is the whole file.
[*range*]dsp[lit][!] [*count*] [/]*pattern*[/]	Like ^W d and ^W ^D, but searches in *range* lines. The default is the whole file.
che[ckpath][!]	List all the included files that could not be found. With the !, list all the included files.

The `path` option is used to search for included files that do not have an absolute pathname. Its default value is `.,/usr/include,,`, which looks in the directory where the edited file resides, in */usr/include*, and in the current directory.

Cursor motion commands for programming

A number of enhanced and new cursor motion commands make it easier to find the opposite ends of matching constructs, as well as to find unmatched constructs that should be matched, for example, `#if` statements that do not have a corresponding `#endif`. Most of these commands may be preceded by a count, which defaults to one if not given.

See Table 11-17 for a list of the extending matching commands.

Table 11-17: vim Extended Matching Commands

Command	Function
%	Extended to match the /* and */ of C comments, and also the C preprocessor conditionals, #if, #ifdef, #ifndef, #elif, #else, and #endif.
[(	Move to the *count*th previous unmatched (.
[)	Move to the *count*th next unmatched).
[{	Move to the *count*th previous unmatched {.
[}	Move to the *count*th next unmatched }.
[#	Move to the *count*th previous unmatched #if or #else.
]#	Move to the *count*th next unmatched #else or #endif.
[*, [/	Move to the *count*th previous unmatched start of a C comment, /*.
]*,]/	Move to the *count*th next unmatched end of a C comment, */.

Autocommands

vim allows you to specify actions that should be executed when a particular event occurs. This facility gives you a great deal of flexibility and control. As always though, with power comes responsibility; the *vim* documentation warns that you should be careful with the autocommand facility so that you don't accidentally destroy your text!

The facility is complicated and detailed. In this section we outline its general capabilities, and provide an example to give you a sense of its flavor.

The autocommand command is named :autocmd. The general syntax is:

```
:au event filepat command
```

The *event* is the kind of event to which this command applies, for example, before and after reading a file (FileReadPre and FileReadPost), before and after writing a file (FileWritePre and FileWritePost), and upon entering or leaving a window (WinEnter and Winleave). There are more defined events, and case in the event name does not matter.

The *filepat* is a shell-style wildcard pattern that *vim* applies to filenames. If they match, then the autocommand will be applied for this file.

The *command* is any *ex* mode command. *vim* has a special syntax for retrieving the different parts of filenames, such as the file's extension, or the name without the extension. These can be used in any *ex* command, but are very useful with autocommands.

Multiple autocommands for the same events and file patterns add commands onto the list. Autocommands can be removed for a particular combination of events and file patterns by appending ! to the :autocmd command.

A particularly elegant example allows you to edit files compressed with the *gzip* program. The file is automatically decompressed when editing starts, and then recompressed when the file is written out (the fourth line is broken for readability):

```
:autocmd! BufReadPre,FileReadPre        *.gz set bin
:autocmd! BufReadPost,FileReadPost      *.gz '[,']!gunzip
:autocmd  BufReadPost,FileReadPost      *.gz set nobin
:autocmd  BufReadPost,FileReadPost      *.gz \
          execute ":doautocmd BufReadPost " . expand("%:r")

:autocmd! BufWritePost,FileWritePost    *.gz !mv <afile> <afile>:r
:autocmd  BufWritePost,FileWritePost    *.gz !gzip <afile>:r

:autocmd! FileAppendPre                 *.gz !gunzip <afile>
:autocmd  FileAppendPre                 *.gz !mv <afile>:r <afile>

:autocmd! FileAppendPost                *.gz !mv <afile> <afile>:r
:autocmd  FileAppendPost                *.gz !gzip <afile>:r
```

The first four commands are for reading compressed files. The first two in this set use ! to remove any previously defined autocommands for compressed files (**.gz*). The compressed file is read into the buffer as a binary file, so the first command turns on the bin (short for binary) option.

vim sets the marks '[and '] to the first and last lines of the just read text. The second command uses this to uncompress the just read file in the buffer.

The next two lines unset the binary option, and then apply any autocommands that apply to the uncompressed version of the file (e.g., syntax highlighting). The %:r is the current filename without the extension.

The next two lines are for writing the compressed file. The first one in this set first removes any previously defined autocommands for compressed files (**.gz*), with these events. The commands invoke a shell to rename the file to not have the .gz extension, and then run *gzip* to compress the file. The <afile>:r is the filename without the extension. (The use of <afile>:r is restricted to autocommands.) *vim* writes the uncompressed buffer to the file with the *.gz* extension, thus the need for the renaming.

The second line in this set runs *gzip* to compress the file. *gzip* automatically renames the file, adding the *.gz* extension.

The last four lines handle the case of appending to a compressed file. The first two of these lines uncompress the file and rename it before appending the contents to the file.

Finally, the last two lines recompress the file after writing to it, so that the uncompressed file is not left lying around.

This section just touches the tip of the iceberg of autocommands. For example, autocommands can be placed into groups, so that they can all be executed or removed together. All of the syntax coloring commands described in the section "Syntax Highlighting" are placed into the `highlight` group. An autocommand then executes all of them together when an appropriate file is read.

As an example, instead of having your *.vimrc* file always execute `set cindent` for smart C indenting, you might use an autocommand to do it just for C source code, like this:

```
autocmd BufReadPre,FileReadPre   *.[chy] set cindent
```

Sources and Supported Operating Systems

vim has its own Internet domain. The best thing to do is start from the home page at *http://www.vim.org/*. There is a FAQ (Frequently Asked Questions) for *vim*, at *http://www.vim.org/faq/*. Of particular interest are several *vim*-related mailing lists; start with *http://www.vim.org/mail.html*.

Instead of just one or two distribution points, there are a number of *ftp* sites that *mirror* the main *vim* distribution site. These are all available as `ftp.country.vim.org`. Replace *country* with a two-letter code from Table 11-18. More details, including other mirror sites, are available via links on the web page, and in the file *ftp://ftp.nl.vim.org/pub/vim/MIRRORS*. The other sites are all mirrors of *ftp.nl.vim.org*. When retrieving files via *ftp*, try to use the one that is closest to you.

Table 11-18: vim Distribution Site Country Codes

Code	Country
au	Australia
ca	Canada
gr	Greece
hu	Hungary
jp	Japan
kr	Korea

Table 11-18: vim Distribution Site Country Codes (continued)

Code	Country
nl	The Netherlands
pl	Poland
us	United States

The source code for *vim* is freely distributable. Distribution is permitted in source and binary form, but if you modify *vim* and distribute it, you must make your changes available to the maintainer for possible inclusion in a subsequent release. *vim* is also "charityware." This was discussed earlier in this chapter.

vim has been ported to the following systems:

- The Amiga. (This is where *vim* was born.)

- The Acorn Archimedes. The last working port was done with Version 2.0. A new port is being done. It will be included in Version 5.2.

- BeOS. As of *vim* Version 5.1, both Intel and non-Intel CPUs are supported.

- MS-DOS.

- The Apple Macintosh. The original port to the Macintosh was for Version 3.0. The 5.x port is still marked as being in an Alpha state.

- MiNT on Atari microcomputers.

- OS/2.

- UNIX. Essentially any UNIX variant should work; *vim* uses GNU Autoconf for configuration.

- VMS.

- Windows 95 and Windows NT. Both console and GUI versions are available. Under Windows 3.1, use the 32-bit DOS version.

The online help documents the peculiarities of the *vim* port to each operating system.

Compiling *vim* is straightforward. Retrieve the distribution via *ftp*. Uncompress and untar it, run the *configure* program, and then run *make*:

```
$ gzip -d < vim-5.1.tar.gz | tar -xvpf -
...
$ cd vim-5.1; ./configure
...
$ make
...
```

vim should configure and build with no problems. Use *make install* to install it.

Should you need to report a bug or problem in *vim*, the person to contact is Bram Moolenaar, at *Bram@vim.org*.

12

vile — vi Like Emacs

vile stands for "vi Like Emacs." It started out as a copy of Version 3.9 of MicroEMACS that was modified to have the "finger feel" of *vi*. There are currently three maintainers: Paul Fox, Tom Dickey, and Kevin Buettner. The current version is 8.0; it is essentially the same as 7.4, but with bug fixes. This chapter was written using *vile*.

Authors and History

Paul Fox describes the early *vile* history this way:

> *vile*'s design goal has always been a little different than that of the other clones. *vile* has never *really* attempted to be a "clone" at all, though most people find it close enough. I started it because in 1990 I wanted to to be able to edit multiple files in multiple windows, I had been using *vi* for 10 years already, and the sources to Micro-EMACS came floating past my newsreader at a job where I had too much time on my hands. I started by changing the existing keymaps in the obvious way, and ran full-tilt into the "Hey! Where's 'insert' mode?" problem. So I hacked a little more, and hacked a little more, and eventually released in '91 or '92. (Starting soon thereafter, major version numbers tracked the year of release: 7.3 was the third release in '97.)

But my goal has always been to preserve finger-feel (as opposed to the display visuals), and, selfishly, to preserve finger-feel most for the commands I use. ☺ *vile* has quite an amazing *ex* mode, that works very well—it just *looks* really odd, and a couple of commands which are beyond the scope of the current parser are missing. For the same reasons, *vile* also won't fully parse existing *.exrc* files, since I don't really think that's so important—it does simple ones, but more sophisticated ones need some tweaking. But when you toss in *vile*'s built-in command/macro language, you quickly forget you ever cared about *.exrc*.

Tom Dickey started working on *vile* in December of 1992, initially just contributing patches, and later doing more significant features and extensions, such as line numbering, name completion, and animating the buffer list window. Tom states that "Integrating features together is more important to my design goals than implementing a large number of features."

In February of 1994, Kevin Buettner started working on *vile*. Initially, he supplied bug fixes for the X11 version, *xvile*, and then improvements, such as scrollbars. This evolved into support for the Motif, OpenLook, and Athena widget sets. Because, surprisingly, the Athena widgets were not "universally available in a bugfree form," he wrote a version that used the raw *Xt* toolkit. This version ended up providing superior functionality to the Athena version. Kevin also contributed the initial support in *vile* for GNU Autoconf.

Currently, *vile* maintenance is done "by committee," with Tom Dickey being the primary maintainer. Paul manages the mailing lists.

For the near term, future work will focus on improving the Perl integration, and enhancing the major mode concept (discussed below).

Important Command-Line Arguments

Although *vile* does not expect to be invoked as either *vi* or *ex*, it can be invoked as *view*, in which case it will treat each file as read-only. Unlike the other clones, it does *not* have a line-editor mode.

Here are the important *vile* command-line arguments:

-? *vile* prints a short usage summary and then exits.

-g *N*
    vile will begin editing on the first file at the specified line number. This can also be given as +*N*.

-s *pattern*
    In the first file, *vile* will execute an initial search for the given pattern. This can also be given as +/*pattern*.

-t *tag*
> Start editing at the specified *tag*. The -T option is equivalent, and can be used when X11 option parsing eats the -t.

-h Invokes *vile* on the help file.

-R Invokes *vile* in "readonly" mode. No writes are permitted while in this mode. (This will also be true if *vile* is invoked as *view*, or if readonly mode is set in the startup file.)

-v Invokes *vile* in "view" mode. No changes are permitted to any buffer while in this mode.

@*cmdfile*
> *vile* will run the specified file as its startup file, and will bypass any normal startup file (i.e., *.vilerc*) or environment variable (i.e., VILEINIT).

Online Help and Other Documentation

vile currently comes with a single (rather large) ASCII text file, *vile.hlp*. The :help command (which can be abbreviated to :h) will open a new window on that file. You can then search for information on a particular topic, using standard *vi* search techniques. Because it is a flat ASCII file, it is also easy to print out and read through.

In addition to the help file, *vile* has a number of built-in commands for displaying information about the facilities and state of the editor. Some of the most useful commands are:

:show-commands
> Creates a new window that shows a complete list of all *vile* commands, with a brief description of each one. The information is placed in its own buffer that can be treated just like any other *vile* buffer. In particular, it is easy to write it out to a file for later printing.

:apropos
> Shows all commands whose names contain a given substring. This is easier than just randomly searching through the help file to find information on a particular topic.

:describe-key
> Prompts you for a key or key sequence, and then shows the description of that command. For instance, the x key will implement the delete-next-character function.

`:describe-function`

> Prompts you for a function name, and then shows the description of that function. For instance, the `delete-next-character` function deletes a given number of characters to the right of the current cursor position.

The `:apropos`, `:describe-function`, and `:describe-key` commands all give the descriptive information, plus all other synonyms (since a function may have more than one name, for convenience), all other keys that are bound to it (since many key sequences may be bound to the same function), and whether the command is a "motion" or an "operator." A good example of this is the output of `:describe-function next-line`:

```
"next-line"                    ^J       j       #-B
    or    "down-arrow"
    or    "down-line"
    or    "forward-line"
(motion:  move down CNT lines )
```

This shows all four of its names and its three key-bindings. (The sequence `#-B` is *vile*'s terminal-independent representation of the up-arrow—a complete list of those names is in the help file.)

The `VILE_STARTUP_PATH` environment variable can be set to a colon-separated search path for the help file.* The `VILE_HELP_FILE` environment variable can be used to override the name of the help file (typically *vile.hlp*).

The combination of online searchable help, built-in command and key descriptions, and command completion makes the help facility straightforward to use.

Initialization

vile and *xvile* perform the following initializations:

1. (*xvile* only) Use the value of the `XVILE_MENU` environment variable for the name of the menu description file, if provided. Otherwise, it uses *.vilemenu*. The purpose of this file is to set the default menus for the X11 interface. You can then add to or override any of these menus in the other startup files.

2. Execute the file named on the command line with `@cmdfile`, if any. Bypass any other initialization steps that would otherwise be done.

3. If the `VILEINIT` environment variable exists, execute its value. Otherwise, look for an initialization file.

---

* Although the help file says that this path is also used when searching for the startup file, the version 7.4 source code disagrees. It is actually the search path used for the `:source` command. In version 8.0, this is fixed—the startup file and `:source` command use the same mechanism.

4. If the `VILE_STARTUP_FILE` environment variable exists, use that as the name of the startup file. If not, on UNIX use *.vilerc*, on other systems use *vile.rc*.

5. Look for the startup file in the current directory, and then in the user's home directory. Use whichever one is found first.

As for *nvi* and *vim*, you can place common initialization actions into your *.exrc* file (i.e., options and commands for UNIX *vi*, and/or the other clones), and have your *.vilerc* file execute `:source .exrc` before or after the *vile*-specific initializations.

Multiwindow Editing

vile is somewhat different from the other clones. It started life as a version of Micro-Emacs, and then was modified into an editor with the "finger-feel" of *vi*.

One of the things that versions of *emacs* have always done is handle multiple windows and multiple files; as such, *vile* was the first *vi*-like program to provide multiple windows and editing buffers.

As in *elvis* and *vim*, the `:split` command* will create a new window, and then you can use the *ex* command `:e filename` to edit a new file in the new window. After that, things become different, in particular the *vi* command mode keys to switch among windows are very different.

```
<preface id="VI6-CH-0">
<title>Preface </title>

<para>
Text editing is one of the most common uses of any computer system, and
<command>vi</command> is one of the most useful standard text editors>
With <command>vi</command> you can create new files, or edit any exist>
file.
</para>
```
`ch00.sgm`   `top`
```
# Makefile for vi book
# Arnold Robbins

CHAPTERS = ch00_6.sgm ch00_5.sgm ch00.sgm ch01.sgm ch02.sgm ch03.sgm \
        ch04.sgm ch05.sgm ch06.sgm ch07.sgm ch08.sgm
APPENDICES = appa.sgm appb.sgm appc.sgm appd.sgm

POSTSCRIPT = ch00_6.ps ch00_5.ps ch00.ps ch01.ps ch02.ps ch03.ps \
        ch04.ps ch05.ps ch06.ps ch07.ps ch08.ps \
```
`=== Makefile =[modified]================================= top ==`

---

* That this works is an artifact of the fact that *vile* allows you to abbreviate commands. The actual command name is `split-current-window`.

The split screen is the result of typing `vile ch00.sgm` followed by `:split` and `:e Makefile`.

Like *vim*, all windows share the bottom line for execution of *ex* commands. Each window has its own status line, with the current window indicated by having its status line filled with equal signs. The status line also acquires an I in the second column when in insert mode, and `[modified]` is appended after the filename when the file has been changed but not yet written out.

vile is also like *emacs* in that commands are bound to key sequences. Table 12-1 presents the commands and their key sequences. In some cases, two sets of key sequences do the same operation, for example, the `delete-other-windows` command.

Table 12-1: vile Window Management Commands

Command	Key Sequence(s)	Function
delete-other-windows	^O, ^X 1	Eliminate all windows except the current one.
delete-window	^K, ^X 0	Destroy the current window, unless it is the last one.
edit-file, E, e find-file	^X e	Bring given (or under-cursor, for ^X e) file or existing buffer into window.
grow-window	V	Increase the size of the current window by *count* lines.
move-next-window-down	^A ^E	Move next window down (or buffer up) by *count* lines.
move-next-window-up	^A ^Y	Move next window up (or buffer down) by *count* lines.
move-window-left	^X ^L	Scroll window to left by *count* columns, half screen if *count* unspecified.
move-window-right	^X ^R	Scroll window to right by *count* columns, half screen if *count* unspecified.
next-window	^X o	Move to the next window.
position-window	z *where*	Reframe with cursor specified by *where*, as follows: center (., M, m), top (RETURN , H, t), or bottom (-, L, b).

Table 12-1: vile Window Management Commands (continued)

Command	Key Sequence(s)	Function
previous-window	^X o	Move to the previous window.
resize-window		Change the current window to *count* lines. *count* is supplied as a prefix argument.
restore-window		Return to window saved with save-window.
save-window		Mark a window for later return with restore-window.
scroll-next-window-down	^A ^D	Move next window down by *count* half screens. *count* is supplied as a prefix argument.
scroll-next-window-up	^A ^U	Move next window up by *count* half screens. *count* is supplied as a prefix argument.
shrink-window	v	Decrease the size of the current window by *count* lines. *count* is supplied as a prefix argument.
split-current-window	^X 2	Split the window in half; a *count* of 1 or 2 chooses which becomes current. *count* is supplied as a prefix argument.
view-file		Bring given file or existing buffer into window, mark it "view-only."
historical-buffer	_	Display a list of the first nine buffers. A digit moves to the given buffer, __ moves to the most recently edited file.
toggle-buffer-list	*	Pop up/down a window showing *all* the *vile* buffers.

GUI Interfaces

The screen shots and the explanation in this section were supplied by Kevin Buettner, Tom Dickey, and Paul Fox. We thank them.

There are several X11 interfaces for *vile*, each utilizing a different toolkit based on the *Xt* library. There is a plain "No Toolkit" version which does not use a toolkit, but has custom scrollbars and a bulletin board widget for geometry management. There are versions which use the Motif, Athena, or OpenLook toolkits. Of these, the "No Toolkit" version is probably best supported since that is the version that some of *vile*'s authors most frequently use. But the Motif and Athena versions have more features, such as menu support.

Fortunately, the basic interface is the same for each of these versions. There is a single top level window which may be split into two or more panes. The panes, in turn, may be used to display multiple views of a buffer or multiple buffers or mixture of both. In *vile* parlance these panes are called "windows," but to avoid confusion, we will continue to call them "panes" in the following discussion.

Building xvile

To build *xvile*, you have to choose which toolkit version to use. This is done when you configure *vile* with the *configure* command. The relevant options are:

`--with-screen=value`
> Specify terminal driver. The default is `tcap`, for the *termcap/terminfo* driver. Other values include `ncurses` (a special case of *terminfo*), `X11`, `OpenLook`, `Motif`, `Athena`, `Xaw`, `Xaw3d`, `neXtaw`, and `ansi`.

`--with-scr=value`
> Same as `--with-screen`.

`--with-x`
> Use the X Window System. This is the "No Toolkit" version.

`--with-Xaw3d`
> Link with *Xaw* 3-D library.

`--with-neXtaw`
> Link with neXt Athena library.

`--with-Xaw-scrollbars`
> Use *Xaw* scrollbars rather than the *vile* custom scrollbars.

Basic Appearance and Functionality

The figures show *xvile*'s Motif interface. It is similar to the Athena interface.

Figure 12-1 shows three panes:

1. The *man* page for *vile*, which shows the use of underlining and boldface.

2. A buffer `misc.c`, from *tin*, which shows syntax highlighting (again, underlining, this time for preprocessor statements, and boldface, for quoted strings).

```
 Xvile  Edit  Buffers  Attributes                              Help
VILE(1)                                                    VILE(1)



NAME
      vile, xvile — VI Like Emacs

SYNOPSIS
      vile [-hVv] [-spattern] [+/pattern] [-ttag] [-gNNN] [+NNN] [@cmdfile]
      [filename]...

DESCRIPTION
      vile is a text editor.  This man page is fairly terse.  More
      information can be obtained from the internal help, available with the
 ────<vile> [read-only view-only] is !man vile | vile-manfilt ───────(6,1) 3% ─
      int line,
      const char *cond)
{
      my_fprintf (stderr, "%s: assertion failure: %s (%d): %s\n", progname, file,>
      my_fflush (stderr);

/*
 * create a core dump
 */
#ifdef HAVE_COREFILE
#    ifdef SIGABRT
         sigdisp(SIGABRT, SIG_DFL);
         kill (process_id, SIGABRT);
#    else
#        ifdef SIGILL
            sigdisp(SIGILL, SIG_DFL);
            kill (process_id, SIGILL);
 ────misc.c [cmode]────────────────────────────────────────────(63,9) 2% ─
Completions prefixed by /tmp/m:
mail.c    main.c    makecfg.c memory.c  misc.c

── [Completions] [view-only] ═══════════════ xvile    version 7.3w (1,1) 33% ═
Find file: m▯
```

Figure 12-1: The vile GUI window

3. A three-line pane, which is active (noted by a darker status line), named [Completions], for filename completions. The pane is coordinated with the minibuffer (the colon command line): the first line reads *Completions prefixed by /tmp/m:*, and the minibuffer reads *Find file: m*. The rest of the pane contains the actual filenames which match. The first line of [Completions] and the contents change as the user completes the filename (and presses TAB to tell vile to show the reduced set of choices).

Figure 12-2 also shows three panes:

1. The [Help] pane, which of course shows the most important feature of an editor (how to exit without modifying your files). ☺

Figure 12-2: Buffers and completions in vile

2. The [Buffer List], which indicates that [Help] is the # (previous)
    buffer. The % (current) buffer is not shown on the list, since only the "visible"
    buffers are displayed in this copy of [Buffer List]. Supplying an argu-
    ment to the * command would have shown the invisible buffers as well.
    Buffers 1 and 2 are charset.c and misc.c. They have been loaded, so
    their sizes (8931 and 54866) are displayed in the [Buffer List]. Buffers 3,
    4, and 5 (color.c, config.c, and curses.c) have not been loaded, so a
    u is displayed in the first column, and the size is shown as zero.

3. The [Completions] buffer is active. This time it displays tag completions
    for the partial match *co*, and the *Completions prefixed* message is not shown
    because the buffer is scrolled down, which is another side effect of pressing

TAB : *vile* cycles through a scrolling action so that all of the choices will be shown even when the window is small. (The v/V commands don't do anything to the [Completions] buffer while the cursor is in the minibuffer; the [Completions] buffer is automatically sized.)

Scrollbars

At the right of each pane is a scrollbar which may be used in the customary fashion to move about in the buffer. Note, however, that the customary fashion varies from toolkit to toolkit. In the Athena and "No Toolkit" version, the middle mouse button may be used to drag the "thumb" or visible indicator around. The left and right mouse buttons move down or up (respectively) in the buffer. The amount moved depends on the location of the mouse cursor on the scrollbar. Placing it near the top will scroll by as little as one line. When placed near the bottom, the text will scroll by as much as a full paneful.

The Motif and OpenLook scrollbars are probably more familiar. The left-most mouse button is used for all operations. Clicking on the little arrows will move up or down by one line. The scrollbar indicator may be dragged in order to move about and scrolling up or down by an entire pane may be accomplished by clicking above or below the indicator. The OpenLook scrollbars provide additional mechanisms for quickly moving to the top or bottom of the buffer.

In each version, there is a small handle above or below (i.e., between) scrollbars which may be used to adjust the size of two adjacent panes. In the "No Toolkit" version of *xvile*, the pane resize handle blends in with the mode line of two adjacent panes. In the other versions, the resize handle is more distinguishable. But in each case, the mouse cursor will change to a heavy vertical double arrow when placed above the resize handle. The windows may be resized by clicking on and dragging the handle.

A pane may be split into two by holding the control key down and clicking the left mouse button on a scrollbar. Then you will have two views of a particular buffer. Other *vile* commands may be used to replace one of the views with another buffer if desired. A pane may be deleted by holding the control key down and clicking the middle mouse button. Sometimes after creating a lot of panes, you find yourself wanting to use all of the window real estate for just one pane. To do this, control-click the right mouse button; all other panes will be removed, leaving the entire *xvile* window containing only the pane on which you clicked.

Setting the cursor position and mouse motions

Within the text area of a pane, the cursor may be set by clicking the left mouse button. This not only sets the cursor position, but also sets the pane in which editing is being done. In order to set just the pane but preserve the old position, click on the mode line below the text you wish to edit.

A mouse click is viewed as a motion just like 4j is considered a motion. To delete five lines, you could enter d4j which will delete the current line and the four below it. You can do the same thing with a mouse click. Position your cursor at the place you want to start deleting from and then press d. After this, click in the buffer at the point to which you wish to delete to. Mouse clicks are real motions and may be used with other operators as well.

Selections

Selections may be made by holding the left mouse button down and dragging with the mouse. Release of the mouse button will cause the selection to be yanked and made available (if desired) for pasting. You can force the selected region to be rectangular by holding the control key down while dragging with the left button depressed. If the dragging motion goes out of the current window, text will be scrolled in the appropriate direction, if possible, to accommodate selections larger than the window. The speed at which the scrolling occurs will increase with the passage of time, making it practical to select large regions of text quickly.

Individual words or lines may be selected by double- or triple-clicking on them.

A selection may be extended by clicking the right mouse button. As with button one, the selection may be adjusted or scrolled by holding the right button down and dragging with it. Selections may be extended in any window open to the same buffer as the one in which the selection was started. That is, if you have two views of a buffer (in two different panes), one containing the start of the buffer, and the other the end, it is possible to select the entire buffer by clicking the left button at the beginning of the pane showing the beginning of the buffer and then clicking the right button in the pane showing the end of the buffer. Also, selections may be extended in a rectangular fashion by holding the control key down in conjunction with the use of the right mouse button.

The middle button is used for pasting the selection. By default, it pastes at the last text cursor position. If the shift key is held down while clicking the middle button, the paste occurs at the position of the mouse cursor.

A selection may be cleared (if owned by *xvile*) by double-clicking on one of the mode lines.

Clipboard

Data may be exchanged between many X applications via the PRIMARY selection. This selection is set and manipulated as described above.

Other applications, most notably OpenLook applications, use the CLIPBOARD selection to exchange data between applications. On many Sun keyboards, selected text is moved to the clipboard by pressing the $\boxed{\text{COPY}}$ key and pasted by pressing the $\boxed{\text{PASTE}}$ key. If you find that you cannot paste text selected in *xvile* into other applications or vice versa, it may well be that these applications use the CLIPBOARD selection instead of the PRIMARY selection. (The other mechanism used among really old applications involves the use of a ring of cut buffers.)

xvile provides two commands for manipulating the clipboard. These are `copy-to-clipboard` and `paste-from-clipboard`. When `copy-to-clipboard` is executed, the contents of the current selection are copied to the special clipboard kill register (denoted by `;` in the register list). When an application requests the clipboard selection, *xvile* gives it the contents of this kill register. The `paste-from-clipboard` command requests clipboard data from the current owner of the CLIPBOARD selection.

Users of Sun systems may want to put the following key bindings in their *.vilerc* file in order to make use of the $\boxed{\text{COPY}}$ and $\boxed{\text{PASTE}}$ keys found on their keyboards:

```
bind-key copy-to-clipboard #-^
bind-key paste-from-clipboard #-*
```

Key bindings are described in detail later in this chapter.

Resources

xvile has many resources which may be used to control appearance and behavior. Font choice is particularly important if you want italic or oblique fonts to be displayed properly. *vile*'s documentation has a complete list of resources as well a sample set of *.Xdefault* entries.

Adding Menus

The Motif and Athena versions have menu support. Menu items, which are user-definable, are read from the *.vilemenu* file, in the current or home directory.

xvile allows three types of menu items:

- Built-in, i.e., specific to the menuing system, such as rereading the *.vilerc* file, or spawning a new copy of *xvile*

- Direct invocation of built-in commands (e.g., displaying the [Buffer List])

- Invocation of arbitrary command strings (e.g., running interactive macros such as a search command)

The distinction between the last two is made because the authors prefer making *vile* able to check the validity of commands before they are executed.

The sidebar in this chapter contains an annotated sample *.vilemenu* file.

Extended Regular Expressions

Extended regular expressions were introduced in the section "Extended Regular Expressions" in Chapter 8. *vile* provides essentially the same facilities as *nvi*'s `extended` option. The syntax is somewhat different though, relying upon additional backslash-escaped characters:

`\|` Indicates alternation, `house\|home`.

`\+` Matches one or more of the preceding regular expression.

`\?` Matches zero or one of the preceding regular expression.

`\(...\)`
> Provides grouping for `*`, `\+`, and `\?`, as well as making matched sub-texts available in the replacement part of a substitute command (`\1`, `\2`, etc.).

`\s \S`
> Match whitespace and non-whitespace characters, respectively.

`\w \W`
> Match "word-constituent" characters (alphanumerics and the underscore, '_') and non-word-constituent characters, respectively. For example, `\w\+` would match C/C++ identifiers and keywords.*

`\d \D`
> Match digits and non-digits, respectively.

`\p \P`
> Match printable and non-printable characters respectively. Whitespace is considered to be printable.

vile allows the escape sequences `\b`, `\f`, `\r`, `\t`, and `\n` to appear in the replacement part of a substitute command. They stand for backspace, formfeed, carriage return, tab and newline, respectively. Also, from the *vile* documentation:

> Note that *vile* mimics *perl*'s handling of `\u\L\1\E` instead of *vi*'s. Given `:s/\(abc\)/\u\L\1\E/` *vi* will replace with *abc* whereas *vile* and *perl* will replace with *Abc*. This is somewhat more useful for capitalizing words.

---

* For the pedantic among you, it also matches identifiers that start with a leading digit; usually this isn't much of a problem.

Example .vilemenu File

```
# lines beginning with 'C' define a menu heading
C:Xvile
# the following four entries are Buttons invoking menu
# system builtins
B:New:new_xvile
B:Edit .vilerc:edit_rc
B:Parse .vilerc:parse_rc
B:Edit .vilemenu:edit_mrc
B:Quit:quit
#
C:Editing
B:Search Forward...:cmd search-forward
B:Search Backward...:cmd search-reverse
# lines beginning with S are separators
S
B:Manual for...:29
S
# where the command to be executed is given as a number, like the
#  two above and the three below, the menu system will translate
#  this to an invocation of the command execute-macro-<number>.
B:Indent Level...:31
B:Window Title...:35
B:Font...:36
#
C:Buffers
# run a command name (in this case "toggle-buffer") by simply
# naming it
B:Toggle Show:toggle-buffer
# one line starting with 'L' is allowed, at the end of a menu --
# it causes a buffer list menu to be created.
L:list_buff
#
C:Fonts
B:5x8:setv $font 5x8
B:7x14:setv $font 7x14
B:8x13:setv $font 8x13
B:8x16:setv $font 8x16
B:9x15:setv $font 9x15
B:10x20:setv $font 10x20
B:12x24:setv $font 12x24
#
C:Attributes
B:C/C++:30
B:Pascal:32
#
```

Example .vilemenu File (continued)

```
C:Help:help
B:About:version
S
B:General:help
B:Bindings:describe-bindings
B:Motions:describe-motions
B:Operators:describe-operators
S
# prefixing a command with "cmd" will force it to be run as from
#  the ':' line, so that it can prompt for input correctly.
B:Apropos...:cmd apropos
B:Apropos...:apropos set
B:On Function...:cmd describe-function
B:On Key...:describe-key &gts
S
B:Settings:setall
B:Variables:show-variables
B:Registers:show-registers
```

Improved Editing Facilities

This section describes the features of *vile* that make simple text editing easier and more powerful.

Command-Line History and Completion

vile stores all your *ex* commands in a buffer named [History]. This feature is controlled with the history option, which is true by default. Turning it off disables the history feature and removes the [History] buffer. The command show-history will split the screen and display the [History] buffer in a new window.

Starting with *vile* 7.4, the colon command line is really a minibuffer. You can use it to recall lines from the [History] buffer and edit them.

You use the ↑ and ↓ keys to scroll backward and forward in the history, and ← and → to move around within the line. Your current delete character (usually BACKSPACE) can be used to delete characters. Any other characters you type will be inserted at the current cursor postion.

You can toggle the minibuffer into *vi* mode by typing the mini-edit character (by default, ^G). When you do this, *vile* will highlight the minibuffer using the mechanism specified by the `mini-hilite` option. The default is `reverse`, for reverse video. In *vi* mode, you can use *vi* style commands for positioning. In Version 8.0, you can also use the `i`, `I`, `a`, and `A` *vi* commands.

An interesting feature is that *vile* will use the history to show you previous data that corresponds to the command you're entering. For instance, after typing `:set` followed by a space, *vile* will prompt you with `Global value:`. At that point, you can use ↑ to see previous global variables that you've set, should you wish to change one of them.

The *ex* command line provides completion of various sorts. As you type the name of a command, you can hit the TAB key at any point. *vile* will fill out the rest of the command name as much as possible. If you type a TAB a second time, *vile* will create a new window showing you all the possible completions.

Completion applies to built-in and user-defined *vile* commands, tags, filenames, modes (described later in this chapter), variables, and to the terminal characters (the character settings such as backspace, suspend, and so on, derived from your *stty* settings).

As a side point, this leads to an interesting phenomenon. In *vi*-style editors, commands may have long names, but they tend to be unique in the first few characters, since abbreviations are accepted. In *emacs*-style editors, command names often are not unique in the first several characters, but command completion still allows you to get away with less typing.

Tag Stacks

Tag stacking is described in the section "Tag Stacks" in Chapter 8. In *vile*, tag stacking is available and straightforward. It is somewhat different than the other clones, most notably in the *vi* mode commands that are used for tag searching and popping the tag stack. Table 12-2 shows the *vile* tag commands.

Table 12-2: vile Tag Commands

Command	Function
ta[g][!] [*tagstring*]	Edit the file containing *tagstring* as defined in the *tags* file. The `!` forces *vile* to switch to the new file if the current buffer has been modified but not saved.
pop[!]	Pops a cursor position off the stack, restoring the cursor to its previous position.
next-tag	Continues searching through the *tags* file for more matches.
show-tagstack	Creates a new window that displays the tag stack. The display changes as tags are pushed onto or popped off of the stack.

The *vi* mode commands are described in Table 12-3.

Table 12-3: vile Command Mode Tag Commands

Command	Function
^]	Look up the location of the identifier under the cursor in the *tags* file, and move to that location. The current location is automatically pushed onto the tag stack.
^T ^X ^]	Return to the previous location in the tag stack, i.e., pop off one element.
^A ^]	Same as the :next-tag command.

As in the other editors, options control how *vile* manages the tag related commands, as shown in Table 12-4.

Table 12-4: vile Options for Tag Management

Option	Function
taglength	Controls the number of significant characters in a tag that is to be looked up. The default value of zero indicates that all characters are significant.
tagignorecase	Makes tag searches ignore case. By default this option is false.
tagrelative	When using a *tags* file in another directory, filenames in that *tags* file are considered to be relative to the directory where the *tags* file is.
tags	Can be set to a whitespace separated list of *tags* files to use for looking up tags. *vile* loads all *tags* files into separate buffers that are hidden by default, but that can be edited if you wish. You can place environment variables and shell wildcards into tags.
tagword	Uses the whole word under the cursor for the tag lookup, not just the sub-word starting at the current cursor position. This option is disabled by default, which keeps *vile* compatible with *vi*.

Infinite Undo

vile is similar in principle but different in practice from the other editors. Like *elvis* and *vim*, there is an undo limit you can set, but like *nvi*, the . command will do the next undo or redo, as appropriate it. Separate *vi* mode commands implement successive undo and redo.

vile uses the undolimit option to control how many changes it will store. The default is 10, meaning that you can undo up to the 10 most recent changes. Setting it to zero allows true "infinite undo," but this may consume a lot of memory.

To start an undo, first use either the u or ^X u commands. Then each successive . command will do another undo. Like *vi*, two u commands just toggle the state of the change; however, each ^X u command does another undo.

The ^X r command does a redo. Typing . after the first ^X r will do successive redos. You can provide a count to the ^X u and ^X r commands, in which case *vile* will perform the requested number of undos or redos.

Arbitrary Length Lines and Binary Data

vile can edit files with arbitrary length lines, and with an arbitrary number of lines.

vile automatically handles binary data. No special command lines or options are required. To enter 8-bit text, type ^V followed by an x and two hexadecimal digits, or a 0 and three octal digits, or three decimal digits.

Incremental Searching

As mentioned in the section "Incremental Searching" in Chapter 8, you perform incremental searching in *vile* using the ^X S and ^X R commands. It is not necessary to set an option to enable incremental searching.

The cursor moves through the file as you type, always being placed on the first character of the text that matches. ^X S incrementally searches forward through the file, while ^X R incrementally searches backwards.

You may wish to add these commands (described below) to your *.vilerc* file to make the more familiar / and ? search commands work incrementally:

```
bind-key incremental-search /
bind-key reverse-incremental-search ?
```

Also of interest is the "visual match" facility, which will highlight *all* occurrences of the matched expression. For a *.vilerc* file:

```
set visual-matches reverse
```

This command directs *vile* to use reverse video for visual matching. Since the highlighting can sometimes be visually distracting, the = command will turn off any current highlighting until you enter a new search pattern.

Left-Right Scrolling

As mentioned in the section "Left-Right Scrolling" in Chapter 8, you enable left-right scrolling in *vile* using :set nolinewrap. Unlike the other editors, left-right

scrolling is the default. Long lines are marked at the left and right edges with <
and >. The value of `sideways` controls the number of characters by which *vile*
shifts the screen when scrolling left to right. With `sideways` set to zero, each
scroll moves the screen by one third. Otherwise the screen scrolls by the desired
number of characters.

Visual Mode

vile is different from *elvis* and *vim* in the way you highlight the text you want to
operate on. It uses the "quoted motion" command, `q`.

You enter `q` at the beginning of the region, any other *vi* motions to get to the
opposite end of the region, and then another `q` to end the quoted motion. *vile*
highlights the marked text.

Arguments to the `q` command determine what kind of highlighting it will do. `1q`
(same as `q`) does an exact highlighting, `2q` does line-at-a-time highlighting, and `3q`
does rectangular highlighting.

Typically, you use a quoted motion in conjunction with an operator, such as `d` or
`y`. Thus, `d3qjjwq` deletes the rectangle indicated by the motions. When used
without an operator, the region is left highlighted. It can be referred to later using
`^S`. Thus, `d ^S` will delete the highlighted region.

In addition, rectangular regions can be indicated through the use of marks.* As
you know, a mark can be used to refer to either a specific character (when
referred to with `` ` ``) or a specific line (when referred to with `'`). In addition, refer-
ring to the mark (say a mark set with `mb`) with `` `b `` instead of `'b` can change the
nature of the operation being done—`d'b` will delete a set of lines, and `` d`b `` will
delete two partial lines and the lines in between. Using the `` ` `` form of mark refer-
ence gives a more "exact" region than the `'` form of mark reference.

vile adds a third form of mark reference. The `\` command can be used as another
way of referring to a mark. By itself, it behaves just like `` ` `` and moves the cursor to
the character at which the mark was set. When combined with an operator, however, the behavior is quite different. The mark reference becomes "rectangular,"
such that the action `d\b` will delete the rectangle of characters whose corners are
marked by the cursor and the character which holds mark `b`.

---

* Thanks to Paul Fox for this explanation.

Keystrokes

ma

```
    The 6th edition of <citetitle>Learning the vi Editor</citetitle>
    brings the book into the late 1990s.
    In particular, besides the &amp;ldquo;original&amp;rdquo; version of
    <command>vi</command> that comes as a standard part of every UNIX system,
    there are now a number of freely available &amp;ldquo;clones&amp;rdquo;
    or work-alike editors.
```

Results

Set mark a at the *b* in *book.*

Keystrokes

3jfr

```
    The 6th edition of <citetitle>Learning the vi Editor</citetitle>
    brings the book into the late 1990s.
    In particular, besides the &amp;ldquo;original&amp;rdquo; version of
    <command>vi</command> that comes as a standard part of every UNIX system,
    there are now a number of freely available &amp;ldquo;clones&amp;rdquo;
    or work-alike editors.
```

Results

Move the cursor to the *r* in *number* to mark the opposite corner.

Keystrokes

^A ~\a

```
    The 6th edition of <citetitle>Learning the vi Editor</citetitle>
    brings the BOOK INTO The late 1990s.
    In particulAR, BESIDES the &amp;ldquo;original&amp;rdquo; version of
    <command>vi</COMMAND> that comes as a standard part of every UNIX system,
    there are nOW A NUMBER of freely available &amp;ldquo;clones&amp;rdquo;
    or work-alike editors.
```

Results

Toggle the case of rectangle bounded with mark a.

The commands which define arbitrary regions and operate upon them are summarized in Table 12-5.

Table 12-5: vile Block Mode Operations

Command	Operation
q	Start and end a quoted motion.
^A r	Open up a rectangle.
>	Shift text to the right. Same as ^A r when the region is rectangular.
<	Shift text to the left. Same as d when the region is rectangular.
y	Yank the whole region. *vile* remembers that it was rectangular.

Table 12-5: vile Block Mode Operations (continued)

Command	Operation
c	Change the region. For a non-rectangular region, delete all the text between the end points and enter insert mode. For a rectangular region, prompt for the text to fill the lines.
^A u	Change the case of the region to all uppercase.
^A l	Change the case of the region to all lowercase.
^A ~	Toggle the case of all alphabetic characters in the region.
^A SPACE	Fill the region with spaces.
p, P	Put the text back. *vile* does a rectangular put if the original text was rectangular.
^A p, ^A P	Force previously yanked text to be put back as if it were rectangular. The width of the longest yanked line is used for the rectangle's width.

Programming Assistance

vile's programming assistance capabilities are discussed in this section.

Edit-Compile Speedup

vile uses two straightforward *vi* mode commands to manage program development, shown in Table 12-6.

Table 12-6: vile Program Development vi Mode Commands

Command	Function
^X !*command* RETURN	Run *command*, saving the output in a buffer named [Output].
^X ^X	Find the next error. *vile* parses the output and moves to the location of each successive error.

vile understands the *Entering directory XXX* and *Leaving directory XXX* messages that GNU *make* generates, allowing it to find the correct file, even if it's in a different directory.

The error messages are parsed using regular expressions in the buffer [**Error Expressions**]. *vile* automatically creates this buffer, and then it uses the buffer when you use ^X ^X. You can add expressions to it as needed, and it has an extended syntax that allows you to specify where filenames, line numbers, columns and so on appear in the error messages. Full details are provided in the online help, but you probably won't need to make any changes, as it works pretty well "out of the box."

vile's error finder also compensates for changes in the file, keeping track of additions and deletions as you progress to each error.

The error finder applies to the most recent buffer created by reading from a shell command. For example, `^X!command` produces a buffer named `[Output]`, and `:e !command` produces a buffer named `[!command]`. The error finder will be set appropriately.

You can point the error finder at an arbitrary buffer (not just the output of shell commands) using the `:error-buffer` command. This lets you use the error finder on the output of previous compiler or *egrep* runs.

Syntax Highlighting

vile relies on help from an external program to provide syntax coloring. In fact, there are three programs: one for C programs, one for Pascal programs, and one for UNIX *man* pages. The *vile* documentation provides this sample macro for use in a *.vilerc* file:

```
30 store-macro
        write-message "[Attaching C/C++ attributes...]"
        set-variable %savcol $curcol
        set-variable %savline $curline
        set-variable %modified $modified
        goto-beginning-of-file
        filter-til end-of-file "vile-c-filt"
        goto-beginning-of-file
        attribute-cntl_a-sequences-til end-of-file
        ~if &not %modified
                unmark-buffer
        ~endif
        %savline goto-line
        %savcol goto-column
        write-message "[Attaching C/C++ attributes...done ]"
~endm
bind-key execute-macro-30 ^X-q
```

This runs *vile-c-filt* over the C source code. This program in turn relies upon the contents of *$HOME/.vile.keywords*, which specifies the attributes to provide to different text. (*B* for bold, *U* for underlined, *I* for italic, and *C* for one of 16 different colors.) This is Kevin Buettner's version:

```
Comments:C2
Literal:U
Cpp:CB
if:B
else:B
for:B
return:B
while:B
```

```
switch:B
case:B
do:B
goto:B
break:B
```

Syntax coloring works on the X11 interface with both Versions 7.4 and 8.0 of *vile*. Getting it to work on a Linux console is a bit more complicated. It depends upon which screen handling interface it was compiled with.

The ncurses library

Configure *vile* with `--with-screen=ncurses` and rebuild. This will then work out of the box.

The termcap library

This is the default way that *vile* is configured. Using this version requires you to have a correct */etc/termcap* entry for the Linux console. The following *termcap* entry works:*

```
console|linux|con80x25|dumb:\
        :do=^J:co#80:li#25:cl=\E[H\E[J:sf=\ED:sb=\EM:\
        :le=^H:bs:am:cm=\E[%i%d;%dH:nd=\E[C:up=\E[A:\
        :ce=\E[K:cd=\E[J:so=\E[7m:se=\E[27m:us=\E[4m:ue=\E[24m:\
        :md=\E[1m:mr=\E[7m:mb=\E[5m:me=\E[m:is=\E[1;25r\E[25;1H:\
        :ll=\E[1;25r\E[25;1H:al=\E[L:dc=\E[P:dl=\E[M:\
        :it#8:ku=\E[A:kd=\E[B:kr=\E[C:kl=\E[D:kb=^H:ti=\E[r\E[H:\
        :ho=\E[H:kP=\E[5~:kN=\E[6~:kH=\E[4~:kh=\E[1~:kD=\E[3~:kI=\E[2~:\
        :k1=\E[[A:k2=\E[[B:k3=\E[[C:k4=\E[[D:k5=\E[[E:k6=\E[17~:\
        :k7=\E[18~:k8=\E[19~:k9=\E[20~:k0=\E[21~:K1=\E[1~:K2=\E[5~:\
        :K4=\E[4~:K5=\E[6~:\
        :pt:sr=\EM:vt#3:xn:km:bl=^G:vi=\E[?25l:ve=\E[?25h:vs=\E[?25h:\
        :sc=\E7:rc=\E8:cs=\E[%i%d;%dr:\
        :r1=\Ec:r2=\Ec:r3=\Ec:\
        :vb=\E[?5h\E[?5l:\
        :ut:\
        :Co#8:\
        :AF=\E[%a+c\036%dm:\
        :AB=\E[%a+c\050%dm:
```

On the one hand, because syntax highlighting is accomplished with an external program, it should be possible to write any number of highlighters for different languages. On the other hand, because the facilities are rather low-level, doing so is not for non-programmers. The online help describes how the highlight filters should work.

The directory *ftp://ftp.clark.net/pub/dickey/vile/utilities* contains user-contributed filters for coloring makefiles, LATEX input, Perl, HTML, and *troff*. It even contains a macro that will color the lines in RCS files according to their age!

---

* This entry courtesy of Kevin Buettner. Note that Linux distributions will vary. This was tested under Redhat Linux 4.2; you may not need to change your */etc/termcap* file.

Interesting Features

vile has a number of interesting features that are the topic of this section.

The vile editing model
> *vile*'s editing model is somewhat different from *vi*'s. Based on concepts from *emacs*, it provides key rebinding and a more dynamic command line.

Major modes
> *vile* supports editing "modes." These are groups of option settings that make it convenient for editing different kinds of files.

The procedure language
> *vile*'s procedure language allows you to define functions and macros that make the editor more programmable and flexible.

Miscellaneous small features
> A number of smaller features make day-to-day editing easier.

The vile Editing Model

In *vi* and the other clones, editing functionality is "hardwired" into the editor. The association between command characters and what they do is built into the code. For example, the x key deletes characters, and the i key enters insert mode. Without resorting to severe trickery, you cannot switch the functionality of the two keys (if it can even be done at all).

vile's editing model, derived from *emacs* through MicroEMACS, is different. The editor has defined, named functions, each of which performs a single editing task, such as `delete-next-character` or `delete-previous-character`. Many of the functions are then bound to keystrokes, such as binding `delete-next-character` to x.

Changing bindings is very easy to do. You use the `:bind-key` command. As arguments, you give it the name of the function, and then the key sequence to bind the function to. You might put the following commands into your *.vilerc* file:

```
bind-key incremental-search /
bind-key reverse-incremental-search ?
```

These commands change the / and ? search commands to do incremental searching.

In addition to pre-defined functions, *vile* contains a simple programming language that allows you to write procedures. You may then bind the command for executing a procedure to a keystroke sequence. GNU *emacs* uses a variant of Lisp for its language, which is extremely powerful. *vile* has a somewhat simpler, less general-purpose language.

Also, as in *emacs*, the *vile* command line is very interactive. Many commands display a default value for their operand, which you can edit if not appropriate, or select by hitting RETURN . As you type *vi* mode editing commands, such as those that change or delete characters, you will see feedback about the operation in the status line.

The "amazing" *ex* mode that Paul referred to earlier is best reflected in the behavior of the :s (substitute) command. It prompts for each part of the command: the search pattern, the replacement text, and any flags.

As an example, let's assume you wish to change all instances of *perl* to *awk* everywhere in your file. In the other editors, you'd simply type :1,$s/perl/awk/g RETURN , and that's what would appear on the command line. The following set of screens describes what you see on the *vile* colon command line *as you type*:

Keystrokes	Results
:1,$s	: 1,$s The first part of the substitute command.
/	substitute pattern: _ *vile* prompts you for the pattern to search for. Any previous pattern is placed there for you to re-use.
perl/	replacement string: _ At the next / delimiter, *vile* prompts you for the replacement text. Any previous text is placed there for you to re-use.
awk/	(g)lobally, ([1-9])th occurrence on line, (c)onfirm, and/or (p)rint result: _ At the final delimiter, *vile* prompts for the optional flags. Enter any desired flags, then RETURN .

The last prompt line is broken for readability. *vile* prints it all on one line.

vile follows through with this style of behavior on all appropriate *ex* commands. For example, the read command (:r) will prompt you with the name of the last file you read. To read that file again, just hit RETURN .

Finally, *vile*'s *ex* command parser is weaker than in the other editors. For example, you cannot use search patterns to specify line ranges (:/now/,/forever/s/perl/awk/g), and the move command (m) is not implemented. In practice, what's not implemented does not seem to hinder you very much.

Major Modes

A *major mode* is a collection of option settings that apply when editing a certain class of file. Many of these options apply on a per-buffer basis, such as the tab-stop settings. The major mode concept was first introduced in *vile* 7.2, and is more fully developed in 7.4 and 8.0.

vile has one pre-defined major mode, cmode, for editing C and C++ programs. With cmode, you can use % to match C preprocessor conditionals (#if, #else, and #endif). *vile* will do automatic source code indentation based on the place-ment of braces ({ and }). And it will do smart formatting of C comments. The tabstop and shiftwidth options are set on a per-major-mode basis as well.

Using major modes, you can apply the same features to programs written in other languages. This example, courtesy of Tom Dickey, defines a new major mode, shmode, for editing Bourne shell scripts. (This is useful for any Bourne-style shell, such as *ksh*, *bash*, or *zsh*.)

```
define-mode sh
set shsuf "\.sh$"
set shpre "^#!\\s*\/.*sh\\>$"
define-submode sh comment-prefix "^\\s*/[:#]"
define-submode sh comments "^\\s*/\\?[:#]\\s+/\\?\\s*$"
define-submode sh fence-if   "^\\s*\\<if\\>"
define-submode sh fence-elif "^\\s*\\<elif\\>"
define-submode sh fence-else "^\\s*\\<else\\>"
define-submode sh fence-fi   "^\\s*\\<fi\\>"
```

The shsuf (shell suffix) variable describes the file name suffix that indicates a file is a shell script. The shpre (shell preamble) variable describes a first line of the file that indicates that the file contains shell code. The define-submode com-mands then add options that apply only to buffers where the corresponding major mode is set. The examples here set up the smart comment formatting and the smart % command matching for shell programs.

The Procedure Language

vile's procedure language is almost unchanged from that of MicroEMACS. Com-ments begin with a semicolon or a double quote character. Environment variable names (editor options) start with a $, user variable names start with %. A number of built-in functions exist for doing comparisons and testing conditions; their names all begin with &. Flow control commands and certain others begin with ~. An @ with a string prompts the user for input, and the user's answer is returned. This rather whimsical example from the *macros.doc* file should give you a taste of the language's flavor:

```
~if &sequal %curplace "timespace vortex"
        insert-string "First, rematerialize\n"
~endif
~if &sequal %planet "earth"       ;If we have landed on earth...
        ~if &sequal %time "late 20th century"  ;and we are then
                write-message "Contact U.N.I.T."
        ~else
                insert-string "Investigate the situation....\n"
                insert-string "(SAY 'stay here Sara')\n"
        ~endif
~elseif &sequal %planet "luna"  ;If we have landed on our neighbor...
        write-message "Keep the door closed"
~else
        setv %conditions @"Atmosphere conditions outside? "
        ~if &sequal %conditions "safe"
                insert-string &cat "Go outside......" "\n"
                insert-string "lock the door\n"
        ~else
                insert-string "Dematerialize..try somewhen else"
                newline
        ~endif
~endif
```

You can store these procedures into a numbered macro, or give them names that can be bound to keystrokes. The above procedure is most useful when using the Tardis *vile* port. ☺

This more realistic example from Paul Fox runs *grep*, searching for the word under the cursor in all C source files. It then puts the results in a buffer named after the word, and sets things up so that the built-in error finder (`^X ^X`) will use this output as its list of lines to visit. Finally, the macro is bound to `^A g`. The `~force` command allows the following command to fail without generating an error message:

```
14 store-macro
        set-variable %grepfor $identifier
        edit-file &cat "!egrep -n " &cat %grepfor " *.[ch]"
        ~force rename-buffer %grepfor
        error-buffer $cbufname
~endm
bind-key execute-macro-14 ^A-g
```

Finally, the `read-hook` and `write-hook` variables can be set to names of procedures to run after reading and before writing a file, respectively. This allows you to do things similar to pre- and post-operation files in *elvis* and the autocommand facility in *vim*.

The language is quite capable, including flow control and comparison features, and variables that provide access to a large amount of *vile*'s internal state. The *macros.doc* file in the *vile* distribution describes the language in detail.

Miscellaneous Small Features

Several other, smaller features are worth mentioning:

Piping into vile

If you make *vile* the last command in a pipeline, it will create a buffer named [Standard Input] and edit that buffer for you. This is perhaps the "pager to end all pagers."

Editing DOS files

When set to true, the dos option causes *vile* to strip carriage returns at the end of a line in files when reading, and to write them back out again. This makes it easy to edit DOS files on a UNIX or Linux system.

Text reformatting

The ^A f command reformats text, performing word wrapping on selected text. It understands C and shell comments (lines with a leading * or #) and quoted email (a leading >). It is similar to the UNIX *fmt* command, but faster.

Formatting the information line

The modeline-format variable is a string which controls the way *vile* formats the mode line. This is the line at the bottom of each window that describes the buffer's status, such as its name, current major mode, modification status, insert versus command mode, and so on.

The string consists of printf(3) style percent-sequences. For example, %b for the buffer name, %m for the major mode, and %l for the line number if ruler has been set. Characters in the string which are not part of a format specifier are output verbatim.

vile has many other features. The *vi* finger-feel makes it easy to move to. The programmability provides flexibility, and its interactive nature and use of defaults is perhaps friendlier for the novice than traditional *vi*.

Sources and Supported Operating Systems

The official WWW location for *vile* is *http://www.clark.net/pub/dickey/vile/vile.html*. The *ftp* location is *ftp://ftp.clark.net/pub/dickey/vile/vile.tar.gz*. The file *vile.tar.gz* is always a symbolic link to the current version.

vile is written in ANSI C. It builds and runs on UNIX, VMS (with both VAX C and DEC C), MS-DOS, Win32 console and Win32 GUI, and OS/2.

Compiling *vile* is straightforward. Retrieve the distribution via *ftp* or from the web page. Uncompress and untar it, run the *configure* program, and then run *make*:

```
$ gzip -d < vile.tar.gz | tar -xvpf -
...
$ cd vile-8.0; ./configure
...
$ make
...
```

vile should configure and build with no problems. Use *make install* to install it.

 If you intend to use a Linux console and want syntax coloring to
work, you may wish to run *configure* with the following option:
--with-screen=ncurses.

Should you need to report a bug or problem in *vile*, send email to the address
vile-bugs@foxharp.boston.ma.us. This is the preferred way to report bugs. If
necessary, you can contact Tom Dickey directly at *dickey@clark.net*.

III

Appendixes

Part III provides reference material that should be of interest to a *vi* user. This part contains the appendixes:

- Appendix A, *Quick Reference*
- Appendix B, *ex Commands*
- Appendix C, *Setting Options*
- Appendix D, *Problem Checklists*
- Appendix E, *vi and the Internet*

Quick Reference

This appendix lists *vi* commands and *ex* commands according to their use.

Table A-1: Movement Commands

Command	Function
Character	
h,j,k,l	Left, down, up, right (←, ↓, ↑, →).
Text	
w,W,b,B	Forward, backward by word.
e,E	End of word.
),(	Beginning of next, previous sentence.
},{	Beginning of next, previous paragraph.
]],[[	Beginning of next, previous section.
Lines	
⌷RETURN⌷	First non-blank character of next line.
0, $	First, last position of current line.
^	First non-blank character of current line.
+, −	First non-blank character of next, previous line.
n |	Column *n* of current line.
H	Top line of screen.
M	Middle line of screen.
L	Last line of screen.
*n*H	*n* (number) of lines after top line.
*n*L	*n* (number) of lines before last line.

Table A-1: Movement Commands (continued)

Command	Function
Scrolling	
CTRL-F , CTRL-B	Scroll forward, backward one screen.
CTRL-D , CTRL-U	Scroll down, up one-half screen.
CTRL-E , CTRL-Y	Show one more line at bottom, top of window.
z RETURN	Reposition line with cursor: to top of screen.
z .	Reposition line with cursor: to middle of screen.
z –	Reposition line with cursor: to bottom of screen.
CTRL-L	Redraw screen (without scrolling).
Searches	
/pattern	Search forward for *pattern*.
?pattern	Search backward for *pattern*.
n, N	Repeat last search in same, opposite direction.
/, ?	Repeat previous search forward, backward.
fx	Search forward for character x in current line.
Fx	Search backward for character x in current line.
tx	Search forward to character before x in current line.
Tx	Search backward to character after x in current line.
;	Repeat previous current-line search.
,	Repeat previous current-line search in opposite direction.
Line number	
CTRL-G	Display current line number.
nG	Move to line number n.
G	Move to last line in file.
:n	Move to line n in file.
Marking position	
mx	Mark current position as x.
`x	Move cursor to mark x.
` `	Return to previous mark or context.
'x	Move to beginning of line containing mark x.
' '	Return to beginning of line containing previous mark.

Table A-2: Editing Commands

Command	Function
Insert	
i, a	Insert text before, after cursor.
I, A	Insert text before beginning, after end of line.
o, O	Open new line for text below, above cursor.
Change	
r	Replace character.
cw	Change word.
cc	Change current line.
cmotion	Change text between the cursor and the target of *motion*.
C	Change to end of line.
R	Type over (overwrite) characters.
s	Substitute: delete character and insert new text.
S	Substitute: delete current line and insert new text.
Delete, move	
x	Delete character under cursor.
X	Delete character before cursor.
dw	Delete word.
dd	Delete current line.
dmotion	Delete text between the cursor and the target of *motion*.
D	Delete to end of line.
p, P	Put deleted text after, before cursor.
"np	Put text from delete buffer number *n* after cursor (for last nine deletions).
Yank	
yw	Yank (copy) word.
yy	Yank current line.
"ayy	Yank current line into named buffer a (a–z). Uppercase names append text.
ymotion	Yank text between the cursor and the target of *motion*.
p, P	Put yanked text after, before cursor.
"aP	Put text from buffer a before cursor (a–z).
Other commands	
.	Repeat last edit command.
u, U	Undo last edit; restore current line.
J	Join two lines.

Table A-2: Editing Commands (continued)

Command	Function
ex edit commands	
:d	Delete lines.
:m	Move lines.
:co or :t	Copy lines.
:.,$d	Delete from current line to end of file.
:30,60m0	Move lines 30 through 60 to top of file.
:.,/*pattern*/co$	Copy from current line through line containing *pattern* to end of file.

Table A-3: Exit Commands

Command	Function
ZZ	Write (save) the file if modified, and quit file.
:x	Write (save) the file if modified, and quit file.
:wq	Write (save) the file unconditionally, and quit file.
:w	Write (save) file.
:w!	Write (save) file, overriding protection.
:30,60w *newfile*	Write from line 30 through line 60 as *newfile*.
:30,60w>> *file*	Write from line 30 through line 60 and append to *file*.
:w %.*new*	Write current buffer named *file* as *file.new*.
:q	Quit file.
:q!	Quit file, overriding protection.
Q	Quit *vi* and invoke *ex*.
:e *file2*	Edit *file2* without leaving *vi*.
:r *newfile*	Read contents of *newfile* into current file.
:n	Edit next file.
:e!	Return to version of current file at time of last write (save).
:e #	Edit alternate file.
:vi	Invoke *vi* editor from *ex*.
:	Invoke one *ex* command from *vi* editor.
%	Current filename (substitutes into *ex* command line).
#	Alternate filename (substitutes into *ex* command line).

Table A-4: Solaris vi Command Mode Tag Commands

Command	Function
^]	Look up the location of the identifier under the cursor in the *tags* file, and move to that location. If tag stacking is enabled, the current location is automatically pushed onto the tag stack.
^T	Return to the previous location in the tag stack, i.e., pop off one element.

Table A-5: Command-Line Options

Command	Function
vi *file*	Invoke *vi* editor on *file*.
vi *file1 file2*	Invoke *vi* editor on files sequentially.
view *file*	Invoke *vi* editor on *file* in read-only mode.
vi -R *file*	Invoke *vi* editor on *file* in read-only mode.
vi -r *file*	Recover *file* and recent edits after a crash.
vi -t *tag*	Look up *tag* and start editing at its definition.
vi -w *n*	Set the window size to *n*; useful over a slow connection.
vi + *file*	Open *file* at last line.
vi +*n file*	Open *file* directly at line number *n*.
vi -c *command file*	Open *file*, execute *command*, which is usually a search command or line number (POSIX).
vi +/*pattern file*	Open *file* directly at *pattern*.
ex *file*	Invoke *ex* editor on *file*.
ex - *file* < *script*	Invoke *ex* editor on *file*, taking commands from *script*; suppress informative messages and prompts.
ex -s *file* < *script*	Invoke *ex* editor on *file*, taking commands from *script*; suppress informative messages and prompts (POSIX).

Table A-6: Other ex Commands

Command	Function
Abbreviations[a]	
:map *x sequence*	Define keystroke *x* as a command *sequence*. *x* can be multiple characters.
:map! *x sequence*	Define *x* as command *sequence* for insert mode.
:unmap *x*	Disable the map *x*.
:unmap! *x*	Disable the insert mode map *x*.
:ab *abbr phrase*	Abbreviate *phrase* as *abbr*; when *abbr* is typed in insert mode, it expands to full words or phrases.

Table A-6: Other ex Commands (continued)

Command	Function
`:unab` *abbr*	Disable abbreviation *abbr*.
Customizing environment:[a]	
`:set` *option*	Activate *option*.
`:set` *option=value*	Assign *value* to *option*.
`:set` *nooption*	Deactivate *option*.
`:set`	Display options set by user.
`:set all`	Display list of all current option settings, both default and those set by the user.
`:set` *option?*	Display value of *option*.
Accessing UNIX	
`:sh`	Invoke shell.
`^D`	Return to editor from shell.
`:!` *command*	Give UNIX *command*.
`:n,m!` *command*	Filter lines *n* to *m* through UNIX *command*.
`:r !`*command*	Read output of UNIX *command* into current file.

[a] In *.exrc* files, omit the colon at the start of *ex* commands.

B

ex Commands

This appendix describes the syntax of *ex* commands and then presents an alphabetical list of *ex* commands.

Command Syntax

To enter an *ex* command from *vi*, use this form:

```
:[address] command [options]
```

address is the line number or range of lines that are the object of *command*. If no address is given, the current line is (usually) the object of the command.

Address Symbols

In *ex* command syntax, *address* can be specified in any of the forms shown in Table B-1.

Table B-1: ex Address Syntax

Address	Includes
1,$	All lines in the file
x,y	Lines *x* through *y*
x;y	Lines *x* through *y*, with current line reset to *x*
0	Top of file
.	Current line
n	Absolute line number *n*
$	Last line
%	All lines; same as 1,$

Table B-1: ex Address Syntax (continued)

Address	Includes
x-n	n lines before x
x+n	n lines after x
-[n]	One or n lines previous
+[n]	One or n lines ahead
'x	Line marked with x
' '	Previous mark
/pat/ or ?pat?	Ahead or back to line where *pat* matches

Option Symbols

In *ex* command syntax, *options* might be any of the following:

! Indicates a variant form of the command, overriding the normal behavior.

count
    The number of times the command is to be repeated. *count* cannot precede the command, because a number preceding an *ex* command is treated as a line address. d3 deletes three lines beginning with the current line; 3d deletes line 3.

file
    The name of a file that is affected by the command. % stands for current file; # stands for previous file.

Alphabetical List of Commands

In this section, the full name of the *ex* command is listed as the keyword. To the right of or below each keyword is the syntax, using the shortest abbreviation possible for that command. A brief description follows the syntax.

abbrev
    ab [string text]

    Define *string* when typed to be translated into *text*. If *string* and *text* are not specified, list all current abbreviations.

append
    [address] a[!]

    text

Append *text* at specified *address*, or at present address if one is not specified. Add a ! to switch the `autoindent` setting that will be used during input. That is, if `autoindent` was enabled, ! disables it.

args

`ar`

Print the members of the argument list (files named on the command line), with the current argument printed within brackets ([ ]).

change

[*address*] c[!]

text

.

Replace the specified lines with *text*. Add a ! to switch the `autoindent` setting during input of *text*.

copy

[*address*] co *destination*

Copy the lines included in *address* to the specified *destination* address. The command t (short for "to") is a synonym for **copy**.

delete

[*address*] d [*buffer*]

Delete the lines included in *address*. If *buffer* is specified, save or append the text to the named buffer. Buffer names are the lowercase letters a–z. Uppercase names append text to the buffer.

edit

e [!][+n] [*filename*]

Begin editing on *filename*. If no *filename* is given, start over with a copy of the current file. Add a ! to edit the new file even if the current file has not been saved since the last change. With the +*n* argument, begin editing on line *n*. Or *n* may be a pattern, of the form / *pattern*.

file

f [*filename*]

Change the name of the current file to *filename*, which is considered "not edited." If no *filename* is specified, print the current status of the file.

global

[*address*]g[!]/*pattern*/[*commands*]

Execute *commands* on all lines which contain *pattern*, or if *address* is specified, all lines within that range. If *commands* are not specified, print all such lines. Add a ! to execute *commands* on all lines *not* containing *pattern*.

insert

> [*address*]i[!]
>
> *text*
>
> .

Insert *text* at line before the specified address, or at present address if none is specified. Add a ! to switch the `autoindent` setting during input of *text*.

join

> [*address*]j[!][*count*]

Place the text in the specified range on one line, with whitespace adjusted to provide two space characters after a period (.), no space characters after a) , and one space character otherwise. Add a ! to prevent whitespace adjustment.

k   [*address*] k *char*

Mark the given *address* with *char*, a single lowercase letter. Return later to the line with 'x. k is equivalent to `mark`.

list [*address*] l [*count*]

Print the specified lines so that tabs display as ^I and the ends of lines display as $.

map

> map *char commands*

Define a macro named *char* in visual mode with the specified sequence of commands. *char* is usually the sequence #*n*, representing a function key on the keyboard, or one or more characters.

mark

> [*address*] ma *char*

Mark the specified line with *char*, a single lowercase letter. Return later to the line with 'x.

move

> [*address*] m *destination*

Move the lines specified by *address* to the *destination* address.

next

> n[!] [[+*n*] *filelist*]

Edit the next file from the command-line argument list. Use `args` to list these files. If *filelist* is provided, replace the current argument list with *filelist* and begin editing on the first file. With the +*n* argument, begin editing on line *n*. Or *n* may be a pattern, of the form */pattern*.

number

   [*address*] nu [*count*]

   Print each line specified by *address*, preceded by its buffer line number. Use # as an alternate abbreviation for **number**.

open

   [*address*] o [/*pattern*/]

   Enter *open* mode (*vi*) at the lines specified by *address*, or at the lines matching *pattern*. Exit open mode with Q.

preserve

   pre

   Save the current editor buffer as though the system was about to crash.

print

   [*address*] p [*count*]

   Print the lines specified by *address*. P is another abbreviation.

put

   [*address*] pu [*char*]

   Restore previously deleted or yanked lines, from named buffer specified by *char*, to the line specified by *address*; if *char* is not specified, the last deleted or yanked text is restored.

quit

   q[!]

   Terminate current editing session. Use ! to discard changes made since the last save. If the editing session includes additional files in the argument list that have not yet been accessed, quit by typing q! or by typing q twice.

read

   [*address*] r *filename*

   Copy the text of *filename* after the line specified by *address*. If *filename* is not specified, the current filename is used.

read

   [*address*] r ! *command*

   Read the output of *command* into the text after the line specified by *address*.

recover

   rec [*filename*]

   Recover *filename* from system save area.

rewind

> `rew[!]`

Rewind argument list and begin editing the first file in the list. Add a ! to rewind even if the current file has not been saved since the last change.

set `se parameter parameter2`

Set a value to an option with each *parameter*, or if no *parameter* is supplied, print all options that have been changed from their defaults. For toggle options, each *parameter* can be phrased as "*option*" or "no*option*," other options can be assigned with the syntax, "*option=value*". The form `set option?` displays the value of *option*.

shell

> `sh`

Create a new shell. Resume editing when the shell is terminated.

source

> `so filename`

Read and execute *ex* commands from *filename*.

substitute

> `[address] s [/pattern/repl/][options]`

Replace each instance of *pattern* on the specified lines with *repl*. If *pattern* and *repl* are omitted, repeat last substitution. An option of `g` substitutes all instances of *pattern* on the line. An option of `c` prompts for confirmation before each change. (Spelling out the command name does not work in Solaris 2.6 *vi*.) See Chapter 6, *Global Replacement*, for full details.

t `[address] t destination`

Copy the lines included in *address to* the specified *destination* address. `t` is equivalent to `copy`.

tag `[address] ta tag`

Switch the focus of editing to *tag*.

unabbreviate

> `una word`

Remove *word* from the list of abbreviations.

undo

> `u`

Reverse the changes made by the last editing command.

unmap

unm *char*

Remove *char* from the list of macros.

v [*address*] v/ *pattern*/[*commands*]

Execute *commands* on all lines *not* containing *pattern*. If *commands* are not specified, print all such lines. v is equivalent to g!.

version

ve

Print the current version number of the editor and the date the editor was last changed. Each clone prints something appropriate.

visual

[*address*] vi [*type*] [*count*]

Enter visual mode at the line specified by *address*. Exit with Q. *type* can be one of −, ^, or . (See the z command). *count* specifies an initial window size.

visual

vi [+*n*] [*filename*]

Begin editing on *filename* in visual mode.

write

[*address*] w[!] [[>>]*filename*]

Write lines specified by *address* to *filename*, or full contents of buffer if *address* is not specified. If *filename* is also omitted, save the contents of the buffer to the current filename. If >> *filename* is used, write contents to the end of the specified *filename*. Add a ! to force the editor to write over any current contents of *filename*.

write

[*address*] w !*command*

Write lines specified by *address* to *command*.

wq

wq[!]

Write and quit the file in one movement. The file is always written.

xit x

Write file if changes have been made to the buffer since last write, then quit.

yank

> [*address*] y [*char*] [*count*]

> Place lines specified by *address* in named buffer indicated by *char*, or if no *char* is specified place in general buffer.

z   [*address*] z [*type*] [*count*]

> Print a window of text with line specified by *address* at the top. *type* can be one of:

> +   Place specified line at the top of the window (default).

> −   Place specified line at the bottom of the window.

> .   Place specified line in the center of the window.

> ^   Print the previous window.

> =   Place specified line in the center of the window and leave the current line at this line.

> *count* specifies the number of lines to be displayed.

!   [*address*] ! *command*

> Execute *command* in a shell. If *address* is specified, apply the lines contained in *address* as standard input to *command*, and replace the lines with the output and error output. (This is called *filtering* the text through the *command*.)

=   [*address*] =

> Print the line number of the line indicated by *address*. Default is line number of last line.

< >

> [*address*] < [*count*]

> or

> [*address*] > [*count*]

> Shift lines specified by *address* in specified direction. Only leading spaces and tabs are added or removed when shifting lines. The shiftwidth option controls the number of columns that are shifted. Repeating the < or > increases the shift amount. For example, :>>> shifts three times as much as :>.

address

> address

> Print the lines specified in *address*.

RETURN

    RETURN

    Print the next line in the file.

&   [*address*] & [*options*] [*count*]

    Repeat the previous substitute command.

~   [*address*] ~ [*count*]

    Replace the last used regular expression (even if from a search, and not from an **s** command) with the replacement pattern from the most recent **s** (substitute) command. See the section "More Substitution Tricks" in Chapter 6 for details.

C

In this appendix:
- *Solaris 2.6 vi Options*
- *nvi 1.79 Options*
- *elvis 2.0 Options*
- *vim 5.1 Options*
- *vile 8.0 Options*

Setting Options

This appendix describes the important **set** command options for Solaris 2.6 *vi*, *nvi* 1.79, *elvis* 2.0, *vim* 5.1, and *vile* 8.0.

Solaris 2.6 vi Options

Table C-1 contains brief descriptions of the important **set** command options. In the first column, options are listed in alphabetical order; if the option can be abbreviated, that abbreviation is shown in parentheses. The second column shows the default setting that *vi* uses unless you issue an explicit **set** command (either manually or in the *.exrc* file). The last column describes what the option does, when enabled.

Table C-1: Solaris 2.6 vi Set Options

Option	Default	Description
autoindent (ai)	noai	In insert mode, indents each line to the same level as the line above or below. Use with the shiftwidth option.
autoprint (ap)	ap	Displays changes after each editor command. (For global replacement, displays last replacement.)
autowrite (aw)	noaw	Automatically writes (saves) the file if changed before opening another file with :n or before giving UNIX command with :!.
beautify (bf)	nobf	Ignores all control characters during input (except tab, newline, or formfeed).

Table C-1: Solaris 2.6 vi Set Options (continued)

Option	Default	Description
directory (dir)	*/tmp*	Names directory in which *ex/vi* stores buffer files. (Directory must be writable.)
edcompatible	noedcompatible	Remember the flags used with the most recent substitute command (global, confirming), and use them for the next substitute command. Despite the name, no actual version of *ed* actually behaved this way.
errorbells (eb)	errorbells	Sounds bell when an error occurs.
exrc (ex)	noexrc	Allows the execution of *.exrc* files that reside outside the user's home directory.
hardtabs (ht)	8	Defines boundaries for terminal hardware tabs.
ignorecase (ic)	noic	Disregards case during a search.
lisp	nolisp	Inserts indents in appropriate lisp format. ( ), { }, [[, and]] are modified to have meaning for lisp.
list	nolist	Prints tabs as ^I; marks ends of lines with $. (Use list to tell if end character is a tab or a space.)
magic	magic	Wildcard characters . (dot), * (asterisk), and [ ] (brackets) have special meaning in patterns.
mesg	mesg	Permits system messages to display on terminal while editing in *vi*.
novice	nonovice	Requires the use of long *ex* command names, such as copy or read.
number (nu)	nonu	Displays line numbers on left of screen during editing session.
open	open	Allows entry to *open* or *visual* mode from *ex*. Although not in Solaris 2.6 *vi*, this option has traditionally been in *vi*, and may be in your UNIX's version of *vi*.
optimize (opt)	noopt	Abolishes carriage returns at the end of lines when printing multiple lines, speeds output on dumb terminals when printing lines with leading whitespace (spaces or tabs).

Table C-1: Solaris 2.6 vi Set Options (continued)

Option	Default	Description
paragraphs (para)	IPLPPPQP LIpplpipbp	Defines paragraph delimiters for movement by { or }. The pairs of characters in the value are the names of *troff* macros that begin paragraphs.
prompt	prompt	Displays the *ex* prompt (:) when *vi*'s Q command is given.
readonly (ro)	noro	Any writes (saves) of a file will fail unless you use ! after the write (works with w, ZZ, or autowrite).
redraw (re)		*vi* redraws the screen whenever edits are made (in other words, insert mode pushes over existing characters, and deleted lines immediately close up). Default depends on line speed and terminal type. noredraw is useful at slow speeds on a dumb terminal: deleted lines show up as @, and inserted text appears to overwrite existing text until you press ESC .
remap	remap	Allows nested map sequences.
report	5	Displays a message on the status line whenever you make an edit that affects at least a certain number of lines. For example, 6dd reports the message "6 lines deleted."
scroll	[½ *window*]	Number of lines to scroll with ^D and ^U commands.
sections (sect)	SHNHH HU	Defines section delimiters for [[and]] movement. The pairs of characters in the value are the names of *troff* macros that begin sections.
shell (sh)	*/bin/sh*	Pathname of shell used for shell escape (: !) and shell command (: sh). Default value is derived from shell environment, which varies on different systems.
shiftwidth (sw)	8	Defines number of spaces in backward (^D) tabs when using the autoindent option, and for the << and >> commands.

Table C-1: Solaris 2.6 vi Set Options (continued)

Option	Default	Description
showmatch (sm)	nosm	In *vi*, when) or } is entered, cursor moves briefly to matching (or {. (If no match, rings the error message bell.) Very useful for programming.
showmode	noshowmode	In insert mode, displays a message on the prompt line indicating the type of insert you are making. For example, "OPEN MODE," or "APPEND MODE."
slowopen (slow)		Holds off display during insert. Default depends on line speed and terminal type.
tabstop (ts)	8	Defines number of spaces that a TAB indents during editing session. (Printer still uses system tab of 8.)
taglength (tl)	0	Defines number of characters that are significant for tags. Default (zero) means that all characters are significant.
tags	*tags /usr/lib/tags*	Defines pathname of files containing tags. (See the UNIX ctags command.) (By default, *vi* searches the file *tags* in the current directory and */usr/lib/tags.*)
tagstack	tagstack	Enables stacking of tag locations on a stack.
term		Sets terminal type.
terse	noterse	Displays shorter error messages.
timeout (to)	timeout	Keyboard maps time out after 1 second.[a]
ttytype		Sets terminal type. This is just another name for term.
warn	warn	Displays the warning message, "No write since last change."
window (w)		Shows a certain number of lines of the file on the screen. Default depends on line speed and terminal type.
wrapscan (ws)	ws	Searches wrap around either end of file.
wrapmargin (wm)	0	Defines right margin. If greater than zero, automatically inserts carriage returns to break lines.

Table C-1: Solaris 2.6 vi Set Options (continued)

Option	Default	Description
writeany (wa)	nowa	Allows saving to any file.

a When you have mappings of several keys (for example, :map zzz 3dw), you probably want to use notimeout. Otherwise you need to type zzz within 1 second. When you have an insert mode mapping for a cursor key (for example, :map! ^[OB ^[ja), you should use timeout. Otherwise, *vi* won't react to ESC until you type another key.

nvi 1.79 Options

nvi 1.79 has a total of 78 options that affect its behavior. Table C-2 summarizes the most important ones. Most options described in Table C-1 are not repeated here.

Table C-2: nvi 1.79 Set Options

Option	Default	Description
backup		A string describing a backup filename to use. The current contents of a file are saved in this file before writing the new data out. For example, a value of "N%.bak" causes *nvi* to include a version number at the end of the file; version numbers are always incremented.
cdpath	environment variable CDPATH, or current directory	A search path for the :cd command.
cedit		When the first character of this string is entered on the colon command line, *nvi* opens a new window on the command history that you can then edit. Hitting RETURN on any given line executes that line. ESC is a good choice for this option. (Use ^v ^[to enter it.)
comment	nocomment	If the first non-empty line begins with /*, //, or #, *nvi* skips the comment text before displaying the file. This avoids displaying long, boring legal notices.
directory (dir)	environment variable TMPDIR, or */tmp*	The directory where *nvi* puts its temporary files.
extended	noextended	Searches use *egrep*-style extended regular expressions.

Table C-2: nvi 1.79 Set Options (continued)

Option	Default	Description
filec		When the first character of this string is entered on the colon command line, *nvi* treats the blank delimited word in front of the cursor as if it had an * appended to it and does shell-style filename expansion. ESC is a also good choice for this option. (Use ^v ^[to enter it.) When this character is the same as for the cedit option, command line editing is performed only when the character is entered as the first character on the colon command line.
iclower	noiclower	Make all regular expression searches case insensitive, as long as the search pattern contains no uppercase letters.
leftright	noleftright	Long lines scroll the screen left to right, instead of wrapping.
lock	lock	*nvi* attempts to get an exclusive lock on the file. Editing a file that cannot be locked creates a read-only session.
octal	nooctal	Displays unknown characters in octal, instead of in hexadecimal.
path		A colon-separated list of directories in which *nvi* will look for the file to be edited.
recdir	*/var/tmp/vi.recover*	The directory where recovery files are stored.
ruler	noruler	Displays the row and column of the cursor.
searchincr	nosearchincr	Searches are done incrementally.
secure	nosecure	Turns off access to external programs via text filtering (:r!, :w!), disables the *vi* mode ! and ^z commands, and the *ex* mode !, shell, stop, and suspend commands. Once set, it cannot be changed.
shellmeta	~{[*?$`'"\	When any of these characters appear in a filename argument to an *ex* command, the argument is expanded by the program named by the shell option.

Table C-2: nvi 1.79 Set Options (continued)

Option	Default	Description
showmode (smd)	noshowmode	Displays a string in the status line showing the current mode. Displays an * if the file has been modified.
sidescroll	16	The number of columns by which the screen is shifted left or right when `leftright` is true.
taglength (tl)	0	Defines number of characters that are significant for tags. Default (zero) means that all characters are significant.
tags (tag)	*tags /var/db/libc.tags /sys/kern/tags*	The list of possible tag files.
tildeop	notildeop	The ~ command takes an associated motion, not just a preceding count.
wraplen (wl)	0	Identical to the `wrapmargin` option, except that it specifies the number of characters from the left margin at which the line will be split. The value of `wrapmargin` overrides `wraplen`.

elvis 2.0 Options

elvis 2.0 has a total of 144 options that affect its behavior. Table C-3 summarizes the most important ones. Most options described in Table C-1 are not repeated here.

Table C-3: elvis 2.0 Set Options

Option	Default	Description
autoiconify (aic)	noautoiconify	Iconify the old window when de-iconifying a new one.
backup (bk)	nobackup	Make a backup file (*xxx.bak*) before writing the current file out to disk.
binary (bin)		The buffer's data is not text. This option is set automatically.
boldfont (xfb)		The name of the bold font.
bufdisplay (bd)	normal	The default display mode for the buffer (`hex`, `html`, `man`, `normal`, or `syntax`).
ccprg (cp)	cc ($1?$1:$2)	The shell command for :cc.
commentfont (cfont)		The name of the font used for comments.

Table C-3: elvis 2.0 Set Options (continued)

Option	Default	Description
directory (dir)		Where to store temporary files. The default is system dependent.
display (mode)	normal	The name of current display mode, set by the :display command.
elvispath (epath)		A list of directories in which to search for configuration files. The default is system dependent.
focusnew (fn)	focusnew	Force keyboard focus into the new window.
functionfont (ffont)		The name of the font used for function names.
gdefault (gd)	nogdefault	Causes the substitute command to change all instances.
home (home)	$HOME	The home directory for ~ in filenames.
italicfont (xfi)		The name of the italic font.
keywordfont (kfont)		The name of the font used for reserved words.
lpcolumns (lpcols)	80	The width of a printer page; for :lpr.
lpcrlf (lpc)	nolpcrlf	The printer needs CR-LF for newline in the file; for :lpr.
lpformfeed (lpff)	nolpformfeed	Send a form-feed after the last page; for :lpr.
lplines (lprows)	60	The length of a printer page; for :lpr.
lppaper (lpp)	letter	The paper size (letter, a4, . . .) for PostScript printers; for :lpr.
lpout (lpo)		The printer file or filter, for :lpr. A typical value might be ❘lpr. The default is system dependent.
lptype (lpt)	dumb	The printer type, for :lpr. The value should be one of: ps, ps2, epson, pana, ibm, hp, cr, bs, or dumb.
lpwrap (lpw)	lpwrap	Simulate line-wrap; for :lpr.
makeprg (mp)	make $1	The shell command for :make.
normalfont (xfn)		The name of the normal font.
otherfont (ofont)		The font used for other symbols.
prepfont (pfont)		The font used for preprocessor commands.
ruler (ru)	noruler	Display the cursor's line and column.
safer (trapunsafe)	nosafer	Be paranoid; use the :safer command to set this, don't do it directly.

Table C-3: elvis 2.0 Set Options (continued)

Option	Default	Description
showmarkups (smu)	noshowmarkups	For the man and html modes, show the markup at the cursor position, but not elsewhere.
sidescroll (ss)	0	The sideways scrolling amount. Zero mimics *vi*, making lines wrap.
stringfont (sfont)		The font used for strings.
taglength (tl)	0	Defines number of characters that are significant for tags. Default (zero) means that all characters are significant.
tags (tagpath)	tags	The list of possible tag files.
tagstack (tsk)	tagstack	Remember the origin of tag searches on a stack.
undolevels (ul)	0	The number of undoable commands. Zero mimics *vi*. You probably want to set this to a bigger number.
variablefont (vfont)		The font used for variables.
warpback (wb)	nowarpback	Upon exit, move the pointer back to the *xterm* which started *elvis*.
warpto (wt)	don't	How ^w ^w forces pointer movement: don't for no movement, scrollbar moves the pointer to the scrollbar, origin moves the pointer to the upper left corner, and corners moves it to the corners furthest from and nearest to the current cursor position. This forces the X display to pan, to make sure the window is entirely onscreen.

vim 5.1 Options

vim 5.1 has a total of 170 options that affect its behavior. Table C-4 summarizes the most important ones. Most options described in Table C-1 are not repeated here.

The summaries in the table here are of necessity very brief. Much more information about each option may be found in the *vim* online help.

Table C-4: vim 5.1 Set Options

Option	Default	Description
background (bg)	dark or light	*vim* tries to use background and foreground colors that are appropriate to the particular terminal.
backspace (bs)	0	Controls whether you can backspace over a newline and/or over the start of insert. Values are: 0 for *vi* compatibility, 1 to backspace over newlines, and 2 to backspace over the start of insert. Using a value of 3 allows both.
backup (bk)	nobackup	Make a backup before overwriting a file, then leave it around after the file has been successfully written. To have a backup file just while the file is being written, use the writebackup option.
backupdir (bdir)	., ~/tmp/, ~/	A list of directories for the backup file, separated with commas. The backup file will be created in the first directory in the list where this is possible. If empty, you cannot create a backup file. The name . (dot) means the same directory as where the edited file is.
backupext (bex)	~	The string which is appended to a file name to make the name of the backup file.
binary (bin)	nobinary	Changes a number of other options to make it easier to edit binary files. The previous values of these options are remembered and restored when bin is switched back off. Each buffer has its own set of saved option values. This option should be set before editing a binary file. You can also use the −*b* command line option.
cindent (cin)	nocindent	Enables automatic smart C program indenting.
cinkeys (cink)	0{,0},:,0#,!^F, o,O,e	A list of keys that, when typed in insert mode, cause reindenting of the current line. Only happens if cindent is on.
cinoptions (cino)		Affects the way cindent reindents lines in a C program. See the online help for details.

Table C-4: vim 5.1 Set Options (continued)

Option	Default	Description
cinwords (cinw)	if, else, while, do, for, switch	These keywords start an extra indent in the next line when smartindent or cindent is set. For cindent this is only done at an appropriate place (inside {...}).
comments (com)		A comma-separated list of strings that can start a comment line. See the online help for details.
compatible (cp)	cp; nocp when a *.vimrc* file is found	Makes *vim* behave more like *vi* in too many ways to describe here. It is on by default, to avoid surprises. Having a *.vimrc* turns off the *vi* compatibility; usually this is a desirable side effect.
cpoptions (cpo)	aABceFs	A sequence of single character flags, each one indicating a different way in which *vim* will or will not exactly mimic *vi*. When empty, the *vim* defaults are used. See the on-line help for details.
define (def)	^#\s*define	A search pattern that describes macro definitions. The default value is for C programs. For C++, use ^\(#\s*define\ |[a-z]*\s*const\s*[a-z]*\). When using the :set command, you need to double the backslashes.
directory (dir)	., ~/tmp, /tmp	A list of directory names for the swap file, separated with commas. The swap file will be created in the first directory where this is possible. If empty, no swap file will be used and recovery is impossible! The name . (dot) means to put the swap file in the same directory as the edited file. Using . first in the list is recommended so that editing the same file twice will result in a warning.
equalprg (ep)		External program to use for = command. When this option is empty the internal formatting functions are used.
errorfile (ef)	errors.err	Name of the errorfile for the quickfix mode. When the *−q* command line argument is used, errorfile is set to the following argument.
errorformat (efm)	(too long to print)	Scanf-like description of the format for the lines in the error file.

Table C-4: vim 5.1 Set Options (continued)

Option	Default	Description
expandtab (et)	noexpandtab	When inserting a tab, expand it to the appropriate number of spaces.
fileformat (ff)	unix	Describes the convention to terminate lines when reading/writing the current buffer. Possible values are dos (CR-LF), unix (LF), and mac (CR). *vim* will usually set this automatically.
fileformats (ffs)	dos,unix	Lists the line-terminating conventions that *vim* will try to apply to a file when reading. Multiple names enable automatic end-of-line detection when reading a file.
formatoptions (fo)	*vim* default: tcq, *vi* default: vt	A sequence of letters which describes how automatic formatting is to be done. See the online help for details.
gdefault (gd)	nogdefault	Causes the substitute command to change all instances.
guifont (gfn)		A comma-separated list of fonts to try when starting the GUI version of *vim*.
hidden (hid)	nohidden	Hides the current buffer when it is unloaded from a window, instead of abandoning it.
hlsearch (hls)	nohlsearch	Highlight all matches of the most recent search pattern.
history (hi)	*vim* default: 20, *vi* default: 0	Controls how many *ex* commands, search strings and expressions are remembered in the command history.
icon	noicon	*vim* attempts to change the name of the icon associated with the window where it is running. Overridden by the iconstring option.
iconstring		String value used for the icon name of the window.
include (inc)	^#\s*include	Defines a search pattern for finding include commands. The default value is for C programs.
incsearch (is)	noincsearch	Enables incremental searching.

Table C-4: vim 5.1 Set Options (continued)

Option	Default	Description
isfname (isf)	@,48-57,/,.,-,_, +,,,$,:,~	A list of characters that can be included in file and path names. Non-UNIX systems have different default values. The @ character stands for any alphabetic character. It is also used in the other is*xxx* options, below.
isident (isi)	@,48-57,_,192-255	A list of characters that can be included in identifiers. Non-UNIX systems may have different default values.
iskeyword (isk)	@,48-57,_,192-255	A list of characters that can be included in keywords. Non-UNIX systems may have different default values. Keywords are used in searching and recognizing with many commands, such as w, [i, and many more.
isprint (isp)	@,161-255	A list of characters that can be displayed directly to the screen. Non-UNIX systems may have different default values.
makeef (mef)	*/tmp/vim##.err*	The errorfile name for the :make command. Non-UNIX systems have different default values. The ## is replaced by a number to make the name unique.
makeprg (mp)	make	The program to use for the :make command. % and # in the value are expanded.
mouse		Enable the mouse in non-GUI versions of *vim*. This works for MS-DOS, Win32, and *xterm*. See the online help for details.
mousehide (mh)	nomousehide	Hides the mouse pointer during typing. Restores the pointer when the mouse is moved.
paste	nopaste	Changes a large number of options so that pasting into a *vim* window with a mouse does not mangle the pasted text. Turning it off restores those options to their previous values. See the online help for details.
ruler (ru)	noruler	Shows the line and column number of the cursor position.
secure	nosecure	Disables certain kinds of commands in the startup file. Automatically enabled if you don't own the *.vimrc* and *.exrc* files.

Table C-4: vim 5.1 Set Options (continued)

Option	Default	Description
shellpipe (sp)		The shell string to use for capturing the output from :make into a file. The default value depends upon the shell.
shellredir (srr)		The shell string for capturing the output of a filter into a temporary file. The default value depends upon the shell.
showmode (smd)	*vim* default: smd, *vi* default: nosmd	Put a message in the status line for insert, replace, and visual modes.
sidescroll (ss)	0	How many columns to scroll horizontally. The value zero puts the cursor in the middle of the screen.
smartcase (scs)	nosmartcase	Overrides the ignorecase option if the search pattern contains uppercase characters.
suffixes	*.bak,~,.o,.h, .info,.swp	When multiple files match a pattern during filename completion, the value of this variable sets a priority among them, in order to pick the one *vim* will actually use.
taglength (tl)	0	Defines number of characters that are significant for tags. Default (zero) means that all characters are significant.
tagrelative (tr)	*vim* default: tr, *vi* default: notr	Filenames in a *tags* file from another directory are taken to be relative to the directory where the *tags* file is.
tags (tag)	*./tags,tags*	Filenames for the :tag command, i.e., add the colon and put the whole thing in courier, separated by spaces or commas. The leading ./ is replaced with the full path to the current file.
tildeop (top)	notildeop	Makes the ~ command behave like an operator.
undolevels (ul)	1000	The maximum number of changes that can be undone. A value of 0 means *vi* compatibility: one level of undo and u undoes itself. Non-UNIX systems may have different default values.

Table C-4: vim 5.1 Set Options (continued)

Option	Default	Description
viminfo (vi)		Reads the *viminfo* file upon startup and writes it upon exiting. The value is complex; it controls the different kinds of information that *vim* will store in the file. See the online help for details.
writebackup (wb)	writebackup	Make a backup before overwriting a file. The backup is removed after the file was successfully written, unless the `backup` option is also on.

vile 8.0 Options

vile 8.0 has a total of 92 options that affect its behavior. Table C-5 summarizes the most important ones. Most options described in Table C-1 are not repeated here.

Table C-5: vile 8.0 Set Options

Option	Default	Description
alt-tabpos	noatp	Controls whether the cursor sits at the left or right end of the whitespace representing a TAB character.
animated	animated	Automatically updates the contents of scratch buffers when their contents would change.
autobuffer (ab)	autobuffer	Uses "most-recently-used" style buffering; the buffers are sorted in order of use. Otherwise, buffers remain in the order in which they were edited.
autosave (as)	noautosave	Automatic file saving. Writes the file after every `autosavecnt` characters of inserted text.
autosavecnt (ascnt)	256	Specifies after how many inserted characters automatic saves take place.
backspacelimit (bl)	backspacelimit	If disabled, then in insert mode you can backspace past the point at which the insert began.
backup-style	off	Controls how backup files are created when writing a file. Possible values are `off` for no backups, `.bak` for DOS style backups, and `tilde` for *emacs* style *hello.c˜* backups under UNIX.

Table C-5: vile 8.0 Set Options (continued)

Option	Default	Description
bcolor		Sets the background color on systems that support it.
check-modtime	nocheck-modtime	Issues a *file newer than buffer* warning if the file has changed since last read or written, and prompts for confirmation.
cmode	off	A built-in major mode for C code.
comment-prefix	^\s*\(\s*[#*>]\)\+	Describes the leading part of a line that should be left alone when reformatting comments. The default value is good for *Makefile*, shell and C comments, and email.
comments	^\s*/\?\(\s*[#*>]\)\+/\?\s*$	A regular expression defining commented paragraph delimiters. Its purpose is to preserve paragraphs inside comments when reformatting.
dirc	nodirc	*vile* checks each name when scanning directories for filename completion. This allows you to distinguish between directory names and filenames in the prompt.
dos	nodos	Strips out the CR from CR-LF pairs when reading files, and puts them back when writing. New buffers for non-existent files inherit the line-style of the operating system, whatever the value of dos.
fcolor		Sets the foreground color on systems that support it.
fence-begin	/*	Regular expressions for the start and end of simple, non-nestable fences, such as C comments.
fence-end	*/	
fence-if	^\s*#\s*if	Regular expression marking the start, "else if," "else," and end of line-oriented, nested fences, such as C-preprocessor control lines.
fence-elif	^\s*#\s*elif\>	
fence-else	^\s*#\s*else\>	
fence-fi	^\s*#\s*endif\>	
fence-pairs	{}()[]	Each pair of characters denotes a set of "fences" that should be matched with %.

Table C-5: vile 8.0 Set Options (continued)

Option	Default	Description
glob	!echo %s	Controls how wildcard characters (e.g., * and ?) are treated in prompts for filenames. A value of off disables expansion, and on uses the internal globber, which can handle normal shell wildcards and ~ notation. The default value for UNIX guarantees compatibility with your shell.
history (hi)	history	Logs commands from the colon command line in the [History] buffer.
horizscroll (hs)	horizscroll	Moving off the end of a long line shifts the whole screen sideways. If not set, only the current line shifts.
linewrap (lw)	nolinewrap	Wraps long logical lines onto multiple screen lines.
maplonger	nomaplonger	The map facility matches against the longest possible mapped sequence, not the shortest.
meta-insert-bindings (mib)	nomib	Controls behavior of 8-bit characters during insert. Normally, key-bindings are only operational when in command mode: when in insert mode, all characters are self-inserting. If this mode is on, and a meta-character (i.e., a character with the eighth bit set) is typed which is bound to a function, then that function binding will be honored and executed from within insert mode. Any unbound meta-characters will remain self-inserting.
mini-edit	^G	The character that toggles the editing mode in the minibuffer.
mini-hilite (mh)	reverse	Defines the highlight attribute to use when the user toggles the editing mode in the minibuffer.
popup-choices (pc)	delayed	Controls the use of a pop-up window for help in doing completion. The value is one of off for no window, immediate for an immediate pop-up, and delayed to wait for a second TAB key.
preamble (pre)		A regular expression describing the first line of filenames for which the corresponding major mode will be set.

Table C-5: vile 8.0 Set Options (continued)

Option	Default	Description
resolve-links	noresolve-links	If set, *vile* fully resolves filenames in cases where some path components are symbolic links. This helps avoid multiple unintentional edits of the same physical file via different pathnames.
ruler	noruler	Shows the current line and column in the status line, as well as what percentage of the current buffer's lines lie in front of the cursor.
showmode (smd)	noshowmode	Display an indicator on the modeline for insert and replace modes.
sideways	0	Prompts for a new value for the sideways scroll offset, which controls by how many characters the screen scrolls to the left or right. The value of 0 moves the screen by one third.
suffixes (suf)		A regular expression describing filenames for which the corresponding major mode will be set. Used as part of the major mode facility, not by itself.
tabinsert (ti)	tabinsert	Allow the physical insertion of tab characters into the buffer. If turned off (notabinsert), *vile* will never insert a TAB into a buffer; instead it will always insert the appropriate number of spaces.
tagignorecase (tc)	notagignorecase	Makes tag searches ignore case.
taglength (tl)	0	Defines number of characters that are significant for tags. Default (zero) means that all characters are significant. This does not effect tags picked up from the cursor, they are always matched exactly. (This is different from the other editors.)
tagrelative (tr)	tagrelative	When using a *tags* file in another directory, filenames in that *tags* file are considered to be relative to the directory where the *tags* file is.
tags	*tags*	A space separated list of files in which to look up tag references.
tagword (tw)	notagword	Uses the whole word under the cursor for the tag lookup, not just the sub-word starting at the current cursor position.

Table C-5: vile 8.0 Set Options (continued)

Option	Default	Description
undolimit (ul)	10	Limits how many changes may be undone. The value zero means "no limit."
unprintable-as-octal (uo)	nonprintable-as-octal	Displays non-printing characters with the eighth bit set in octal. Otherwise, uses hexadecimal. Non-printing characters whose eighth bit is not set are always displayed in control character notation.
visual-matches	none	Controls highlighting of all matching occurrences of a search pattern. The possible values are none for no highlighting, or underline, bold, and reverse for those kinds of highlighting. Colors may also be used on systems that support it.
xterm-mouse	noxterm-mouse	Allows use of the mouse from inside an *xterm*. See the online help for details.

Problem Checklists

This appendix consolidates the problem checklists that are provided throughout the text. Here they are presented in one place for ease of reference.

Problems Opening Files

✓ *When you invoke* vi, *the message* [open mode] *appears.*

Your terminal type is probably incorrectly identified. Quit the editing session immediately by typing :q Check the environment variable $TERM. It should be set to the name of your terminal. Or ask your system administrator to provide an adequate terminal type setting.

✓ *You see one of the following messages:*

```
Visual needs addressable cursor or upline capability
Bad termcap entry
Termcap entry too long
terminal:  Unknown terminal type
Block device required
Not a typewriter
```

Your terminal type is either undefined, or there's probably something wrong with your *terminfo* or *termcap* entry. Enter :q to quit. Check your $TERM environment variable, or ask your system administrator to select a terminal type for your environment.

✓ *A* [new file] *message appears when you think a file already exists.*

You are probably in the wrong directory. Enter :q to quit. Then check to see that you are in the correct directory for that file (enter pwd at the UNIX prompt). If you are in the right directory, check the list of files in the directory (with ls) to see whether the file exists under a slightly different name.

✓ *You invoke* vi, *but you get a colon prompt (indicating that you're in* ex *line-editing mode).*

You probably typed an interrupt before *vi* could draw the screen. Enter *vi* by typing vi at the *ex* prompt (:).

✓ *One of the following messages appears:*

```
[Read only]
File is read only
Permission denied
```

"Read only" means that you can only look at the file; you cannot save any changes you make. You may have invoked *vi* in *view* mode (with view or vi -R), or you do not have write permission for the file. See the section "Problems Saving Files" below.

✓ *One of the following messages appears:*

```
Bad file number
Block special file
Character special file
Directory
Executable
Non-ascii file
file non-ASCII
```

The file you've called up to edit is not a regular text file. Type :q! to quit, then check the file you wish to edit, perhaps with the *file* command.

✓ *When you type* :q *because of one of the above difficulties, the message appears:*

```
No write since last change (:quit! overrides).
```

You have modified the file without realizing it. Type :q! to leave *vi*. Your changes from this session will not be saved in the file.

Problems Saving Files

✓ *You try to write your file, but you get one of the following messages:*

```
File exists
File file exists - use w!
[Existing file]
File is read only
```

Type :w! *file* to overwrite the existing file, or type :w *newfile* to save the edited version in a new file.

✓ *You want to write a file, but you don't have write permission for it. You get the message "Permission denied."*

Use `:w newfile` to write out the buffer into a new file. If you have write permission for the directory, you can use `mv` to replace the original version with your copy of it. If you don't have write permission for the directory, type `:w pathname/file` to write out the buffer to a directory in which you do have write permission (such as your home directory, or */tmp*).

✓ *You try to write your file, but you get a message telling you that the file system is full.*

Type `:!rm junkfile` to delete a (large) unneeded file and free some space. (Starting an *ex* command with an exclamation point gives you access to UNIX.)

Or type `:!df` to see whether there's any space on another file system. If there is, choose a directory on that file system and write your file to it with `:w pathname`. (`df` is the UNIX command to check a *d*isk's *f*ree space.)

✓ *The system puts you into open mode and tells you that the file system is full.*

The disk with *vi*'s temporary files is filled up. Type `:!ls /tmp` to see whether there are any files you can remove to gain some disk space.* If there are, create a temporary UNIX shell from which you can remove files or issue other UNIX commands. You can create a shell by typing `:sh`; type CTRL-D or `exit` to terminate the shell and return to *vi*. (On most UNIX systems, when using a job-control shell, you can simply type CTRL-Z to suspend *vi* and return to the UNIX prompt; type `fg` to return to *vi*.) Once you've freed up some space, write your file with `:w!`.

✓ *You try to write your file, but you get a message telling you that your disk quota has been reached.*

Try to force the system to save your buffer with the *ex* command `:pre` (short for `:preserve`). If that doesn't work, look for some files to remove. Use `:sh` (or CTRL-Z if you are using a job-control system) to move out of *vi* and remove files. Use CTRL-D (or `fg`) to return to *vi* when you're done. Then write your file with `:w!`.

---

* Your *vi* may keep its temporary files in */usr/tmp*, */var/tmp*, or your current directory; you may need to poke around a bit to figure out where exactly you've run out of room.

Problems Getting to Visual Mode

✓   *While editing in* vi, *you accidentally end up in the* ex *editor.*

A Q in the command mode of *vi* invokes *ex.* Any time you are in *ex*, the command vi returns you to the *vi* editor.

Problems with vi Commands

✓   *When you type commands, text jumps around on the screen and nothing works the way it's supposed to.*

Make sure you're not typing the J command when you mean j.

You may have hit the ⌊CAPS⌋ key without noticing it. *vi* is case-sensitive. That is, uppercase commands (I, A, J, etc.) are different from lowercase commands (i, a, j), so all your commands are being interpreted not as lowercase but as uppercase commands. Press the ⌊CAPS⌋ key again to return to lowercase, press ⌊ESC⌋ to ensure that you are in command mode, then type either U to restore the last line changed or u to undo the last command. You'll probably also have to do some additional editing to fully restore the garbled part of your file.

Problems with Deletions

✓   *You've deleted the wrong text and you want to get it back.*

There are several ways to recover deleted text. If you've just deleted something and you realize you want it back, simply type u to undo the last command (for example, a dd). This works only if you haven't given any further commands, since u only undoes the most recent command. On the other hand, a U will restore the line to its pristine state; the way it was before *any* changes were applied to it.

You can still recover a recent deletion, however, by using the p command, since *vi* saves the last nine deletions in nine numbered deletion buffers. If you know, for example, that the third deletion back is the one you want to restore, type:

    "3p

to "put" the contents of buffer number 3 on the line below the cursor. This works only for a deleted *line*. Words, or a portion of a line, are not saved in a buffer. If you want to restore a deleted word or line fragment, and u won't work, use the p command by itself. This restores whatever you've last deleted.

vi and the Internet

Sure, vi is friendly. It's just particular about who it makes friends with.

Being the "standard" UNIX screen editor since at least 1980 has enshrined *vi* firmly in UNIX culture.

vi helped build UNIX, and UNIX in turn built the foundation for today's Internet. Thus, it was inevitable that there be at least one Internet web site devoted to *vi*. This appendix describes some of the *vi* resources that are available for the *vi* connoisseur.

Where to start: There is surely no activity with more built-in obsolescence than publishing World Wide Web sites in a printed book. We have tried to publish URLs that we hope will have a reasonable lifetime.

In the meantime, the "Tips" section of the *elvis* documentation lists interesting *vi*-related web sites (that's where we started), and the USENET *comp.editors* newsgroup is also a good place to look.

vi Web Sites

There are two primary *vi*-related web sites, the *vi Lover's Home Page*, by Thomer M. Gil, and the *Vi Pages*, by Sven Guckes. Each contains a large number of links to interesting *vi*-related items.

The vi Lover's Home Page

You will find the *vi Lover's Home Page* at *http://www.thomer.com/thomer/vi/vi.html*. This site contains the following items:

- A table of all known *vi* clones, with links to the source code or binary distributions

- Links to other *vi* sites, including the *Vi Pages*, by Sven Guckes

- A large number of links to *vi* documentation, manuals, help, and tutorials, at a number of different levels

- *vi* macros for writing HTML documents and solving the Towers of Hanoi, and *ftp* sites for other macro sets

- Miscellaneous *vi* links: poems, a story about the "real history" of *vi*, *vi* versus *emacs* discussions, and *vi* coffee mugs (see below)

There are other things there too; this makes a great starting point.

The Vi Pages

The *Vi Pages* can be found at *http://www.math.fu-berlin.de/~guckes/vi*. This site contains the following items:

- A detailed comparison of options and features among different *vi* clones

- Screen shots of different versions of *vi*

- A table listing many *vi* clones, as well as a list with contact information (name, address, URL) for the clones

- Pointers to several FAQ (Frequently Asked Questions) files

- Some cute quotes about *vi*, such as the one that opened this chapter

- Other links, including a link to the *vi* coffee mugs

The *vi Lover's Home Page* refers to this web site as "the only Vi site on this planet better than the one you're looking at." This site too is well worth checking out.

VI Powered!

One of the cuter items we found is the *VI Powered* logo (Figure E-1). This is a small GIF file you can add to your personal web page to show that you used *vi* to create it.

The original home page for the *VI Powered* logo is *http://www.abast.es/~avelle/vi.html*. This page is written in Spanish. The English home page is at *http://www.darryl.com/vi.html*. Instructions for adding the logo are at *http://www.darryl.com/addlogo.html*. Doing so consists of several simple steps:

1. Download the logo. Enter *http://www.darryl.com/vipower.gif* into your (graphical) web browser, and then save it to a file.

Figure E-1: VI Powered!

2.   Add the following code to your web page in an appropriate place:

```
<A HREF="http://www.darryl.com/vi.html">
<IMG SRC="vipower.gif">
</A>
```

This puts the logo into your page and makes it into a hypertext link, that when selected will go to the *VI Powered* home page. You may wish to add an `ALT="This Web Page is vi Powered"` attribute to the `<IMG>` tag, for users of non-graphical browsers.

3.   Add the following code to the `<HEAD>` section of your web page:

```
<META name="editor" content="/usr/bin/vi">
```

Just as the Real Programmer will eschew a WYSIWYG word processor in favor of *troff*, so too, Real Webmasters eschew fancy HTML authoring tools in favor of *vi*. You can use the *VI Powered* logo to display this fact with pride.

You can find additional logos at *http://www.vim.org/pics.html* ("made in *vi*," "designed in *vi*," and so on). One of these may suit your fancy better than the *VI Powered* logo.

vi for Java Lovers

Despite the title, this subsection is about the java you drink, not the Java you program in.*

Our hypothetical Real Programmer, while using *vi* to write her C++ code, her *troff* documentation, and her web page, undoubtedly will want a cup of coffee now and then. She can now drink her coffee from a mug with a *vi* command reference printed on it!

The URL is *http://www.vireference.com/vimug.htm*. The mugs come in sets of four, with a concise *vi* command summary printed on the mug. The web site has pricing and shipping information; you might want to split a set of four with one or more friends.

---

* Although it's fitting, somehow, that Java came from Sun Microsystems, where Bill Joy, *vi*'s original author, is a founder and vice president.

Online vi Tutorial

The two home pages have a large number of links to documentation on *vi*. Of special note, though, is a nine-part online tutorial from *Unix World* magazine, by Walter Zintz. The starting off point is *http://www.wcmh.com/uworld/archives/95/ tutorial/009/009.html*. (You're probably better off just following the link from one of two *vi* home pages.) The tutorial covers the following topics:

- Editor fundamentals

- Line-mode addresses

- The g (global) command

- The substitute command

- The editing environment (the **set** command, tags, and **EXINIT** and *.exrc*)

- Addresses and columns

- The replacement commands, r and R

- Automatic indentation

- Macros

Also available with the tutorial is an online quiz that you can use to see how well you've absorbed the material in the tutorial. Or you can just try the quiz directly, to see how well we've done with this book!

Amaze Your Friends!

In the long term, perhaps the most useful items are in the collection of *vi* related information in the *alf.uib.no ftp* archives. The original archives are at *ftp://afl.uib.no/pub/vi*. We had little success with this site, however the archives are mirrored at *ftp://ftp.uu.net/pub/text-processing/vi*. The file *INDEX* in that directory describes what's in the archives, and lists additional mirrors that may be geographically closer to you.

Unfortunately, these files were last updated in May of 1995. Fortunately, *vi*'s basic functionality has not changed, and the information and macros in the archive are still useful. The archive has four subdirectories:

docs
    Documentation on *vi*, also some *comp.editors* postings.

macros
    vi macros.

comp.editors

> Various materials posted to *comp.editors*.

programs

> Source code for *vi* clones for various platforms (and other programs). Take things from here with caution, as much of it is out of date.

The *docs* and *macros* are the most interesting. The *docs* directory has a large number of articles and references, ranging from beginner's guides, explanations of bugs, quick references, and many short "how to" kinds of articles (e.g., how to capitalize just the first letter of a sentence in *vi*). There's even a song about *vi*!

The *macros* directory has over 50 files in it that do different things. We mention just three of them. (Files whose names end in *.Z* are compressed with the UNIX *compress* program. They can be uncompressed with either *uncompress* or *gunzip*.)

evi.tar.Z

> An *emacs* "emulator." The idea behind it is to turn *vi* into a modeless editor (one that is always in input mode, with commands done with control keys). It is actually done with a shell script that replaces the EXINIT environment variable.

hanoi.Z

> This is perhaps the most famous of the unusual uses of *vi*; a set of macros that solve the Towers of Hanoi programming problem. This program simply displays the moves, it does not actually draw the disks. For fun, we have reprinted it in the sidebar.

turing.tar.Z

> This program uses *vi* to implement an actual Turing machine! It's rather amazing to watch it execute the programs.

There are many, many more interesting macros, including Perl and RCS modes and even a Word Star emulator.

Tastes Great, Less Filling

We can't discuss *vi* as part of UNIX culture without acknowledging what is perhaps the longest running debate in the UNIX community,* *vi* versus *emacs*.

Discussions about which is better have cropped up on *comp.editors* (and other newsgroups) for years and years. You will find summaries of some of these discussions in the *ftp* archives described above. You will find pointers to more recent versions on the web pages.

---

* OK, it's really a religious war, but we're trying to be nice. (The other religious war, BSD vs. System V, was settled by POSIX. System V won, although BSD received significant concessions. ☺)

The Towers of Hanoi, vi Version

```
" From: gregm@otc.otca.oz.au (Greg McFarlane)
" Newsgroups: comp.sources.d,alt.sources,comp.editors
" Subject: VI SOLVES HANOI
" Date: 19 Feb 91 01:32:14 GMT
"
" Submitted-by: gregm@otc.otca.oz.au
" Archive-name: hanoi.vi.macros/part01
"
" Everyone seems to be writing stupid Tower of Hanoi programs.
" Well, here is the stupidest of them all: the hanoi solving
" vi macros.
"
" Save this article, unshar it, and run uudecode on
" hanoi.vi.macros.uu. This will give you the macro file
" hanoi.vi.macros.
" Then run vi (with no file: just type "vi") and type:
"       :so hanoi.vi.macros
"       g
" and watch it go.
"
" The default height of the tower is 7 but can be easily changed
" by editing the macro file.
"
" The disks aren't actually shown in this version, only numbers
" representing each disk, but I believe it is possible to write
" some macros to show the disks moving about as well. Any takers?
"
" (For maze solving macros, see alt.sources or comp.editors)
"
" Greg
"
" ----------- REAL FILE STARTS HERE ---------------
set remap
set noterse
set wrapscan
" to set the height of the tower, change the digit in the following
" two lines to the height you want (select from 1 to 9)
map t 7
map! t 7
map L 1G/t^MX/^0^M$P1GJ$An$BGC0e$X0E0F$X/T^M@f^M@h^M$A1GJ@f0l$Xn$PU
map g IL
map I KMYNOQNOSkRTV
map J /^0[^t]*$^M
map X x
map P p
map U L
map A "fyl
```

The Towers of Hanoi (continued)

```
map B "hyl
map C "fp
map e "fy2l
map E "hp
map F "hy2l
map K 1Go^[
map M dG
map N yy
map O p
map q tllD
map Y o0123456789Z^[0q
map Q 0iT^[
map R $rn
map S $r$
map T ko0^M0^M^M^[
map V Go/^[
```

Some of the better arguments in favor of *vi* are:

- *vi* is available on every UNIX system. If you are installing systems, or moving from system to system, you might have to use *vi* anyway.

- You can usually keep your fingers on the home row of the keyboard. This is a big plus for touch typists.

- Commands are one (or sometimes two) regular characters; they are much easier to type than all of the control- and meta-characters that *emacs* requires.

- *vi* is generally smaller and less resource-intensive than *emacs*. Startup times are appreciably faster, sometimes up to a factor of 10.

- Now that the *vi* clones have added features like incremental searching, multiple windows and buffers, GUI interfaces, syntax highlighting and smart indenting, and programmability via extension languages, the functional gap between the two editors has narrowed significantly, if not disappeared entirely.

To be complete, two more items should be mentioned. First, there are actually two versions of *emacs* that are popular: the original GNU *emacs*, and *xemacs*, which is derived from an earlier version of GNU *emacs*. Both have advantages and disadvantages, and their own sets of devotees.*

Second, while GNU *emacs* has always had *vi*-emulation packages, until recently, they have not been very good. This has changed. The "viper mode" is reputed to

---

* Who undoubtedly share a joint distaste for *vi*! ☺

be an excellent *vi* emulation. It can serve as a bridge for learning *emacs* for those who are interested in doing so.

To conclude, always remember that you are the final judge of a program's utility. You should use the tools that make you the most productive, and for many tasks, *vi* and its clones are excellent tools.

vi Quotes

Finally, here are some more *vi* quotes, courtesy of Bram Moolenaar, *vim*'s author:

> THEOREM: *vi* is perfect.

> PROOF: VI in roman numerals is 6. The natural numbers less than 6 which divide 6 are 1, 2, and 3. 1 + 2 + 3 = 6. So 6 is a perfect number. Therefore, *vi* is perfect.

> — Arthur Tateishi

A reaction from Nathan T. Oelger:

> So, where does the above leave *vim?* VIM in roman numerals might be: (1000 − (5 + 1)) = 994, which happens to be equal to 2*496+2. 496 is divisible by 1, 2, 4, 8, 16, 31, 62, 124, and 248 and 1+2+4+8+16+31+62+124+248 = 496. So, 496 is a perfect number. Therefore, *vim* is twice as perfect as *vi*, *plus* a couple extra bits of goodies. ☺

> That is, *vim* is *better* than perfect.

Sven Guckes points out a nice quote from the Tigger's Song in *Winnie the Pooh and Tigger Too*:

> The wonderful thing about Tiggers
> Is Tiggers are wonderful chaps
> They're loaded with *vim* and *vig*or ...

This quote seems to sum it up for the true *vi* lover.

> To me *vi* is zen. To use *vi* is to practice zen. Every command is a koan. Profound to the user, unintelligible to the uninitiated. You discover truth every time you use it.

> — Satish Reddy

Index

About the Author

Linda Lamb is an editor with O'Reilly & Associates, currently working on a new series of in-depth, consumer health books called Patient-Centered Guides. She has worked with O'Reilly for fourteen years in various guises, including technical writer, editor of technical books, and marketing manager. *vi* is still her favorite text editor, by far. It's fast, powerful, and ergonomic.

Arnold Robbins, an Atlanta native, is a professional programmer and technical author. He has been working with UNIX systems since 1980, when he was introduced to a PDP-11 running a version of Sixth Edition UNIX. He was forced to learn *vi* around 1983 when his graduate school's VAX UNIX system did not have a port of the locally written screen editor, and has been using it ever since. He has also been a heavy *awk* user since 1987, when he became involved with *gawk*, the GNU project's version of *awk*. As a member of the POSIX 1003.2 balloting group, he helped shape the POSIX standard for *awk*. He is currently the maintainer of *gawk* and its documentation. The documentation is available from the Free Software Foundation (*http://www.gnu.org*) and has also been published by SSC (*http://www.ssc.com*) as *Effective AWK Programming*. He is also co-author of the second edition of O'Reilly's *sed & awk*. Since late 1997, he and his family have been living happily in Israel.

Colophon

Our look is the result of reader comments, our own experimentation, and feedback from distribution channels. Distinctive covers complement our distinctive approach to technical topics, breathing personality and life into potentially dry subjects.

The animal featured on the cover of *Learning the vi Editor* is a tarsier, a nocturnal mammal related to the lemur. Its generic name, Tarsius, is derived from the animal's very long ankle bone, the tarsus. The tarsier is a native of the East Indies jungles from Sumatra to the Philippines and Sulawesi, where it lives in the trees, leaping from branch to branch with extreme agility and speed.

A small animal, the tarsier's body is only six inches long, followed by a ten inch tufted tail. It is covered in soft, brown or grey silky fur, has a round face, and huge eyes. Its arms and legs are long and slender as are its digits which are tipped with rounded, fleshy pads to improve the tarsier's grip on trees. Tarsiers are active only at night, hiding during the day in tangles of vines or in the tops of tall trees. They subsist mainly on insects, and, though very curious animals, tend to be loners.

Edie Freedman designed the cover of this book, using a 19th-century engraving from the Dover Pictorial Archive. The cover layout was produced by Kathleen Wilson, using QuarkXPress 3.32 with ITC Garamond font from Adobe.

Nicole Gipson Arigo was the production editor and project manager. Jane Ellin proofread the book. Claire Cloutier LeBlanc, Madeleine Newell, Melanie Wang, and Sheryl Avruch provided quality control reviews. Seth Maislin wrote the index, and Robert Romano created the illustrations in Adobe Photoshop 4.0 and Macromedia Freehand 7.0. The inside layout was designed by Edie Freedman and Nancy Priest and was formatted in SGML by Len Muellner and Chris Maden, using ITC Garamond Light and ITC Garamond Book fonts. This colophon was written by Michael Kalantarian.

Whenever possible, our books use a durable and flexible lay-flat binding. If the page count exceeds the lay-flat binding's page limit, then perfect binding is used.

 # More Titles from O'Reilly

UNIX Basics

Learning the UNIX Operating System, 4th Edition

By Jerry Peek, Grace Todino & John Strang
4th Edition December 1997
106 pages, ISBN 1-56592-390-1

If you are new to UNIX, this concise introduction will tell you just what you need to get started and no more. The new fourth edition covers the Linux operating system and is an ideal primer for someone just starting with UNIX or Linux, as well as for Mac and PC users who encounter a UNIX system on the Internet. This classic book, still the most effective introduction to UNIX in print, now includes a quick-reference card.

Learning the Korn Shell

By Bill Rosenblatt
1st Edition June 1993
360 pages, ISBN 1-56592-054-6

A thorough introduction to the Korn shell, both as a user interface and as a programming language. This book provides a clear explanation of the Korn shell's features, including ksh string operations, co-processes, signals and signal handling, and command-line interpretation. Learning the Korn Shell also includes real-life programming examples and a Korn shell debugger (kshdb).

Learning GNU Emacs, 2nd Edition

By Debra Cameron, Bill Rosenblatt & Eric Raymond
2nd Edition September 1996
560 pages, ISBN 1-56592-152-6

Learning GNU Emacs is an introduction to Version 19.30 of the GNU Emacs editor, one of the most widely used and powerful editors available under UNIX. It provides a solid introduction to basic editing, a look at several important "editing modes" (special Emacs features for editing specific types of documents, including email, Usenet News, and the World Wide Web), and a brief introduction to customization and Emacs LISP programming. The book is aimed at new Emacs users, whether or not they are programmers. Includes quick-reference card.

Volume 3M: X Window System User's Guide, Motif Edition, 2nd Edition

By Valerie Quercia & Tim O'Reilly
2nd Edition January 1993
956 pages, ISBN 1-56592-015-5

The X Window System User's Guide, Motif Edition orients the new user to window system concepts and provides detailed tutorials for many client programs, including the xtermterminal emulator and the twm, uwm, and mwmwindow managers. Later chapters explain how to customize the X environment. Revised for Motif 1.2 and X11 Release 5.

Using csh and tcsh

By Paul DuBois
1st Edition August 1995
242 pages, ISBN 1-56592-132-1

Using csh and tcsh describes from the beginning how to use these shells interactively to get your work done faster with less typing. You'll learn how to make your prompt tell you where you are (no more pwd); use what you've typed before (history); type long command lines with few keystrokes (command and filename completion); remind yourself of filenames when in the middle of typing a command; and edit a botched command without retyping it.

Web Programming

ASP in a Nutshell

By A. Keyton Weissinger
1st Edition February 1999
426 pages, ISBN 1-56592-490-8

This detailed reference contains all the information Web developers need to create effective Active Server Pages (ASP) applications. It focuses on how features are used in a real application and highlights little-known or undocumented aspects, enabling even experienced developers to advance their ASP applications to new levels.

O'REILLY®

TO ORDER: **800-998-9938** • **order@oreilly.com** • **http://www.oreilly.com/**
OUR PRODUCTS ARE AVAILABLE AT A BOOKSTORE OR SOFTWARE STORE NEAR YOU.
FOR INFORMATION: **800-998-9938** • **707-829-0515** • **info@oreilly.com**

Web Programming

CGI Programming with Perl, 2nd Edition

By Shishir Gundavaram
2nd Edition July 2000 (est.)
450 pages (est.), ISBN 1-56592-419-3

Completely rewritten, this comprehensive explanation of CGI for those who want to provide their own Web servers features Perl 5 techniques and shows how to use two popular Perl modules, CGI.pm and CGI_lite. It also covers speed-up techniques, such as FastCGI and mod_perl, and new material on searching and indexing, security, generating graphics through ImageMagick, database access through DBI, Apache configuration, and combining CGI with JavaScript.

Dynamic HTML: The Definitive Reference

By Danny Goodman
1st Edition July 1998
1088 pages, ISBN 1-56592-494-0

Dynamic HTML: The Definitive Reference is an indispensable compendium for Web content developers. It contains complete reference material for all of the HTML tags, CSS style attributes, browser document objects, and JavaScript objects supported by the various standards and the latest versions of Netscape Navigator and Microsoft Internet Explorer.

PHP Pocket Reference

By Rasmus Lerdorf
1st Edition January 2000
120 pages, ISBN 1-56592-769-9

The *PHP Pocket Reference* is a handy quick reference for PHP, an open-source, HTML-embedded scripting language that can be used to develop web applications. This small book acts both as a perfect tutorial for learning the basics of PHP syntax and as a reference to the vast array of functions provided by PHP.

JavaScript: The Definitive Guide, 3rd Edition

By David Flanagan
3rd Edition June 1998
800 pages, ISBN 1-56592-392-8

This third edition of the definitive reference to JavaScript covers the latest version of the language, JavaScript 1.2, as supported by Netscape Navigator 4 and Internet Explorer 4. JavaScript, which is being standardized under the name ECMAScript, is a scripting language that can be embedded directly in HTML to give Web pages programming-language capabilities.

Learning VBScript

By Paul Lomax
1st Edition July 1997
616 pages, Includes CD-ROM
ISBN 1-56592-247-6

This definitive guide shows Web developers how to take full advantage of client-side scripting with the VBScript language. In addition to basic language features, it covers the Internet Explorer object model and discusses techniques for client-side scripting, like adding ActiveX controls to a Web page or validating data before sending it to the server. Includes CD-ROM with over 170 code samples.

How to stay in touch with O'Reilly

1. Visit Our Award-Winning Web Site

http://www.oreilly.com/

★ "Top 100 Sites on the Web" —*PC Magazine*
★ "Top 5% Web sites" —*Point Communications*
★ "3-Star site" —*The McKinley Group*

Our web site contains a library of comprehensive product information (including book excerpts and tables of contents), downloadable software, background articles, interviews with technology leaders, links to relevant sites, book cover art, and more. File us in your Bookmarks or Hotlist!

2. Join Our Email Mailing Lists

New Product Releases

To receive automatic email with brief descriptions of all new O'Reilly products as they are released, send email to:
listproc@online.oreilly.com
Put the following information in the first line of your message (*not* in the Subject field):
subscribe oreilly-news

O'Reilly Events

If you'd also like us to send information about trade show events, special promotions, and other O'Reilly events, send email to:
listproc@online.oreilly.com
Put the following information in the first line of your message (*not* in the Subject field):
subscribe oreilly-events

3. Get Examples from Our Books via FTP

There are two ways to access an archive of example files from our books:

Regular FTP

- ftp to:
  ftp.oreilly.com
  (login: anonymous
  password: your email address)
- Point your web browser to:
  ftp://ftp.oreilly.com/

FTPMAIL

- Send an email message to:
  ftpmail@online.oreilly.com
  (Write "help" in the message body)

4. Contact Us via Email

order@oreilly.com
To place a book or software order online. Good for North American and international customers.

subscriptions@oreilly.com
To place an order for any of our newsletters or periodicals.

books@oreilly.com
General questions about any of our books.

software@oreilly.com
For general questions and product information about our software. Check out O'Reilly Software Online at **http://software.oreilly.com/** for software and technical support information. Registered O'Reilly software users send your questions to: **website-support@oreilly.com**

cs@oreilly.com
For answers to problems regarding your order or our products.

booktech@oreilly.com
For book content technical questions or corrections.

proposals@oreilly.com
To submit new book or software proposals to our editors and product managers.

international@oreilly.com
For information about our international distributors or translation queries. For a list of our distributors outside of North America check out:
http://www.oreilly.com/www/order/country.html

5. Work with Us

Check out our website for current employment opportunites:
www.jobs@oreilly.com
Click on "Work with Us"

O'Reilly & Associates, Inc.
101 Morris Street, Sebastopol, CA 95472 USA
TEL   707-829-0515 or 800-998-9938
       (6am to 5pm PST)
FAX   707-829-0104

International Distributors

UK, EUROPE, MIDDLE EAST AND AFRICA (EXCEPT FRANCE, GERMANY, AUSTRIA, SWITZERLAND, LUXEMBOURG, LIECHTENSTEIN, AND EASTERN EUROPE)

INQUIRIES
O'Reilly UK Limited
4 Castle Street
Farnham
Surrey, GU9 7HS
United Kingdom
Telephone: 44-1252-711776
Fax: 44-1252-734211
Email: information@oreilly.co.uk

ORDERS
Wiley Distribution Services Ltd.
1 Oldlands Way
Bognor Regis
West Sussex PO22 9SA
United Kingdom
Telephone: 44-1243-779777
Fax: 44-1243-820250
Email: cs-books@wiley.co.uk

FRANCE

INQUIRIES
Éditions O'Reilly
18 rue Séguier
75006 Paris, France
Tel: 33-1-40-51-52-30
Fax: 33-1-40-51-52-31
Email: france@editions-oreilly.fr

ORDERS
GEODIF
61, Bd Saint-Germain
75240 Paris Cedex 05, France
Tel: 33-1-44-41-46-16 (French books)
Tel: 33-1-44-41-11-87 (English books)
Fax: 33-1-44-41-11-44
Email: distribution@eyrolles.com

GERMANY, SWITZERLAND, AUSTRIA, EASTERN EUROPE, LUXEMBOURG, AND LIECHTENSTEIN

INQUIRIES & ORDERS
O'Reilly Verlag
Balthasarstr. 81
D-50670 Köln
Germany
Telephone: 49-221-973160-91
Fax: 49-221-973160-8
Email: anfragen@oreilly.de (inquiries)
Email: order@oreilly.de (orders)

CANADA (FRENCH LANGUAGE BOOKS)

Les Éditions Flammarion ltée
375, Avenue Laurier Ouest
Montréal (Québec) H2V 2K3
Tel: 00-1-514-277-8807
Fax: 00-1-514-278-2085
Email: info@flammarion.qc.ca

HONG KONG

City Discount Subscription Service, Ltd.
Unit D, 3rd Floor, Yan's Tower
27 Wong Chuk Hang Road
Aberdeen, Hong Kong
Tel: 852-2580-3539
Fax: 852-2580-6463
Email: citydis@ppn.com.hk

KOREA

Hanbit Media, Inc.
Chungmu Bldg. 201
Yonnam-dong 568-33
Mapo-gu
Seoul, Korea
Tel: 822-325-0397
Fax: 822-325-9697
Email: hant93@chollian.dacom.co.kr

PHILIPPINES

Global Publishing
G/F Benavides Garden
1186 Benavides Street
Manila, Philippines
Tel: 632-254-8949/637-252-2582
Fax: 632-734-5060/632-252-2733
Email: globalp@pacific.net.ph

TAIWAN

O'Reilly Taiwan
No. 3, Lane 131
Hang-Chow South Road
Section 1, Taipei, Taiwan
Tel: 886-2-23968990
Fax: 886-2-23968916
Email: taiwan@oreilly.com

CHINA

O'Reilly Beijing
Room 2410
160, FuXingMenNeiDaJie
XiCheng District
Beijing, China PR 100031
Tel: 86-10-66412305
Fax: 86-10-86631007
Email: beijing@oreilly.com

INDIA

Computer Bookshop (India) Pvt. Ltd.
190 Dr. D.N. Road, Fort
Bombay 400 001 India
Tel: 91-22-207-0989
Fax: 91-22-262-3551
Email: cbsbom@giasbm01.vsnl.net.in

JAPAN

O'Reilly Japan, Inc.
Yotsuya Y's Building
7 Banch 6, Honshio-cho
Shinjuku-ku
Tokyo 160-0003 Japan
Tel: 81-3-3356-5227
Fax: 81-3-3356-5261
Email: japan@oreilly.com

ALL OTHER ASIAN COUNTRIES

O'Reilly & Associates, Inc.
101 Morris Street
Sebastopol, CA 95472 USA
Tel: 707-829-0515
Fax: 707-829-0104
Email: order@oreilly.com

AUSTRALIA

Woodslane Pty., Ltd.
7/5 Vuko Place
Warriewood NSW 2102
Australia
Tel: 61-2-9970-5111
Fax: 61-2-9970-5002
Email: info@woodslane.com.au

NEW ZEALAND

Woodslane New Zealand, Ltd.
21 Cooks Street (P.O. Box 575)
Waganui, New Zealand
Tel: 64-6-347-6543
Fax: 64-6-345-4840
Email: info@woodslane.com.au

LATIN AMERICA

McGraw-Hill Interamericana
Editores, S.A. de C.V.
Cedro No. 512
Col. Atlampa
06450, Mexico, D.F.
Tel: 52-5-547-6777
Fax: 52-5-547-3336
Email: mcgraw-hill@infosel.net.mx